Making the Most of the Water We Have: The Soft Path Approach to Water Management

Making the Most of the Water We Have: The Soft Path Approach to Water Management

Edited by David B. Brooks, Oliver M. Brandes
and Stephen Gurman

publishing for a sustainable future

London • Sterling, VA

First published by Earthscan in the UK and USA in 2009

ISBN: 978-1-84407-754-0

Typeset by MapSet Ltd, Gateshead, UK
Cover design by Clifford Hayes

For a full list of publications please contact:

Earthscan
Dunstan House
14a St Cross St
London, EC1N 8XA, UK
Tel: +44 (0)20 7841 1930
Fax: +44 (0)20 7242 1474
Email: earthinfo@earthscan.co.uk
Web: **www.earthscan.co.uk**

22883 Quicksilver Drive, Sterling, VA 20166-2012, USA

Earthscan publishes in association with the International Institute for
Environment and Development

A catalogue record for this book is available from the British Library

Library of Congress Cataloging-in-Publication Data

Making the most of the water we have : the soft path approach to water
management / edited by David B. Brooks, Oliver M. Brandes, and Stephen
Gurman.
   p. cm.
  Includes bibliographical references and index.
  ISBN 978-1-84407-754-0 (hardback)
  1. Water resources development–Environmental aspects. 2. Water-
supply–Management–Environmental aspects. I. Brooks, David, B., 1934– II.
Brandes, Oliver M., 1972– III. Gurman, Stephen.
  TD195.W3M35 2009
  363.6'1–dc22
                             2009005726

Mixed Sources
Product group from well-managed
forests and other controlled sources
www.fsc.org Cert no. SGS-COC-2953
© 1996 Forest Stewardship Council
FSC

I do not know much about gods; but I think that the river
Is a strong brown god – sullen, untamed and intractable,
Patient to some degree, at first recognised as a frontier;
Useful, untrustworthy, as a conveyor of commerce;
Then only a problem confronting the builder of bridges.
The problem once solved, the brown god is almost forgotten
By the dwellers in cities – ever, however, implacable.
Keeping his seasons and rages, destroyer, reminder
Of what men choose to forget. Unhonoured, unpropitiated
By worshippers of the machine, but waiting, watching and waiting...

———

The river is within us, the sea is all about us ...

T. S. Eliot, 'The Dry Salvages' in *Four Quartets*, 1941

Contents

List of Figures, Tables and Boxes

Figures

Tables

Boxes

List of Contributors

Editors

Oliver M. Brandes is a political ecologist who serves as Associate Director for the University of Victoria's POLIS Project on Ecological Governance. He has a background in law, economics and ecological restoration, and leads the POLIS Water Sustainability Project. His work focuses on practical aspects of sustainable water resource management and ecologically based legal and institutional reform: omb@uvic.ca

David B. Brooks, who was educated in geology and economics, retired several years ago after 14 years with Canada's International Development Research Centre. He now serves as Senior Advisor – Fresh Water for Friends of the Earth – Canada. His main research interests lie in the linkages between environmental protection, on the one hand, and the use of minerals, energy and water, on the other: david.b.brooks34@gmail.com

Stephen Gurman is a consultant with experience in environment and development, project management, community development and communications. He has worked with Canadian and international NGOs, CIDA and Industry Canada and spent five years in Africa with a Canadian volunteer-sending organization. Stephen has a Mechanical Engineering degree from McGill University (1972): steve.gurman@sympatico.ca

Contributing authors

Sara Ahmed has been working on the political economy of water in India for the past 20 years. After obtaining her PhD from Cambridge University (1991), Sara taught at the Institute of Rural Management, Anand, India. She is currently working with IDRC, New Delhi, and her primary responsibility will be to develop, with her team, a research programme for South Asia that addresses critical questions of food and water security in the context of climate change, adaptation and growing conflict: sahmed@idrc.org.in

Henning Bjornland holds two academic positions; he is a Canada Research Chair in Water and the Economy – International at University of Lethbridge, Alberta, Canada and an Associate Research Professor at the University of

South Australia. He has researched water management and policy issues in Australia since 1993 and in Canada since 2005: henning.bjornland@uleth.ca

Graham Daborn was Professor of Biology at Acadia University and the first Director of the Arthur Irving Academy for the Environment. Previously (1984–2004) he was the Director of the Acadia Centre for Estuarine Research. He is currently co-chair of the Program Management Committee for the Canadian Water Network: graham.daborn@acadiau.ca

Kurtis Elton holds a Bachelor of Arts & Science from McGill University, where he majored in chemistry. He is currently studying at the University of Waterloo as a Master's candidate in the Faculty of Environment, and enjoys drawing cerebral comics for the school's newspaper: kelton@envmail.uwaterloo.ca

Peter H. Gleick is co-founder and president of the Pacific Institute for Studies in Development, Environment, and Security in Oakland, California. His research and writing address the critical connections between water and human health, the hydrologic impacts of climate change, sustainable water use, privatization and globalization, and international conflicts over water resources. He was named a MacArthur Fellow in October 2003 and was elected to the US National Academy of Sciences: pgleick@pipeline.com

Andrew Hellebust, P.Eng., received training in chemical engineering and biology at the Bachelor's level at the University of Toronto and at the Master's level at Princeton University. Since 1994, he has worked in the field of small-scale and decentralized water and wastewater treatment and is president of Rivercourt Engineering Inc. He balances consulting, design and research in his practice and is a research associate with the Centre for Alternative Wastewater Treatment at Fleming College, Lindsay, Ontario: ahellebust@rivercourt.ca

Elizabeth Hendriks completed a Masters in Environment Studies from the University of Waterloo during which she received a Water Policy Fellowship from the Walter and Duncan Gordon Foundation. She is currently a research associate managing a two-year research project on the role of residential home builders in the uptake of water efficiency innovation: hendriks.elizabeth@gmail.com

Susan Holtz currently works with the Canadian Institute for Environmental Law and Policy as senior policy analyst. She has done projects on many aspects of energy, environment and sustainable development, including being one of the Canadian soft energy path analysts, as well as part of the Canadian water soft path study team: cielap@cielap.org

Lisa Isaacman is a conservation scientist with a Bachelors of Science in Environmental Sciences from the University of Guelph and a Masters of Environmental Studies from Dalhousie University. Her diverse areas of interest include habitat and wildlife protection, environmental policy and stewardship: isaacman@dal.ca

Inga Jacobs is a Researcher in the Water Governance Systems Research Group at the Council for Scientific and Industrial Research in South Africa. She is currently completing her PhD at the School of International Relations, University of St Andrews, Scotland in Transboundary Cooperative Management and Water Politics in Africa: Ijacobs@csir.co.za

Sarah Jordaan is a PhD candidate at the University of Calgary in both Energy and Environmental Systems and Environmental Design. Her first degree was in Physics from Memorial University of Newfoundland. Her research interests lie in assessing land use of energy developments from a life cycle perspective: smjordaa@ucalgary.ca

Paul Kay is Chair, Department of Environment and Resource Studies, University of Waterloo. Since his PhD (Geography, University of Wisconsin-Madison), he has studied climatic variability and water resources from a variety of angles in a variety of settings: pkay@fes.uwaterloo.ca

Simone Klawitter has more than 10 years experience with governmental and non-governmental water agencies, as policy advisor, consultant and academic. She specializes in water economics with focus on water pricing, utility regulation, institutional development, and innovative financing instruments. After many years in the Middle East she now works as financial advisor in Southern Africa on behalf of the German Development Cooperation. She has studied physics and law and holds a PhD in economics: mail@klawitter-berlin.com

Geoff Kuehne has had a 25-year career as a wheat/sheep farmer in South Australia. After selling his farm in 2000, he completed an MBA, and then a PhD researching irrigators' management behaviour. His research interest focuses on identifying and exploring how farmers' non-profit-maximizing values influence their behaviour: Geoff.Kuehne@csiro.au

Carol Maas is the Director of Innovation for the POLIS Water Sustainability Project and is the primary investigator for the water–energy nexus research theme. She is a professional engineer with 10 years of water and wastewater engineering background, including consulting, R&D and process engineering: c.maas@polisproject.org

Tony Maas is Senior Freshwater Policy Advisor with World Wildlife Fund – Canada. Prior to joining WWF, Tony worked extensively on developing the water soft path concept with the University of Victoria's POLIS Project on Ecological Governance. He has studied Environmental Science at Royal Roads University in Victoria and Water Governance at the University of Waterloo.

Robert Sandford is the Chair of the Canadian Partnership Initiative in support of the United Nations International 'Water for Life' Decade; a member of the Advisory Committee for the Rosenberg International Forum on Water Policy; and Director of the Western Watersheds Climate Research Collaborative, a research and public policy consortium of universities, research institutions and government agencies involved in water and water-related climate research in the river basins that originate in Canada's western mountains: sandford@telus-planet.net

Carla Stevens specializes in integrated land use and watershed management. She has worked in the non-government, provincial government and private sectors in Canada. Her research and work experience in alternative approaches to watershed management led to her desire to address the challenges of implementing innovative water management policy: carla.m.a.stevens@gmail.com

Anthony Turton is a water resource specialist focusing on water and human health risks from radionuclide and heavy metal contamination from the gold mining industry in South Africa. He is a Director of TouchStone Resources (Pty) Ltd that works at the interface between new water, new energy and socio-economic development: tony@anthonyturton.com

Gareth Walker holds a BSc in Physics and an MSc in Water Science and Policy. He is currently a research associate with Waterwise, an independent non-governmental organization with a remit to reduce water consumption within the UK. Past work has included developing Waterwise policy on water affordability and economic incentives for efficiency. His current focus is on the water, energy and carbon relationships in domestic consumption: gwalker@water-wise.org.uk

Sarah E. Wolfe is an Assistant Professor in the Department of Environment and Resource Studies at the University of Waterloo, Canada. Her doctoral research examined the interplay between social networks, knowledge and water demand management in southern Africa and Canada (Ontario). Sarah's current research examines tacit knowledge and water efficiency innovations in the residential building sector; upcoming research will explore the gender dimensions of Canadian water policy.

Foreword

Soft Path Approach in Water Resources Management and Policy Reform

Water users and water managers need all the help they can get if they are to avoid destroying the capacity of our water environments to provide secure water services. As we begin a new century, after nearly 150 years of 'modern' water engineering efforts, major flaws are beginning to appear in what has seemed a water management success story. Today's populations and their water consuming ways are exerting unprecedented pressures on the world's surface and groundwater resources. Society and its political leaders obstinately refuse to engage effectively with the dangers resulting from the rising trend in collective global water consumption. We are still living with our beliefs and biases that water should be free in our homes and, where possible, for our livelihoods. Our startling lack of response to the dangers that face us seems to indicate that we are ill-equipped to evaluate risks of the type and scale that human demands are placing on our environment. 'It is a miracle that we get anything right' (Ferguson, 2009). The analysis of approaches to managing water resources in this useful book highlights the risks of our water consuming ways. It emphasizes the role of human behaviour in overusing and spoiling the diminishing supply of fresh water resources upon which we all depend, and, per contra, how human ingenuity can get us out of the trap we have built for ourselves.

Demand management is one dimension of the rich soft path approach. Demand management policies and demand management practices address the issue of water use efficiency – more output per drop and more jobs per drop. They promote measures that achieve technical and economic efficiency by improving the returns to water from investing in technologies that increase efficiency and reduce waste. Water efficiency can be doubled and water pollution significantly reduced by technically efficient measures.

Still more powerful is the soft path approach of allocative efficiency. This approach has vastly more potential to increase returns to water than the hard path technical approaches. However, experience shows that, though the soft approach is economically rational, it is also politically contentious. The soft path approach requires that water users change the way they use and manage water. At home people can shower rather than bathe, remove thirsty plants from the garden, cease watering the garden altogether and generally use water more carefully. They can be given incentives to use less by being charged higher prices for metered water. But while introducing properly maintained water metering and billing systems always induces a modest reduction in use, users do not welcome them. Politicians are predictably wary of such reforms.

The forces that have put the hard path approaches in place are deeply entrenched – professionally, institutionally and politically. It has been difficult for soft path approaches to make inroads as they are often associated with unpopular changes in the ways of using water. Unpopular measures incur political prices. Invisible, 'politics-lite' soft path policies and practice have been adopted much more readily – if unconsciously. They have been very effective in the second half of the 20th century in improving returns to water. They have been much more significant than consciously deployed soft path measures.

The soft path approaches that have reallocated water from low return to high return activities – from low-value to high-value crop production and from relatively low-value irrigation to very high-value industries and services – have had unintended consequences. Of course, they have had efficiency impacts. Even more important they have brought water and food security to regions that are seriously water scarce. Water reallocated in diversifying industrial economies enables the *water scarce* to trade their way to water and food security. Singapore, Israel and Malta are examples. Invisibly and silently, and without destabilizing political conflicts, economic diversification reallocated water to activities and sectors that brought very high returns to scarce water.

But soft path approaches are not just about economic efficiency and improving economic returns to water. As Canadian author Margaret Atwood emphasizes, 'The economy is a wholly owned subsidiary of the environment.' The soft path approach is not just about more crop and jobs per drop. It also addresses the issues of the sustainable management of water. More care per drop is also a high priority as it prevents the irreversible impairment of surface water and groundwater. The soft path approach also recognizes the water–energy nexus. This nexus is associated with *three weddings* and *avoiding two funerals*. The weddings are first, the production of *clean* energy from water; second, the production of usable water with *clean* energy; and third, the extraordinary role of *economic diversification, socio-economic development* and *trade* in enabling environments and economies to be sustainable. The first funeral to be avoided is the destruction of the atmosphere through the profligate use of fossil energy; the second is avoiding serious impairment of the aquatic environment as a consequence of using it as a sink for industrial and agricultural pollution.

The book provides a timely review of how political economies worldwide have been introducing soft path approaches. It is immensely strengthened by authors who introduced the idea to the water sector and diffused it among water scientists, engineers and planners. Many of them have written chapters in this book.

The term soft path has proved to be a *sticky idea* that has begun to gain currency. For those managing water and engaging in its contentious allocative politics, the term draws attention to the existence of alternatives to the familiar supply-side approaches. The soft path approach is intuitively holistic and requires that water users as well as water professionals be informed and engaged with the ecology of water and with the multiplicity of stakeholders who use water. It is precautionary because it helps society avoid the funerals of the degraded water environment and of the poisoned atmosphere by recognizing the air/water/energy nexus. Finally, the soft path approach is timely and appropriate in that it fosters the good governance of water in ways that constructively engage the social solidarities involved in the use and management of water.

Professor Tony Allan
King's College London and the School of Oriental and African Studies,
University of London, UK

References

Ferguson, N. (2009) 'This much I know', *The Observer Magazine*, 18 January, p10

Acknowledgements

This book began as a series of conversations in 2003 about how environmental non-governmental groups might expand the typically constrained discussion about water policy to a more holistic alternative. A clear recurring theme in the discussions was a belief that by putting emphasis on *why we were using so much water* as opposed to *how we might use it better* might provide a real opportunity to create a more sustainable future. The issues centred on the human role in choosing how to use water instead of just on the technologies we had come to depend upon. Several people, including Peter Gleick in the United States and Harry Swain in Canada suggested that we adapt Amory Lovins' soft energy path to fresh water. Early work was done at Friends of the Earth – Canada in collaboration with Gregory Rose, Rob de Loë, Robert Patrick and, more generally on water sustainability, with Keith Ferguson and Michael M'Gonigle at the University of Victoria's POLIS Project on Ecological Governance. Initial support for an in-depth analysis of soft path applications in Canada was arranged by Jennifer Moore in Environment Canada and later by the ongoing and even courageous support of Brenda Lucas at the Gordon Foundation. Though not directly related to the production of this book, they all deserve some credit for the material that appears in it.

The book itself also has had significant support from a variety of people not only providing research and design and technical support, but also review, encouragement and development of ideas and concepts through thoughtful discussion, including notably Rod Dobell, Susanne Porter-Bopp, Ellen Reynolds, Ray Travers, Jennifer Wong and Ann Zurbrigg at the University of Victoria's POLIS Project for Ecological Governance. Nicola Ross and Marcia Ruby were critical in arranging initial publication of our research results in the July 2007 issue (vol 33, no 4) of the Canadian environmental journal, *Alternatives*, and also granted permission for us to use some figures that were originally prepared for that issue. Beatrice Olivastri and Karen Cartier at Friends of the Earth – Canada provided ongoing support throughout the whole process from tentative explorations to completion of the manuscript. Tim Morris at the Gordon Foundation provided funding for a mid-project meeting of the three editors at the offices of the Foundation in Toronto. Others who were involved with preparation of material leading up the book included Lynn Barber, Matt Binstock, Anja Grauenhorst, Alina Michalska and Nabeela

Rahman. For suggesting Canadian poems from which to select quotations, we thank Toby Brooks and Sheila Forsyth.

Our long-time colleague Diane Beckett deserves special thanks for taking on the task of reading the whole text through and getting her overall review and comments back to us in the shortest possible time.

House of Anansi Press kindly gave us permission to use material in Chapter 3 that had previously been published in an article by Susan Holtz and David Brooks entitled 'Reverse Engineering: Soft Energy Paths' in the 2003 book, *Fueling the Future: How the Battle Over Energy is Changing Everything*. The journal *Water International* gave us permission to use material in Chapter 7 that had previously been submitted to the journal for publication as an article by David Brooks and Susan Holtz. Finally, we express our thanks to Tim Hardwick at Earthscan for his general monitoring of our process through to publication, and for patiently answering our interminable series of questions about format.

David B. Brooks, Oliver M. Brandes and Stephen Gurman

List of Acronyms and Abbreviations

ALUS	Alternative Land Use Services
BAU	business as usual
CAWP	Coalition Against Water Privatisation (South Africa)
CMA	Catchment Management Agency
CMHC	Canada Mortgage and Housing Corporation
CoAG	Council of Australian Governments
CRD	Capital Regional District
CSIR	Council for Scientific and Industrial Research (South Africa)
CSIRO	Commonwealth Scientific and Industrial Research Organisation
CWWA-WEN	Canadian Water and Wastewater Association's Water Efficiency Network
Defra	Department for Food, Environment and Rural Affairs
DWAF	Department of Water Affairs and Forestry (South Africa)
DWI	Drinking Water Inspectorate
EA	Environment Agency
EEB	European Environmental Bureau
ELV	Emission Limited Values
ENGOs	environmental non-government organizations
EQS	Environmental Quality Standards
ERR	Earthquake Reconstruction and Rehabilitation
EU	European Union
FCM	Federation of Canadian Municipalities
GDP	gross domestic product
GLC	Great Lakes Commission
GLSLRB	Great Lakes–St Lawrence River Basin
GMID	Goulburn-Murray Irrigation District
GNP	gross national product
GVRD	Greater Vancouver Regional District
GWP	Global Water Partnership
GWSSB	Gujarat Water Supply and Sewerage Board
IDRC	International Development Research Centre (Ottawa)

IJC	International Joint Commission
IWRM	Integrated Water Resources Management
LCA	life cycle assessment
LCD	litres per capita-day
MDB	Murray-Darling Basin
MDBMC	Murray-Darling Basin Ministerial Council
MENA	Middle East and North Africa
Mm^3	million cubic metres
NGOs	non-governmental organizations
NRTEE	National Round Table on the Environment and the Economy
NWI	National Water Initiative (CoAG)
O&M	operations and maintenance
OECD	Organisation for Economic Co-operation and Development
Ofwat	Water Services Regulatory Authority
OPEC	Organization of Petroleum Exporting Countries
RMI	Rocky Mountain Institute
RSC	rural service council (South Africa)
SOPPECOM	Society for Promoting Participative Ecosystem Management (Pune)
SPA	soft path analysis
THM	trihalomethanes
TISS	Tata Institute of Social Studies (Mumbai)
UN	United Nations
UNDP	United Nations Development Programme
UNESCO	United Nations Educational, Social and Cultural Organization
WAGRICO	Water Resources Management in Cooperation with Agriculture project
WASMO	Water and Sanitation Management Organisation (India)
WDM	water demand management
WEDO	Women's Environment and Development Organization
WEPs	Water Efficiency Plans/Policies
WFD	Water Framework Directive (EU)
WHO	World Health Organization
WMAs	water management areas
WRI	World Resources Institute
WRPC	Water Resources Policy Commissions
WSEP	Water Strategy Expert Panel
WSP	water soft paths
WUAs	water user associations

Introduction

1
Why a Water Soft Path, and Why Now

Oliver M. Brandes, David B. Brooks and Stephen Gurman

*Two roads diverged in a wood, and I took the one less
     traveled by,
And that has made all the difference.*

Robert Frost

Water is essential for all life. An adequate supply of water has been critical to the foundation and success of civilization, from the first agricultural societies more than 5000 years ago to the industrialized mega-cities of today. But water is not always a blessing. Human societies have often been faced with water challenges – often too little and periodically too much. Long-term droughts, in particular, have had major impacts on the development of societies, as shown by some of the myths that pervade ancient literature. Until recently, however, concern about adequacy of the water supply on a *global scale* did not exist.

For the past 2500 years, perhaps longer, the practice of water management has been about the design and construction of an ever-larger and more complex infrastructure for water supply; building dams and reservoirs, digging or drilling wells, building cisterns and extending aqueducts, canals and pipelines to cities, factories and farms. This historical supply-oriented model is highly linear, with water literally flowing through our built infrastructure on a one-way course. At the tail-end of this system millions of litres of waste water are carried away from those cities, farms, factories and generating stations (and not always treated) to flow back into our rivers, lakes and oceans.

There is much to celebrate with the achievement of this approach, including the widely accessible and high-quality drinking water and reliable sanitation that has allowed communities in middle- and high-income countries around the world to flourish. Vast amounts of clean water have been made available, whether for domestic needs in cities, for agriculture and industry or for more discretionary uses such as municipal gardens and parks, car washes and swimming pools.

Unfortunately, the era of 'endless' fresh water is coming to an end. Contrary to popular perceptions of water availability, less than 1 per cent of global water resources are actually fresh and renewable (Pielou, 1998). Moreover, geographic, geologic and economic considerations put much of that (relatively small) quantity out of our reach. We have already exploited the most easily accessible sources of fresh water and costs to develop additional supplies are increasing every year (Serageldin, 1995). By the turn of the new millennium, several fast-growing regions of the world were already withdrawing two-fifths to three-fifths of all available water (Raskin et al, 1996).

As a consequence, concern is increasing that the availability of water will become the greatest natural resource challenge of the 21st century. Humanity is currently facing the combined effects of a changing climate, ever-increasing urbanization and expanding population with impacts on the environment magnified by the quest for economic growth. Equally important, but less often noted, is the growing recognition that current water management practices are simply unsustainable and cannot continue to deliver the benefits they have in the past.

Take the case of Canada, commonly viewed as one of the most 'water-rich' countries in the world – a country in which most citizens have a strong belief in their entitlement to potable water (Biro, 2007; Sprague, 2007). In reality, even Canada is not exempt from water resource limitations. Much of that nation's fresh water is located in the Great Lakes, a non-renewable relic of melting continental glaciers. Only a small fraction of the total in the lakes is available for use without impairing their capability to provide the ongoing ecological goods and services that are the foundation for the prosperity of the surrounding region.

Approximately 60 per cent of the rest of the water in Canada flows northward toward Hudson's Bay or the Arctic Ocean, well beyond the reach of even the longest currently feasible pipeline (Sprague, 2007). Even if such pipelines *were* possible, the huge investment required to build them, in addition to the ongoing cost of energy to operate them, would make such a project unattractive to investors as well as violating a general societal reluctance to allow inter-basin transfers of water. Times have changed: Not so long ago it was believed that all water flowing to the sea was fully available for our use and, in fact, would be 'wasted' if not used for human benefit. Today, in contrast, a growing proportion of society understands that much of this supposedly available water must be left in place to support crucial ecological services such as waste dilution, habitat protection, flood control (in wetlands) and other ecosystem functions (Millennium Ecosystem Assessment, 2005; Katz, 2006).

Current water management practices are at an impasse and the symptoms of a 'sick' system are everywhere. Rivers that once ran free and clear are now sluggish or brackish. Water tables are falling. Aquatic habitat is no longer able to support the variety of flora and fauna that it once did. It is becoming increasingly common to find potential sources of water that are too polluted for most uses and communities are often forced to rely on water supplies that are unsafe for domestic use. Human society is thus faced with a serious conundrum. Our ability to provide an inexhaustible supply of 'cheap', safe, fresh water can no longer be met using the old methods, yet we are told that the demand for water will continue to grow.

Box 1.1 summarizes the kinds of water supply problems people and governments around the world are facing. The much-quoted statement by Marq de Villiers (1999) – 'The trouble with water is that they are not making any more of it' – is all too true, and its effects are upon us today. Even acknowledging that the global water cycle continues – the same amount of water flows now as in prehistoric times – is of little help when several regions of the world are withdrawing two-fifths to three-fifths of all available water (Raskin et al, 1996).

Going beyond concrete and steel

Peter Gleick was the first person to explicitly put forward the soft path for water as a paradigm shift in water management practice that would focus on demand rather than supply (1998). Since then there have been a number of others, including the majority of authors in this book, who have been promoting the adoption of a whole new approach to management – one that goes beyond simply 'saving water' and emphasizes *reducing demand* rather than *increasing supply*. This approach manages people – not the watersheds that house them – as the priority.

To find a lasting balance between a resilient and prosperous society, and a healthy and productive environment, a 21st-century approach to water management must move from a focus on large centralized reservoirs, higher capacity pumps and longer pipelines towards an emphasis on decentralized, smaller scale built infrastructure, alternative sources, such as rainwater collection, greater reliance on reuse and recycling, pricing and economic incentives and highly improved efficiency in water use, as the starting point.

This type of demand-oriented approach, often called *water demand management*, is a strategy that recognizes limits to the amount of water that can be withdrawn from nature and that searches for cost-effective measures to cut water use. Greater efficiency – 'more crop per drop' in the jargon of irrigation – can reduce the demand for water and save money. Common demand management measures for the home include full-cost pricing keyed to the amount withdrawn or used, water saving appliances, low-flow taps, shower-heads and toilets, and drip or sprinkler irrigation. For example, well-designed, low-flow toilets can cut water use by about 75 per cent per flush, with further

Box 1.1 The problem

Peter Gleick

During the industrial revolution and population explosion of the 19th and 20th centuries, tens of thousands of monumental engineering projects were built to manage the natural hydrologic cycle and make water available to hundreds of millions of people. Thanks to improved sewer systems, cholera, typhoid and other water-related diseases, once endemic throughout the world, have largely been conquered in the more industrialized nations. Vast cities, incapable of surviving on local resources, have bloomed in the desert with water brought from hundreds and even thousands of miles away. Food production has kept pace with soaring populations largely because of irrigation systems that now produce 40 per cent of the world's food. Nearly one-fifth of all of our electricity is produced by turbines spun by the power of falling water.

But this supply-based approach has its limitations. As the easy sources of water have been tapped, new projects become more ambitious, intrusive and capital-intensive, and their costs, never small, become more evident. Half the world's population still suffers with water services inferior to those available to the ancient Greeks and Romans. One billion people lack access to clean drinking water; more than two and a half billion people do not have improved sanitation services (World Health Organization, 2008). Preventable water-related diseases still kill an estimated 10,000–20,000 children each day, and the latest evidence suggests that we are falling behind in efforts to solve these problems.

The effects of our water policies extend beyond human health. Tens of millions of people have been displaced from their homes – often with little warning or compensation – to make way for the reservoirs behind dams. Certain irrigation practices degrade soil quality and reduce agricultural productivity, threatening to bring an end to the Green Revolution. Groundwater continues to be pumped faster than it is naturally replenished in both developed and developing nations of the world. And disputes over shared water resources have led to violence and continue to raise local, national and even international tensions (see the 'Water Conflict Chronology' at www.worldwater.org).

Negative impacts on natural habitat are also significant. More than 20 per cent of all freshwater fish species are now threatened or endangered because dams and water withdrawals have destroyed the free-flowing river ecosystems where they thrive (Ricciardi and Rasmussen, 1999). On the Columbia and Snake Rivers in the US, 95 per cent of the juvenile salmon trying to reach the ocean do not survive passage through the numerous dams and reservoirs that block their way. More than 900 dams on rivers in New England and Europe block Atlantic salmon from their spawning grounds, and their populations have fallen to less than 1 per cent of historic levels. Perhaps most infamously, the Aral Sea in central Asia has been devastated because water policies in the former Soviet Union (and largely continued by current governments in the region) cut off most of the inflow. Twenty-four species of fish formerly found in the Aral Sea and nowhere else are now thought to be extinct.

We can no longer look to the past policies as a guide to future sustainable water management.

reductions possible if reclaimed wastewater, rather than drinking water, is used for flushing.

Increasing water costs greatly expand the potential for demand management. In fact, experts believe that cost-effective water savings of 20 to 40 per cent are readily available. A recent study of water use in California by the Pacific Institute (Gleick et al, 2003) and in Canada (Brandes et al, 2007) show that total urban (residential, commercial, institutional and most industrial) water use could comfortably be cut by at least 30 per cent using existing ('off-the-shelf') technologies that are cheaper than new supplies of water. Equally important, this 'additional water' can be obtained more quickly than any new supply project can be built and brought on stream. The gains are great enough to eliminate the need for any new supply projects for the next several decades, even if California and urban centres in Canada continue to grow at their current rapid pace.

Demand management is, in fact, already used frequently by water system operators, especially in more progressive and integrated organizations but, in general, is usually employed only as a secondary or temporary option until additional supplies are secured. Most people are rarely aware of the need to moderate their water use until, usually in mid-summer, periods of low rainfall deplete reserves or reduce flow in wells, and temporary restrictions are imposed – typically just on lawn watering or washing cars and sidewalks with a hose. Such 'rationing' is almost invariably coupled with demands to build a larger supply system rather than an analysis of ways in which water demand could be reduced to more closely match availability. A striking parallel exists between this approach to water use and that for electricity and gasoline, both of which generally continue to be underpriced, at least in North America.

Demand management can no longer be viewed as a second-best or a temporary option. Moderating demand must become the priority for water managers, with new supply treated as the *back-up option* that is used only when absolutely necessary. In the face of current uncertainty and change, such as looming energy limits, rapidly changing climate and ever-increasing population and urbanization, reducing the demand for water through efficiency and conservation will simply be the best 'source' of 'new' water most communities have.

Travelling along the spectrum of water management

Demand management, as it is commonly practised today, starts from an emphasis on water efficiency and simple technical fixes (eg, low-flow shower heads, fixtures and appliances) and basic economic incentives (eg, volume-based pricing). Demand reductions achieved in this manner can typically be accomplished at less cost, more quickly and with less environmental damage, than any supply alternative. These savings can be characterized as the 'low hanging fruit' of demand management, and they will always have a role to play in any sustainable water management strategy.

These conventional efforts, though relatively simple, have a fundamental limitation. Because they are based on an *anthropocentric view* rather than an *ecosystem perspective*, they focus more on measures for water use efficiency, as defined by short-term cost effectiveness, than on long-term ecological sustainability. Moving towards a new water management paradigm will require society to ensure that there is a balance between water use and ecological sustainability over the longer term. This kind of comprehensive and integrated approach is called the *water soft path* and is the focus of this book.

Whereas 'traditional' water demand management is generally restricted to water efficiency, water soft paths (WSP) encourage *both* water efficiency and water conservation – two terms that are often used interchangeably but that are really different concepts (Brooks, 2005). Briefly, water efficiency focuses on ways to reduce the amount of water used to accomplish a specific task; water conservation focuses on ways to change the task so that use of water is reduced much further or eliminated entirely.

The key distinction between traditional programmes and WSP is highlighted by the core questions they pose. Demand management focuses on questions that begin with *How* – How to accomplish the same thing with less water? The soft path, in contrast, focuses on *Why* – Why use water to do this in the first place?

Why, for example, do we use water to carry away our waste? Demand management would urge low-flow toilets, but waterless or fully integrated resource recovery systems are available – perhaps not for homes (because of the technical requirements and the need for regular maintenance), but certainly for larger buildings, or networked systems that might exist at the neighbourhood scale. Why do we use half the potable water that is piped to a house in the summer for watering lawns and gardens and washing cars (and all too often the sidewalk (pavement))? Demand management would urge more efficient sprinklers with automatic shut-offs, maybe even watering on alternate days. The soft path goes further: recycling water from bathtubs and washing machines or, better yet, planting greenery that is drought resistant and that requires little or no watering once it is established, a technique called xeriscaping.[1]

By focusing on 'why', the soft path greatly increases the number of possible solutions. The approach is, of course, broadly applicable, not just to houses and gardens, but also large buildings, factories and farms – indeed across sectors – to entire cities and even complete watersheds and basins. Soft paths are therefore 'soft' partly because they require less steel, concrete and other resource-intensive inputs, but mainly because they depend on human ingenuity to find ways around current natural resource use patterns without losing the benefits of economic development that have improved the quality of life for so many people. The role of water management changes from just building and maintaining water supply infrastructure to also providing water related services, such as new forms of sanitation, drought-resistant landscapes, urban redesign for conservation and rain-fed ways to grow crops.

The ultimate goal of WSP is to permit economic and social development at rates, and by means, that are compatible with long-term ecological sustainability and democratic decision-making. Instead of relying exclusively on the use of physical infrastructure – pipes and pumps – to manage water demand, it looks at ways in which social engineering can be used to change water consumption patterns. This approach would engage individuals, businesses, communities and governments in a wide-ranging analysis of local water consumption patterns and the environmental impacts (upstream and downstream) associated with this level of use. The objective is to strike a balance between water consumption and the long-term preservation of the environment.

Widening the audience for water soft paths

This book is designed not only to introduce but also to promote the WSP concept as a viable alternative to the current approach to water management. While the principles involved with the concept are already gaining ground, they have mainly been communicated to niche audiences through articles in professional journals and focused presentations at conferences in Canada, the US and Europe; they have only begun to receive wider attention by more general water management professionals and the public.

The only complete analysis of water soft path options for specific ecological, economic and social settings has been undertaken in Canada, with that study presented in Part II of the book. Despite limited general exposure, the

---

BOX 1.2 SPECTRUM OF WATER MANAGEMENT

Oliver M. Brandes and David B. Brooks

This box illustrates the differing characteristics of supply management, demand management and soft paths across several key aspects, with Figure 1.1 demonstrating this relationship diagrammatically, revealing the likely water use outcome under each of those patterns of water management. This graphic clearly demonstrates that the soft path approach reaches a potentially sustainable level of water use because it is specifically designed that way from the start – ensuring that our demands on water as a source and the supporting environment as a sink do not exceed the carrying capacity of the ecosystem. How one gets to that position is the major concern of the analysis and, as is suggested (by the two lines) in this graphic, there is no uniquely appropriate soft path from here to there.

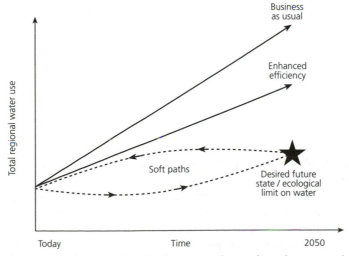

Figure 1.1 *Planning for the future with a soft path approach*

Box 1.2 *continued*

Policy	Dominant discipline	Range of policy choices	Fundamental question	Planning process	Outcome
Supply management	Engineering	Policies based on presumed need for new infrastructure.	How can we meet projected water needs given current trends in water use and population growth?	Planners extrapolate from current consumption patterns to determine future 'requirements' and then locate and develop new sources of supply to meet this projected demand.	Construction of dams, pipelines, canals, wells, desalination systems, and inter-basin transfers, where necessary.
Demand management	Economics	Policies based on short-term cost–benefit calculations.	How can we reduce needs for water to conserve the resource, save money and reduce environmental impacts?	Planners incorporate efficiency and information programmes together with improved pricing patterns to maximize use of existing infrastructure. Increasing capacity is only one option among others in a least-cost approach.	Efficiency gains through technical fixes and consumer education.
Soft path	Multi-disciplinary	Policies based on stakeholder consultation and political review.	How can we deliver services currently provided by water in ways that recognize the need for economic, social and ecological sustainability?	Planners model a sustainable future state for water use with attention to long-term economic and social prosperity. They then 'backcast' to devise a feasible and desirable path to reach that state. Ecological sustainability is fundamental to all economic, political and socio-cultural choices.	Options to reduce water use through innovation, conservation, water reallocation and changing patterns of use and reuse. More water is left in situ.

Source: Brandes and Brooks, 2007

concept of WSP is gaining momentum. A number of communities, notably those faced with an apparent need for expensive additions to their water supplies, have begun to explore the potential of WSP methodology to defer, perhaps permanently, new construction and to save money, while responding to public demands for environmental protection. Ecological sustainability remains somewhat lower on the list of priorities, but they are nevertheless moving in the right direction to achieve it.

As explored in Chapter 3 (Holtz and Brooks) the soft path for water concept is adapted from the energy field. Amory Lovins coined the term 'soft energy path' in a 1976 *Foreign Affairs* article and went on, in subsequent publications, to develop a whole new approach to energy planning. In fact, Lovins used the same quotation from Robert Frost to head his *Foreign Affairs* article that we have used to head this chapter, as it so appropriately captures the changes that he then wanted for energy, and that we, today, want for fresh water.

Four principles that make soft paths different

Soft path thinking seeks to be as open as possible about the principles on which the concept is based and that drive soft path analysis. Four principles stand out as specifically distinguishing the soft path from conventional water planning and management:

1 treating water as a service rather than an end in itself;
2 making ecological sustainability a fundamental criterion;
3 matching the quality of water delivered to that needed by the use;
4 planning from the future back to the present.

Treating water as a service
Of all the innovations that Lovins brought to the field of energy analysis, perhaps the most significant was his recognition that energy is not needed for itself, but for the services it can provide; that is, that it is an intermediate rather than a final good. The same is true for water, or at least for most water. Instead of being viewed as an end product, most water is the means society uses to accomplish specific tasks, such as carrying away wastes, cooling motors or promoting plant growth. Drinking water is a quantitatively small but obviously critical exception; in that case, water is an end in itself. Changing the concept of energy or water from *ends* to *means* is critical to all soft path thinking, and it recognizes that water has been seen differently, at different times, and by different groups, throughout history (Linton, 2009).

This change of perspective liberates water planners and managers from the constraints of merely supplying more water and permits them to innovate by identifying alternatives to water-based services. One example of this approach would be to ask whether flushing toilets is an objective in itself or whether we are really looking at how to remove human waste. Another would redefine the objective of irrigating crops to one of growing food. If this approach allows us to meet our actual needs using less supplied water, we have the potential to cut costs, protect the environment and enhance local control.

When water is viewed as a service, it becomes easier for managers to expand their focus beyond traditional technologies and infrastructure. They are more likely to innovate and engage broader society by, for example, promoting education and social marketing, urban redesign for conservation and different modes of farm management. Changing practices and behaviour offers an increased range of options to reduce water use while maintaining desired services.

Ensuring ecological sustainability

Ecosystems are paramount in any discussion of water use but their position is typically ignored because they cannot speak for themselves. Soft paths recognize *ecosystems* as legitimate 'users' of fresh water and aim to include the value of water needed to sustain ecosystems (and indeed all of us) in the overall assessment of water supply costs. The work of the Millennium Ecosystem Assessment (2005) validates this approach. For example, the Assessment looked at the ecosystem services provided by wetlands and attempted to calculate the economic value of unconverted wetlands versus that of converted wetlands. It was found that the *total economic value* of unconverted wetlands is often greater than that of converted wetlands – that is leaving water in its natural state may be more beneficial to society than extracting it for commercial use. It certainly is a superior option for the plants and animals that inhabit that ecosystem.

Conventional cost–benefit analysis is not sufficient to ensure basic ecological resilience and ecosystem health. Therefore, in soft path studies, environmental constraints are built in from the start to limit the amount of water withdrawn from natural sources and to establish conditions on the quality of water returned to nature. Of the many possible soft paths that exist, each is tested for its effects, and any option – be it source or use – that puts environmental sustainability at risk must be rejected. Major inter-basin transfers of water are not considered acceptable; they contradict the objective of living with the water you have. Similarly, if there are water resources that are valued for their beauty or for their cultural or religious significance, they must be placed off-limits for development. Cost–benefit analysis is only employed once a number of viable options are found, to help identify those that would be cheaper to follow or have other advantages.

Conserving quality as well as quantity

Water quality requirements vary with end-use. A contaminant that is toxic for one use may be benign or even beneficial for another. We don't want animal waste in our drinking water, for example, but we eagerly seek it for gardens and farms. Yet, in most of the Western world, we still flush toilets with drinking water and also use it, in many areas, for irrigating gardens and crops. For both economic and physical reasons, it is almost as important to conserve the quality of water as to conserve its quantity. High-quality water (think of it as drinking water) occurs much less frequently in nature and is much more expensive to deliver to users than lower quality water. Fortunately, we only need small quantities of this high-quality water (mainly for households and special industrial tasks), but huge quantities of lower quality water (such as for irrigation on farms and cooling at generating stations and industrial plants).

Soft path options are designed from the start to match the quality of water supplied to the quality required by the specific end-use. The goal is to create circular cascading systems so that wastewater from one use becomes the input for another use – for example, from rainwater capture to the washing machine and then to the garden, or from cooling systems to water for cleaning or other industrial uses, then treated and recirculated.

Looking ahead by working backwards

Soft paths require a set of policy changes and programme plans that will, over time, move society along the road toward water sustainability in patterns that are consistent with economic prosperity and a high quality of life. The way that route is built is another unique characteristic of the soft path approach. Traditional economic or development planning starts from the present and projects forward to the future. Soft path planning does just the opposite. First it defines a sustainable and desirable future state for society, at least as far as water sources and uses are concerned. It then works backward to identify policies and programmes that will connect the future to the present. This technique is called '*backcasting*' in obvious contrast to forecasting, and it is the most important and the most challenging part of soft path analysis and planning.

Backcasting is not so strange an exercise as might first appear. Think of planning a holiday. One does not leave home and wander aimlessly. Rather, you first choose a destination and then plan your itinerary according to a specific set of priorities. Are you interested in travelling on the more scenic routes or do you want to make the trip in the shortest time possible? Are there other travel options that you need to take into account? Backcasting is a similar iterative process. You do it over and over until reasonably satisfied that the goal can be achieved in the most cost-effective and agreeable way possible. Suppose a community decides that no new water sources will be developed before 2050. The desired condition in this case is that all future water needs for population and economic growth will be met through efficiency and conservation. The initial choice sets in motion the strategic thinking needed to implement policy and programme alternatives to ensure that this end result can be met. But the destination and the goal are clear.

By their very nature, soft paths are a long-term approach to water management. They do not ignore the past we have come from, and they allow time for gradual replacement of the existing physical infrastructure, a factor that can be determined, with a reasonable degree of accuracy, by engineering and economic considerations. This longer time horizon also allows for the gradual evolution of new norms of behaviour or forms of social 'infrastructure', neither of which is easy to anticipate when thinking about the future. Due to the long time frame involved, soft path scenarios for water must also allow for the possible impacts of climate change, such as changing precipitation patterns, longer drought periods, and increased rates of evaporation. The process of developing scenarios by working back from the future allows these kinds of potential impacts to be incorporated in water planning today, but also adjusted over time.

Soft paths and values

The analysis underlying soft path planning does not generally yield a single, best path. Rather there are likely to be a number of paths that vary in the specific social patterns assumed and the specific applications of water use permitted, both of which are of course highly political choices. Notwithstanding the above limitations, soft path analysis has significant benefits. It can be used to identify possible paths, describe their advantages and disadvantages (and, if quantifiable, their benefits and costs), and suggest the likely level of social acceptance and political feasibility associated with each path. It is up to society as a whole, operating through democratic and participatory means, to choose the path most appropriate to its collective values, which is not the task of the analyst.

The strategies that emerge from a soft path plan are explicitly value laden. Supply-based policies are also value laden, but these values are less obvious because they are based on existing policies and status quo approaches. Soft path strategies pay attention to costs but also include ecological sustainability and societal engagement as fundamental criteria. The soft path defines a future, sustainable society in value terms. Implicit in this approach is the assumption that the decisions we make today – identifying new actions, policies and reforms – can, in fact, influence future water consumption patterns and the institutional arrangements that drive them.

As with any strategic plan, soft path planning is not designed to be a one-time event. Rather, it is an iterative process in which assumptions are revisited regularly as new industries arrive, values shift and climate changes. Periodic review (every five or so years) will identify new options and result in policy refinements. However, if the strategy and goals are clear from the start, the smaller adjustments, such as updating demand management technologies or population growth rates, will be relatively easy to accommodate.

Three aspects of soft path thinking

All soft paths, whether for energy, water or any other natural resource, have three key aspects:

1 *human vision* of a different future in which human activity and ecological protection exist in a mutually supportive and sustainable way;
2 *analytical method* for defining and demonstrating the 'feasibility' – a term that itself requires careful definition – of a route between the present and the envisioned future;
3 *planning tool* for water managers, engineers, planners, politicians and community leaders to discuss, design and ultimately implement steps that

will move communities, companies and organizations along the route toward that desired future.

These three aspects provide the organizing structure for this book.

Part I: Water Soft Paths as Human Vision

The vision goes back many millennia. Classical religious texts are highly sensitive to environmental issues, and those originating in the Middle East, as with the Hebrew Bible and the Koran, are particularly so with respect to water. Unfortunately, environmental aspects of the religious vision were neglected for most of the last two millennia. Only in the second half of the 20th century did it again came to the fore, heralded by such seminal works as Aldo Leopold's *A Sand County Almanac*, Rachel Carson's *Silent Spring*, and Jay Forrester's *Limits to Growth*, among others. Because they embody the philosophy of sustainability, soft paths are more than just 'how to'; they are incomplete and likely to be ineffective unless they incorporate the vision that must guide society as it faces the challenges of the 21st century. In a general sense, the vision guiding the water soft path can be seen as the water component of a broader vision of sustainability for a community, a city or a nation. Because soft paths focus on demand, they are inevitably inward looking and focus on a particular jurisdiction or region or watershed. As such, they are equally incomplete and likely to be ineffective if they do not also incorporate important social goals such as full employment and equitable distribution of political and economic power, and attention to issues of governance such as ensuring democratic and participatory decision-making, and community engagement.

This vision aspect of the soft path is captured in Part I of this book which explores the philosophical and theoretical underpinning of soft paths and, in so doing, provides the foundation for the remainder of the book. In Chapter 2, Robert Sandford uses the analogy of a 'perfect storm' to illustrate how human use, overuse and abuse of natural resources are contributing to climate change, and how the resulting ecological effects are likely to work in a vicious circle to magnify the adverse impacts on most life forms, and on our economy in the absence of immediate changes of the type proposed by soft paths. He challenges us to 'follow the water' suggesting its importance in our broader social and ecological systems. The focus turns more directly to the origins of soft path thinking in Chapter 3 where Susan Holtz and David Brooks, who were collaborators on the Canadian soft energy study in the early 1980s, describe how the concept of water soft paths evolved from work on soft energy paths; they go on to review the history of soft energy paths to illustrate some of the opportunities and pitfalls for water soft paths.

Unfortunately, the route toward water soft paths is anything but smooth. In Chapter 4, Peter Gleick identifies a number of misconceptions and misunderstandings about water soft paths, all of which are both widely held and demonstrably wrong. Wrong they may be, but, as he also points out, they continue to inhibit the adoption and impede the implementation of water soft path policies. In Chapter 5, Oliver Brandes looks at the emerging field of ecological governance and shows why it has much to offer in overcoming persistent institutional and social gridlock as well as in helping to move society towards sustainability. This chapter shows how the development of water soft path strategies can act as a catalyst in this process. The adoption of a sustainable water management model will almost certainly discomfit entrenched interests and will displace workers in some industries, but the inevitable upheaval will only worsen the longer we remain fixated on past practices and status quo options. Finally, with Chapter 6 Susan Holtz concludes the section on the vision aspect of the water soft path by looking at water policy as it is commonly conceived. She suggests that the most crucial institutional reform needed involves the relationship between water management and land use planning which falls under the purview of municipal or rural district levels of government. She notes that senior levels of government must play their part by developing appropriate water use standards, policies and guidelines to support efforts at the lower levels.

Part II: Water Soft Paths as Analytical Method

The analytical method for water soft paths is much younger than the vision. As noted above, it was initially developed for energy in the 1970s. Later, as the concept of sustainable development gained currency in the late 1980s, soft paths became its analytics. The objective of this analysis was to show that the water soft path could move beyond its philosophical roots to practical applications of sustainability on the ground. An Annex to the book provides a step-by-step summary of how soft path studies are undertaken; some readers may prefer to read this annex prior to the more detailed discussions in the chapters that follow.

The first complete application of the general soft path analysis anywhere in the world was undertaken in Canada between 2005 and 2007 for one generalized urban area, one watershed and one province, and this study provides the content for Part II of this book. In effect, the chapters in Part II represent a set of case studies of water soft path analysis at three geographic and administrative levels, each with advantages and disadvantages. Taken together, they show that, despite serious deficiencies in our information about how water is used, it is possible to carry out a meaningful soft path analysis and to derive relevant policy conclusions.

Chapter 7 by David Brooks and Susan Holtz describes the methodology of soft path analysis. The chapter first shows how the principles of water soft path analysis differ from conventional natural resource studies in general and from soft energy analysis in particular. After defining the conceptual differences between soft paths and demand management, the chapter concludes by introducing the Canadian water soft path study. Those who want a brief overview of the Canadian study could read just this section.

Chapter 8 by Carol Maas and Tony Maas provides the first published description of the model developed at the University of Victoria's POLIS

Project to help with urban analysis in several parts of the study. Dubbed 'Scenario Builder', the model facilitates a systematic determination of water savings possible when integrating a range of urban water efficiency and conservation measures into a comprehensive plan. In recent years the Scenario Builder has been expanded to calculate the differences in greenhouse gas emissions associated with each scenario as a further incentive to help drive water conservation (see poliswaterproject.org).

Chapters 9, 10 and 11 present, respectively, the urban, watershed and provincial dimensions of the water soft path study.

- In Chapter 9, Oliver Brandes and Tony Maas at the University of Victoria investigate future water use in an urban centre that grows from a population of 200,000 in 2005 to 300,000 in 2050. Their work is based on a variety of real cases across Canada and is probably applicable to much of the developed world. The study shows that the goal of 'no new water' is achievable, even under conditions of significant population growth. A powerful conclusion can be drawn from this work: Existing urban water use patterns and habits need not dictate the future.
- In Chapter 10, Lisa Isaacman and Graham Daborn at Acadia University look at water use in the Annapolis Valley of Nova Scotia as an illustration of water issues found in rural, agricultural areas of Canada. Located in a maritime region, superficial views suggest that water resources are adequate. However, seasonal rainfall variations and increased demand deplete aquifers and degrade surface water. As shown by their analysis, the application of soft path measures together with better use of rainwater would all but eliminate the prospect of unsustainable water use.
- In Chapter 11, Paul Kay and Elizabeth Hendricks at the University of Waterloo ask whether water soft path planning could enable Ontario, Canada's most industrialized province, to avoid the need for new water sources until, at least, 2031. They found that, even with soft path policies, both the agricultural and the industrial sectors might use more water in 2031 than today. Therefore, to achieve the goal of no new water by 2031, the province would have to induce farms and industrial plants to adopt more water conserving methods or encourage a shift in crop choice and industrial structure.

Part III: Water Soft Paths as Planning Tool

Part III takes up the story of the way in which the vision and the analysis of soft paths can be converted to planning tools, first in urban areas and later elsewhere. Its focus is the practical application and implications of the soft path approach. This section also provides the opportunity to look at soft path thinking in other parts of the world: the US and some other relatively rich countries, as well as a number of developing countries. The point in these chapters is not to look for current formal applications of soft path analysis, but to identify the kinds and sources of emerging thinking that not only contain aspects of the soft path thinking but could also support future soft path innovations.

In Chapter 12, Sarah Jordaan, Carla Stevens and David Brooks categorize the kinds of institutional barriers that slow down, and in some cases block, policies aimed at promoting efficiency and encouraging conservation. They define barriers as specific impediments that make it difficult or undesirable to implement policies, yet are correctable by appropriate government or institutional action.

In Chapter 13, Sarah Wolfe and Kurtis Elton point out that soft path elements of water management have not received much attention from municipal planners and engineers. In order to investigate this gap, they surveyed specific water management strategies already undertaken by municipalities and the extent to which they fit within a soft path framework. Informed by a theoretical structure based on social capital and the nature of intrinsic knowledge, the responses to the survey indicate that the foundations for a shift toward a soft path do exist in municipal water practitioner networks, and that aspirations for a sustainable future are more widely shared than is apparent.

Chapter 13 is complemented by Chapter 14 in which Andrew Hellebust reviews opportunities for designing and building less water-intensive buildings and neighbourhoods. Even at the one-building scale that characterizes most wastewater reuse projects in Canada, unexpected benefits have become apparent, including reduced life cycle costs, longer life of existing infrastructure and reduced time in the approval process. However, big gains will only come when reuse is employed at the block or even community scale. The water and nutrients contained in wastewater are resources that can benefit agriculture and the environment, but technology has to shift focus from dilution to recovery.

The next three chapters go beyond the specific practical applications of the concept and reveal the extent to which elements of water soft path thinking are taking hold around the globe. Peter Gleick begins with a review in Chapter 15 of water soft path approaches in the US, where an active debate about future water policy is driven by both shortages and environmental concerns. He notes that, for the first time in history, water use in the US is declining – not just in per capita or per dollar terms but in absolute numbers. He also demonstrates the immediate gains available from demand management; for example, the State of California could reduce water use by 30 per cent or more at lower cost and in far less time than building new capacity.

Chapter 16 extends the review globally and contains short reviews of the initial (and typically implicit) elements of water soft path thinking in three OECD countries or regions:

- Gareth Walker reviews recent experience with water privatization in England, and suggests that the government needs to embrace water soft path policies and adapt its regulatory approach to them if privatization is to overcome social and environmental externalities as well as financing problems related to valuing capital and operational costs.

- Simone Klawitter focuses on several aspects of the European Water Directive, currently being implemented across the European Community to achieve a more demand-oriented water policy, and finds that many aspects are indeed conceptually and practically consistent with the approach outlined in this book.
- Henning Bjornland and Geoff Kuehne describe how multi-year drought in Australia is driving innovative solutions such as water markets as part of a broader reform that puts the limits on excessive use of water and protection of aquatic ecosystems in the forefront.

Chapter 17 contains short reviews of the initial (and at this time very limited) elements of water soft path thinking in three developing countries or regions:

- Inga Jacobs and Tony Turton review recent water history in South Africa, and particularly the dominance of irrigation as a form of water use; they find substantial change in the institutions managing water, and wider recognition of the need to protect water in situ, but that more fundamental reforms are still forthcoming.
- Sara Ahmed looks at one region of India where the key issues are equity, both among classes and between sexes. She emphasizes effects that long-standing inequity have had on water productivity, and on the varying effects – mostly good, but some less so – reform will have for women.
- David Brooks writes on the Middle East and North Africa, where water scarcity has been a chronic problem throughout written history; he finds that demand management and participatory irrigation management are gaining ground, but not nearly fast enough to overcome current problems and certainly not fast enough to be described as a water soft path.

Conclusion

The book concludes with a look back and a look forward by David Brooks, Oliver Brandes and Stephen Gurman in which they ask: 'What have we really learned from the concept of water soft paths?', and 'How might the future differ from the past if the soft path approach is adopted?' They emphasize that citizens and their governments must be willing to rethink the ways in which our freshwater resources are supplied, distributed and, most importantly, used, to avoid an arid future of our own making. In their view only the soft path offers a way to guide current water management practice onto a sustainable path for long-term ecological and social prosperity. They recognize, however, that soft paths, which require deeper changes in lifestyles and livelihoods than more conventional demand management approaches, should be applied with great caution in those parts of the world where equity in access to water and democratic decision-making cannot be assured. Though they believe strongly in the potential for water soft paths and ecological governance, they conclude that parallel social and political values, including democratic decision-making, equity in political and economic power, and broad public participation in decisions about water use and environmental protection, are not just equally important, but inherent components of water soft paths.

Note

1 Sandra Postel (1997, p159) describes xeriscaping as follows: 'From the Greek word *xeros*, meaning dry, Xeriscaping designs draw on a wide variety of attractive indigenous and drought-tolerant plants shrubs and ground cover to replace the thirsty green lawns found in most suburbs. A Xeriscaped yard typically requires 30–80 per cent less water than a conventional one, and can reduce fertilizer and herbicide use as well. One study in Navato, California found the Xeriscaped landscaping cuts water use by 54 per cent, fertilizer use by 61 per cent and herbicide use by 22 per cent.'

References

Biro, A. (2007) 'Half-empty or half-full? Water politics and the Canadian National Imaginary', in K. Bakker (ed) *Eau Canada: The Future of Canada's Water*, UBC Press, Vancouver, BC

Brandes, O. M. and Brooks, D. B. (2007) *The Soft Path for Water in a Nutshell*, Friends of the Earth Canada, Ottawa, ON, and POLIS Project on Ecological Governance, University of Victoria, Victoria, BC

Brandes, O. M., Maas, T., Mjolsness, A. and Reynolds, E. (2007) *A New Path to Water Sustainability for the Town of Oliver, BC – Soft Path Case Study*, POLIS Project on Ecological Governance, University of Victoria, Victoria, BC

Brooks, D. B. (2005) 'Comment on "Using economic instruments for water demand management: Introduction"', *Canadian Water Resources Journal*, vol 30, no 3, pp263–264

Gleick, P. H. (1998) 'The changing water paradigm: A look at twenty-first century water resources development', *Water International*, vol 25, no 1, pp127–138

Gleick, P. H., Haasz, D., Henges-Jeck, C., Srinivasan, V., Wolff, G., Cushing, K. and Mann, A. (2003) *Waste Not, Want Not: The Potential for Urban Water Conservation in California*, Pacific Institute for Studies in Development, Environment, and Security, Oakland, CA

Katz, D. (2006) 'Going with the flow: Preserving and restoring instream water allocations', in P. H. Gleick (ed) *The World's Water: 2006–2007*, Island Press, Washington, DC

Linton, J. (2009) *What Is Water? The History and Crisis of a Modern Abstraction*, UBC Press, Vancouver, BC

Lovins, A. B. (1976) 'Energy strategy: The road not taken', *Foreign Affairs*, vol 55, no 1, pp186–218

Millennium Ecosystem Assessment (2005) *Ecosystems and Human Well-Being: Wetlands and Water-Synthesis*, World Resources Institute, Washington, DC

Pielou, E. C. (1998) *Fresh Water*, University of Chicago Press, Chicago

Postel, S. (1997) *Last Oasis: Facing Water Scarcity*, W. W. Norton and Company, New York City

Raskin, P., Hansen, E. and Margolis, R. M. (1996) 'Water and sustainability: Global patterns and long-range problems', *Natural Resources Forum*, vol 20, no 1, pp1–15

Ricciardi, A. and Rasmussen, J. B. (1999) 'Extinction rates of North American fresh water fauna', *Conservation Biology*, vol 13, no 5, pp1220–1222

Serageldin, I. (1995) *Toward Sustainable Development of Water Resources*, World Bank, Washington, DC

Sprague, J. (2007) 'Great wet North? Canada's myth of water abundance', in K. Bakker (ed) *Eau Canada: The Future of Canada's Water*, UBC Press, Vancouver, BC

de Villiers, M. (1999) *Water*, Stoddart Publishing, Toronto

World Health Organization (2008) *UN Global Water Annual Assessment of Sanitation and Drinking Water*, Pilot report, World Health Organization, Geneva, www.who.int/water_sanitation_health/glaas_2008_pilot_finalreport.pdf

Part I
Water Soft Paths as Human Vision

2
Avoiding the Perfect Storm: Weathering Climate Change by Following its Effects on Water Resources

Robert W. Sandford

> *To date we have been as effective at curbing global warming as the old League of Nations was at preventing the Second World War.*
>
> Robert Strom

Circulating dangerously around the climate change threat are all the interpenetrating elements required to create a perfect storm of cascading global environmental, economic, social cum political circumstances. It is the duty of our generation to do everything we can to avoid creating that storm and to minimize its effects if we can't prevent it. One of the best ways of doing that is to protect our water resources.

The perfect storm in myth and fact

The notion of a perfect storm emerged into popular culture in 1997 with the appearance of Sebastion Junger's non-fiction work of the same name, which was also made into a popular Hollywood movie. The book is about the 'Halloween Nor'easter' as the locals called it – a storm that struck the east coast of North America in October of 1991. The story revolves around the crew of the fishing boat, the *Andrea Gail*, who were out for swordfish nearly

1000 kilometres off the coast of Massachusetts when the storm formed. It is a riveting story based on the hard facts of autumn seas.

It should be noted that it wasn't Sebastian Junger who first described the 1991 tempest as 'the perfect storm'. It was the US National Weather Service that gave it that name and created its legend. In the history of American weather observation, no one had ever seen anything quite like it.[1]

It was on 28 October 1991 that an extra-tropical cyclone developed along a cold front that had, in typical fashion, moved northward off the north-east coast of the US. This low, however, wasn't the only storm that existed at the time in the great expanse that is the Atlantic. Hurricane Grace, which had formed on 27 October from a pre-existing subtropical storm, was moving north-westward.

Grace was a large system and, though she remained far offshore, she was already generating 5-metre swells offshore of North Carolina. At first it looked as if she would just stay out there until she lost strength and dissipated, but then something unusual happened. A National Oceanic and Atmospheric Administration weather satellite observed that after their brief introduction Grace immediately took more than a passing interest in the stormy stranger that appeared to be dangling the prospect of a tempestuous union before her. The next day they embraced. Then the extra-tropical storm absorbed the hurricane. The two were suddenly one.

The combined storm was a colossus. The captain and crew of *Andrea Gail* were not the only ones surprised and then overwhelmed by the hurricane's intensity. The storm combined with high tides to cause extraordinary damage to infrastructure not designed for such extremes. Coastal flooding occurred along the Atlantic shoreline from Canada all the way down the American coast to as far south as Puerto Rico, the Dominican Republic and the Bahamas. Never before had weather and climate scientists on this continent seen so many seemingly disparate circumstances come together so perfectly to create such violent weather on such a massive scale.

The 1991 Halloween Nor'easter remained the perfect storm until 2005 when it was overshadowed by Hurricane Katrina, which flattened 250 kilometres of Gulf Coast coastline before turning the Mississippi River back on itself, destroying much of New Orleans. Some will argue that's a different story. But maybe it was simply a warning of other perfect storms to come.

The threat of global climate change

Another kind of perfect storm is gathering about us. This storm is not entirely natural in that we have had a hand in creating it. The perfect storm to which this essay refers is the one forming as wide-ranging human environmental impacts merge and converge on a warming globe.

Though weather and climate are different, all perfect storms have one thing in common. When conditions are just right, circumstances can align to create a serial combination of vulnerabilities that lead straight to disaster. We know all about the elements converging in our time to create this tempest. We are fully aware of the global environmental impacts caused by unrestrained growth of human populations and material desire. The converging trade-offs of food security, industrial development, habitat and biodiversity loss and destruction of ocean ecosystems have been expertly described and explained. We have been bickering over what to do about these issues for 50 years.

What is new about climate change is that in synergistic combination with other wide-ranging impacts, warming temperatures threaten to exacerbate already serious problems. Climate change is poised to absorb into itself the hurricane that we have already created through population explosion, landscape change and global water scarcity. At the moment, climate change also appears poised to overwhelm institutional structures designed for an earlier, more climatically stable era of human existence. Poverty, deteriorating environmental conditions, jealously protected private property precedents, short-sighted economic and market imperatives, self-centred social preferences, unbelievable waste, the increasingly atomized and contaminated nature of public discourse and the reduced capacity of contemporary political frameworks to function in a timely manner in addressing urgent issues are all lining up globally in just the right way to create a hurricane of their own, just waiting to be absorbed into the perfect storm of global warming.

Contributing elements of a perfect storm

As evidenced by the difficulty we have had in coming to a consensus on the fact that global warming is even happening, there are aspects of the global climate change problem that put into bold relief profound weaknesses in the capacity of our society to organize around threats of this magnitude.

First of all, the most rapidly occurring and accelerating changes are taking place in parts of the world where there are the fewest people, at the poles and in the highest mountain ranges. Changes that always seem – to North Americans at least – to be occurring elsewhere in the world are happening when the fewest people are up or about – at night and in winter. Because greenhouse gases trap the heat radiated by the earth, the greenhouse effect is most noticeable when there is the least heat from the sun, which is at night and in winter.

There has also never been a time in history when so many people have congregated in cities where they are far less likely to be in contact with changes in natural rhythms. In addition, people spend more time than ever inside houses, offices, restaurants, planes and cars. We are shielded from obvious evidence of climate change by the elaborate global infrastructure that envelops us when we travel.

Global warming is also happening at a time in history – and is in part caused by – a degree of human physical mobility never before imagined. Our mobility presents unique challenges. If you have never lived in a place for more than five years, how would you know if the climate of that place was changing? We live in the first era in the history of our species in which we need scientists to tell us spring is coming earlier and fall later. (Then, as if offended with the suggestion that we should have figured this out for ourselves, we often dismiss and sometimes censor them for telling us so.)

Another factor contributing to the perfect storm coalescing around climate change is the fact that the most significant potential impacts of climate change are at present barely discernable. The reason for this is that small temperature changes have the greatest impact at the most fundamental levels at which our ecosystems function.

Very small changes in temperature are magnified in significance at the molecular and cellular interface. These changes will alter first what happens at the viral level and then extend into the huge universe that is bacterial life; then move upward into the insect kingdom. At this level small temperate differences are often barriers to species ranges at both microbiological and macrobiotic levels.[2]

The impacts of rising temperature regimes are already moving erratically up the life chain to affect the physiology and then the behaviour and range of plants and animals. In many of the world's forests, clear-cutting is resulting in more rapid ecological change than in the past as startling arrays of invasive plants and animals take advantage of the changes induced by climate change and scramble to colonize freshly disturbed landscapes (Hellum, 2008).

Very small changes in temperature also affect the water–ice interface which impacts soil temperature and moisture retention, which in turn affects the timing and extent of water supply (Armstrong and Brun, 2008). Changes in the dynamics of the water–ice interface could have huge impacts, particularly in circumpolar countries where this interface defines many ecological circumstances.

Gambling with our future

We know that it is entirely possible that an increase in global atmospheric temperature can trigger feedbacks that will make global warming its own cause – and this is the most frightening aspect of the influence humans are having on climate (Strom, 2008; Broecker and Kunzig, 2008). We know what these feedbacks are but we still don't know if or when they will kick in.[3]

We still think that if we simply develop a few new emissions reduction technologies that the thermostat will stop rising. In nature, however, one thing is inevitably connected and leads to another. We do not know enough about either climate or ecological systems to predict exactly what will happen at a great many levels. We do know, however, that by the time the average person fully grasps these changes for what they really mean, they will already be of significant magnitude and irreversible in direction. When that happens we will have created a perfect storm.

Observers have called the 20-year Intergovernmental Panel on Climate Change's ongoing assessment of global climate change the greatest peer-reviewed research project in the history of science. This massive research initiative has resulted at last in a consensus on the fact that climate change is happening and that we are driving a good measure of the warming we are experiencing. Unfortunately, our society isn't very well structured to deal with long-term problems of this scope. Economic agendas and other issues always seem to be far more pressing. However, the real cost is paid by the environment, and over the long run, those impacts cost the global economy far more than what is spent to rescue our economy from its periodic crises.

Additionally, climate change does not fall easily within existing risk management frameworks and processes. Over the past two decades, planning processes in North America and abroad have come to be dominated by strategic planning directives and language that favour a short-term focus on immediately measurable results and accompanying results-based reward structures (Korton, 2001; Dessler and Parson, 2006). This direction in corporate strategic planning has also been adopted by governments at all levels.

The net impact has been the contraction of planning horizons from multiyear to annual to quarterly down to monthly and even weekly performance parameters that, by design, ignore long-term trends until they become urgent immediate threats. This short-term focus is a disaster when it comes to managing creeping, long-term challenges such as climate change. By the time global warming becomes an urgent threat it will have become a colossus and we will not have the tools to deal with it.

Following water towards understanding and adaptation

We know that our planet's remaining, relatively intact, functioning ecosystems slow and can even moderate the impacts of climate change. We know also that water plays an important function in this process (Daily, 1997). What is happening to our water resources on a global scale is widely regarded as a measure of what is happening to both our landscapes and to our climate. If they are not indeed different manifestations of the same thing, then water and climate are at least married.

As climate change clearly threatens to impact how much water is available and when, we should carefully examine the link between them. Land, water and climate are reflections of one another. By managing one, we are in effect managing the other. For that reason alone we need to take land use impacts seriously. And the best measure of how well we are doing in the management of land use is expressed by local water quality and supply.

This suggests an immediate need for additional monitoring and interpretation of expanded hydro-meteorological data; enhanced understanding of present and future surface and groundwater flow regimes; and support for aquatic ecosystem research. Only through better, more thorough monitoring can we develop modelling techniques that will allow us to more effectively predict and slow climate change impacts on global water availability. It will also be important to strengthen mechanisms for resolving potential and actual conflicts over water allocation and use.

Valuing eco-hydrological services

At present there are a great many benefits of biodiversity that remain external to present economic models and not yet assigned market prices, but that are nonetheless highly valued. Examples of ecosystem services that depend on healthy biodiversity include pollination, biological water filtration, detoxification and breakdown of wastes, suppression of pests and diseases, nutrient conversions, maintenance of soil cover, perpetuation of healthy wildlife populations and fish stocks.

Law makers and public policy scholars around the world are reacting to ground-breaking research that indicates that natural ecosystems may be far more important to our global economy than many of us may have appreciated (Safriel, 2008). The hydro-ecological principle at the core of this insight is breathtakingly simple: nature has survival value to people and much of that survival value is defined by the fact that nature is our only provider of water. In order to provide water and other critical benefits to people, nature, however, needs water, too. We need water to prime the pump – so to speak – and the hydrological cycle is a very large pump.

It follows then – and this is the important and painfully obvious part – that, if we want it to continue to receive valuable ecosystem services on a free basis, nature must be regarded in the context of water resources management decision-making as a legitimate water customer in its own right.

Current eco-hydrological research underscores much of what humans have known intuitively for generations. Healthy aquatic ecosystems contribute far more than we ever understood to the production of water through the hydrological cycle as well as to the self-purifying power of healthy wetlands, lakes and rivers. Intact aquatic ecosystems function synergistically with neighbouring terrestrial complexes to provide regulating services such as those that control rainwater capture, enhance the storage of water in ecosystems, and facilitate the gradual release of the water that perpetuates stream flow throughout the year.

These functions in turn are responsible for the primary production of organisms that make life on Earth possible and that form the foundation of more complex ecosystems that lead to higher life forms and relationships. Together, primary production and soil formation are the basis of the biodiversity that is at the heart of the relative ecosystem stability that has defined our planet's atmospheric composition. Our atmospheric composition is in turn the foundation of the relative climate stability upon which our civilization has relied to sustain population growth and increasing economic prosperity over the past several hundred years. Natural ecosystem function is also the foundation of the ecological diversity that makes agricultural food production for our growing populations possible.

As we come to realize the importance of water's role in the stabilization of natural and agricultural ecosystems, we begin to see the ways in which our numbers may be altering the very systems upon which we depend to sustain planetary conditions, as we know them. Currently, global human population growth is the highest in places where there is the least water. About 40 per cent of the surface of the solid Earth receives so little precipitation that natural ecosystem function is limited by water availability (Safriel, 2008). Thus we find that globally, a third of humanity is now competing directly with nature for water.

Storm clouds on the horizon

The current global water crisis has been brought about as a result of the tripling of demand for water over the last 50 years. As Lester Brown (2008) of the Earth Policy Institute has pointed out, the drilling of millions of irrigation wells has pushed water withdrawals far beyond recharge rates in many places, in effect leading to groundwater mining. The failure to limit pumping to the sustainable yield of aquifers means that water tables are now falling in countries in which half the world's population lives; including three of the world's greatest grain producers – China, India and the US. Since the over-pumping of aquifers is occurring in many countries simultaneously, the depletion of aquifers and resulting grain harvest reductions could come at roughly the same time. The accelerating depletion of aquifers worldwide means that this day could come about soon, creating the potential for almost unimaginable food scarcity.

Researchers at the Brace Centre for Water Resources Management at McGill University in Montreal have calculated that, to meet the food demands that are projected to exist in the world in 2025, we will need to put an additional 2000 cubic kilometres of water into irrigation (Madramootoo, 2004). This amount is roughly equivalent to 24 times the average flow of the Nile. Given current water use patterns, the population that is projected to exist on the planet in 2050 will require 3800 cubic kilometres of water per year, which is close to all the freshwater that can presently be withdrawn on Earth.

This would mean that the world would lose most of the important environmental services that aquatic ecosystems currently provide on our behalf. Clearly, that is just not going to happen. Something has to give – and that is exactly what is happening.

We are beginning to observe that rapidly expanding urban centres have begun to compete with agriculture for both land and water on a global basis. Agriculture has, in turn, begun to compete with nature for land and water. We are increasingly concerned that we cannot meet both agricultural and urban needs while at the same time providing enough water to ensure the perpetuation of natural ecosystem function. As a consequence of growing populations and increased competition for land and water, humanity is converging upon the need to make uncommonly difficult public policy trade-offs that have never had to be made on a global scale before:

- If we provide to nature the water it needs to perpetuate our planetary life-support system, then much of that water will have to come at the expense of agriculture, which means that many people will have to starve to meet ecosystem protection goals.

- If, on the other hand, we provide agriculture all the water it needs to have any hope of feeding the populations that are projected to exist even in 2025, then we must expect ongoing deterioration of the biodiversity-based ecosystem function that has generated Earth's current conditions, upon which our society depends both for its stability and sustainability.

Getting our global house in order

To avoid making climate change into a perfect storm we have to get our global house in order. Having our house in order means achieving a meaningful level of sustainability. There are at least three major problem areas that need to be addressed if we are to achieve anything close to the level of sustainability that will allow us to adapt to climate change.

Challenge 1: Acknowledging the seriousness of the problem

The first challenge we have to address is our own perception of the seriousness of the problem. We are deluding ourselves when we think that we have the water–climate nexus in hand. We think that, because we can afford to engineer our way out of short-term water availability and quality issues, we are creating a sustainable water management future. There is no guarantee that this is so.

We have, over the last century, destroyed a great deal of our planet's natural aquatic ecosystem function and replaced it wherever possible or necessary with technology. However, artificial technological replacements for natural and passively managed ecosystem function invariably turn out to be expensive and inferior to ecosystem-provided goods and services. If eco-hydrology has anything to teach us, it is that there are things nature does on our behalf that we don't know how and can't afford to do for ourselves. What we are effectively doing is putting nature and all of humanity on dialysis.

The cumulative effects of our global engineering efforts on our planet's life support function are increasingly measurable. The point is not that we should stop relying on engineering solutions. We can't go back now. If anything we need solid engineering solutions more than ever. The point is that we need to improve our understanding not just of fundamental eco-hydrological function, but of the expanded services that our natural, agricultural and urban ecosystems might be able to provide in the future and engineer toward realization of that potential. But here's the kicker. We then have to reserve enough water through our management mechanisms to make sure these ecosystems have the water they need to perform these functions – and to do so both under current circumstances and under the altered circumstances in which we may have to live as a consequence of higher mean global temperatures.

We need to encourage the ongoing, interdisciplinary collaboration between eco-hydrology and engineering. The protection of our water resources in the face of a changing global climate gives us a damn good reason for doing so.

Challenge 2: Valuing emerging eco-hydrological perspectives

The second challenge we need to address relates to what we must do to make room for emerging eco-hydrological considerations in the way we manage water. Until we do this, we will continue to make public policy choices based on false assumptions that will have undesirable ecological, social and political consequences in the future.

Current developments in our global market economy put into relief lessons we might learn from advanced research into eco-hydrological relations in natural systems. Unlike our economy in the last few years, nature's economy is highly self-regulated. Every component influences and therefore regulates every other. The more complex the system, the greater the number of self-regulatory elements it possesses. The greater the number of contributing and regulating influences in a system, the greater the resilience of that system to extreme disruption.

Biodiversity works to prevent natural economies from being overwhelmed by singular events. Because of this feedback, life on this planet has been able to bounce back from at least five major astrophysical and geomorphological events that threatened to wipe out almost all planetary ecosystem function in the Earth's past (Ward, 2007). However, biodiversity-based ecosystem productivity operates at its own slow pace, which is often deemed too slow to satisfy human needs. In many parts of the world, hydrological cycles no longer produce enough water to meet human supply needs, nor are natural aquatic and terrestrial ecosystems able to store, purify and transport water fast enough to provide enough clean water where we want it when we need it.

To overcome these natural ecosystem limitations we have, over time, employed engineering solutions that aim to achieve the goal of optimizing water supply and water quality assurance to meet our own very specific needs. Though they often enhance the reliability and safety of water supply, those engineering solutions often directly affect natural hydrological cycles and diminish beneficial natural ecosystem functioning. It is also important to remember that natural and aquatic ecosystems do not exist just to supply and purify water for human use.

Challenge 3: We must improve processes of governance

The third big challenge we face relates to governance (Brandes, Chapter 5 in this book). Many prominent scientists and public policy scholars, around the world, fear that our environmental problems could get away from us simply because we failed to build a strong enough bridge between science and public policy. If we are to achieve anything resembling long-term sustainability, science needs to find better ways to give decision-makers the perspectives and language they need to craft durable public policy options in a timely and effective manner. It is not just local issues to which policy-makers must be attuned. We also have to provide political leaders at all levels the perspectives they need to act upon knowledge about what is happening *elsewhere* that may affect them in their unique local context.

Very real problems exist globally that are associated with jurisdictional fragmentation, weak regulatory strictures and the absence of proper monitoring. There is a growing sense in some influential quarters that our global water management problems will go away if we simply let the marketplace do its magic. Though one cannot object to markets as a means for managing increasingly scarce water resources, we know from international example that even carefully developed water markets cannot make up for failures of government to offer the kind of appropriate oversight that can only emerge through strong regulatory frameworks (Ingram, 2008).

As we have seen abundantly recently in the US, the market serves itself first and does not serve the common good unless government demands that it do so. As the famous economist John Maynard Keynes said half a century ago, the market is an excellent servant but a terrible master. In our efforts to confront well-identified future challenges, we need to aim for far more than just market efficiency (Whitely et al, 2008).

As University of Arizona water scholar Helen Ingram has written, before we contemplate the need for better water policy on a global basis, we must ask ourselves some fundamental questions: What is our water policy really about? Is it about market efficiency? Is it about decentralization and local participation in water resource decision-making? Is it about sustainability? Or should it be about all of these things together?

Towards a new world water ethic

What we need is a new global water ethic that encourages harmonization of regional, national and local water resource aspirations. Under the aegis of that ethic, we need to ensure formal representation for the environment itself and ways to advocate for nature's own need for water so as to perpetuate biodiversity-based, ecosystem productivity.

If we can balance the water availability and quality needs of nature, agriculture and our cities, many other things we need to do, including achieving sustainability, may very well fall into line. And most importantly, we may be able to avoid turning climate change into a perfect storm.

Notes

1 The National Ocean and Atmospheric Administration in the US still maintains a website explaining the nature and character of that remarkable combination of weather events: www.ncdc.noaa.gov/oa/satellite/satelliteseye/cyclones/pfctstorm91/pfctstorm.html
2 Perhaps the most obvious case where minor changes in temperature have dramatically affected ecosystem composition are those regions of North America where pine-bark beetle (*Dendroctonus ponderosae*) populations have exploded resulting in the devastation of millions of hectares of mountain forest. While the range of this species was largely inhibited historically by regular winter temperatures below −40°C, warmer winters have allowed this pest to advance its

range northward where there are now concerns it may jump to jack-pine species and threaten the entire northern boreal forest.

3 Those with an interest in leading-edge research currently being undertaken on climate change feedbacks in the Arctic may wish to familiarize themselves with the research presently being conducted as part of the Improved Processes and Perameterisation for Prediction in Cold Regions (IP3) scientific research in Canada. Among the many projects being undertaken as part of this major research project is a study on the rate of loss of permafrost in the Yukon Territory. Research conducted by Dr William Quinton of Wilfrid Laurier University and others indicates that most of the permafrost in this part of the Arctic is at a mean annual temperature of −0.1°C to −0.2°C. At the rate of melt that has been observed between 1947 and 2000, it was estimated that it would take 90 years for permafrost in the study area to disappear. At the rate of melt that has been witnessed between 2000 and 2008, however, the permafrost in the study area is not expected to last more than 30 years (see www.usask.ca/ip3/).

References

Armstrong, R. L. and Brun, E. (2008) *Snow and Climate: Physical Processes, Surface Exchange and Modeling*, Cambridge University Press, Cambridge

Broecker, W. S. and Kunzig, R. (2008) *Fixing Climate: What Past Climate Changes Reveal About the Current Threat – And How To Counter It*, Hill and Wang (Farrar, Straus and Giroux), New York, NY

Brown, L. (2008) *Plan B 3.0: Mobilizing To Save Civilization*, Earth Policy Institute, W. W. Norton, New York, NY; see especially ch 4, 'Emerging water shortages', pp68–84

Daily, G. (1997) *Nature's Services: Societal Dependence on Natural Ecosystems*, Island Press, Washington, DC; see ch 5, 'The interaction of climate and life', pp71–72

Dessler, A. and Parson, E. A. (2006) *The Science and Politics of Global Climate Change: A Guide to the Debate*, Cambridge University Press, Cambridge

Hellum, A. K. (2008) *Listening To Trees*, NeWest Press, Edmonton, AB

Ingram, H. (2008) *Institutional Challenges in Providing for Environmental Water*, Iranian-US Workshop on Water Management, Rosenberg International Forum on Water Policy and the US National Academy of Science, University of California at Irvine; available at www.rosenberg.ucanr.org/

Korton, D. C. (2001) *When Corporations Rule the World*, 2nd Edition, Berrett-Koehler, Bloomfield, CT

Madramootoo, C. (2004) *Confronting Water Scarcity in Agriculture*, a paper presented at the Confronting Water Scarcity Conference, University of Lethbridge, Lethbridge, AB

Safriel, A. (2008) *Balancing Water for People and Nature*, paper presented at Rosenberg International Forum on Water Policy held in Zaragoza, Spain; available at www.rosenberg.ucanr.org/forum6

Strom, R. (2008) *Hot House: Global Climate Change and the Human Condition*, Copernicus Books (Springer-Verlag), New York, NY

Ward, P. (2007) *Under a Green Sky: Global Warming, the Mass Extinctions of the Past and What They Can Tell Us About Our Future*, Smithsonian Books, Washington, DC

Whitely, J. M., Ingram, H. and Perry, R. (2008) *Water, Place, and Equity*, MIT Press, Cambridge, MA

3

In the Beginning: Soft Energy Paths

Susan Holtz and David B. Brooks

The economy is a wholly owned subsidiary of the environment.
Margaret Atwood

By the early years of the 1970s, the environmental movement in North America and Western Europe was on its way to becoming a cultural and political force.[1] Increasing public concern about environmental degradation had resulted in new legislation, new government agencies and a multitude of new environmental non-government organizations (ENGOs). Names such as Greenpeace and Friends of the Earth became known throughout OECD countries and, in almost every city or region, local groups became active. No longer made up mainly of university students and activists, these groups also included academics and even a few business executives able to use science and economics to argue persuasively for the environmental agenda (Leiss, 1979). And, no less important, the United Nations (UN) had begun to react with the first of a series of global conferences (Stone, 1973; Ward, 1976).

At the same time, this period also witnessed a huge increase in the number of proposals for new energy mega-projects. These projects ranged from hydro dams in wilderness areas, to oil and gas production in the Arctic, to new coal mines, uranium mines and nuclear generating stations. As might be expected, environmentalists and other locally affected groups started to become concerned about these proposed projects and their impacts, social and economic as well as biophysical. And some of these groups and individuals began to raise fundamental questions about the actual need for so much energy. Could there really be a demand for as many as 30 nuclear reactor units in the Canadian Maritime provinces by 2000, as an Atomic Energy of Canada Ltd projection had suggested?

True, for the two preceding decades, energy demand had been growing rapidly, fuelled by low oil prices and the post-war economic expansion. For energy project proponents, and many economic commentators, the parallel link between growth in energy use and growth in gross domestic product (GDP) seemed not only strong historically but self-evidently necessary. Of course these new supply projects would be needed!

Then in 1973 came the first energy crisis (more accurately, 'oil crisis'). With little warning, the Arab oil producers embargoed the US for some months, and the Organization of Petroleum Exporting Countries (OPEC) declared they would no longer negotiate but would instead adopt a take-it-or-leave-it approach to oil pricing. By the end of 1974 the price of a barrel of oil was eight times higher than it had been five years earlier (Stobaugh and Yergin, 1983, p4). The resulting impacts shocked the Western world, both economically and politically. Higher home heating bills, long line-ups at the gas (petrol) pump and higher costs for many goods and services brought the situation home to consumers. Almost overnight, politicians and business leaders became concerned about the security of national energy supplies, and many people called on governments to accelerate plans for new domestic energy sources. Toward the end of 1978 and into 1979, tight oil supplies and political events in the Middle East brought a second series of major oil price hikes, which added to the political and economic consternation.

The stage was thus set in 1973 for the fierce battles that erupted throughout the following decade between environmentalists opposed to new mega-projects and mainstream interests who insisted on the crucial need to increase domestic energy supplies. The intensity of the debate was not lessened because both sides had valid points to make. It had become clearer than ever before how dependent the very fabric of society was on energy, and that disruptions in supply and/or sudden price increases could threaten a country's social and political stability and economic well-being.

At the same time, massive new energy projects undeniably did impose substantial and highly visible social, economic and environmental costs. In addition, mounting scientific evidence had begun to show that some health and ecological impacts could also be subtle and distant in time and space from their point of origin. For example, ionizing radiation risks, relevant to the nuclear industry, came under review in the early 1970s for possible upward revision for future cancers and genetic effects, and acid precipitation was found to damage forests hundreds of kilometres from the coal-fired power plants whose emissions were the source of the problem. The real impact boundaries for energy use and energy projects were turning out to be much larger than had once been assumed.

This intellectual impasse about energy policy was the catalyst that led to the concept of *soft energy paths*. The term is taken from analyst Amory B. Lovins' first major essay on the subject, 'Energy strategy: The road not taken?', which was published in the prestigious journal *Foreign Affairs* (Lovins, 1976, pp186–218) and subsequently elaborated in a book (Lovins, 1977). Lovins drew two opposing pictures of the energy future. One relied on centralized, large-scale, capital-intensive technologies to meet unconstrained, rapidly rising demand (the 'hard path'). The other emphasized radical improvements in energy efficiency as the primary focus, with new supply coming mainly from smaller-scale renewable sources (the 'soft path').

Lovins and other soft path analysts around the world took both sides of the energy security versus environment debate absolutely seriously. They accepted that decision-makers must consider and plan for energy security, and that economics did matter. Above all, when challenged as to how, exactly, the demand for energy was going to be met, soft path proponents did not simply point generally to more environmentally benign renewable technologies and conservation. A substantive response required hard numbers. This requirement was met by the soft path analysts: their conceptual analysis was extended to incorporate more economics (Ross and Williams, 1981) and, in a dozen or more mainly industrialized countries, scenarios were developed that provided comprehensive, quantitative energy supply-and-demand balances based on these alternative technologies (see Bibliography in Bott et al, 1983).

Never before – and not again until water soft paths were studied nearly 30 years later – had environmentalists created such a concrete vision for an entire sector of the economy. Analytically, it meant designing scenarios that took into account real-world constraints, and, in creating those scenarios, making choices that were not always ideal, yet kept sight of overriding environmental and social goals. For social critics, this was not the most comfortable approach to take, nor was it necessarily the most effective way to stop a specific project. However, in the context of sustainable development – a more inclusive concept which came well over a decade later (World Commission, 1987) – this provided a valuable model for public policy debate, especially when dealing with issues involving a multitude of problems, varying consequences of dealing with them, and no single best route to achieving economic, social and environmental goals.

How does the soft path differ from conventional thinking?

Soft paths, regardless of whether they focus on energy or water or anything else, differ from conventional approaches to natural resource planning and management in important ways. For historical interest and the light that hindsight can shed, this chapter will focus on the details of soft *energy* paths. However, the comments can, for the most part, be generalized to all soft path work. As it happens, energy policy choices at this time are again taking place against a background of rising oil prices, awareness of physical as well as geopolitical limitations on future supplies and concerns about climate change. These issues reflect the same themes as those earlier energy debates and a wider understanding of the soft energy path approach is remarkably relevant in the current energy policy arena.

Our main point here is to explain the origin and illustrate the application of soft path ideas. In Chapter 6 we will emphasize specific differences that arise when soft path concepts are applied to water rather than energy. For the moment, we will only note that, in the shift from energy to water, a minor change in terminology was necessary. The term 'soft water' had long been used to refer to water that is low in carbonates, and that therefore produces suds in the kitchen and does not leave scale deposits on industrial boilers. To avoid confusion, the noun and adjective were reversed; 'soft energy paths' are comparable with 'water soft paths'.

What, then, are the differences between soft paths and conventional thinking about energy policy?

First, soft energy paths do not look to increasing supply as the primary way to 'fuel the future'. Rather, they ask what kinds of services are needed for a given society at some given future time. We will elaborate the point about 'services' later. It is sufficient to emphasize here that *demand reduction* through different kinds of efficiency improvements and alternative choices is always the first priority.

Second, and even more fundamental, soft energy paths are not primarily about technology. They are about *values*. A soft strategy is driven by a set of choices that explicitly take into account key environmental, economic and social considerations. The decisions about what considerations to incorporate are profoundly normative; thus, a different set or weighting of these values-based choices would mean a different outcome for the strategy. Of course, no approach to energy policy is value-free. However, most policy analysts treat values implicitly by burying them in the analysis. In contrast, soft path analysts not only clearly identify those values, but also insist that they should be the starting point for the analysis, along with the values-related implications that are *de facto* results of all energy decisions.

Third, a soft path approach relies on a soft path *strategy* – choices based on an analytically rigorous overview of a given jurisdiction's energy demand and supply for a specified future period. Unlike advocates for some particular technology, such as hydrogen or nuclear power, who see that source as *the* answer for the energy future, soft path analysts evaluate the usefulness of all technologies within the overall picture of the entire energy sector.

This approach includes looking at what, when and where different categories of energy services are required. It also means reviewing cost, timing and political, social and environmental consequences of available options as comprehensively as possible. It includes using some 'less bad' fossil fuels, notably natural gas, that are needed as transitional sources on the way to better alternatives. The ecological dictum that 'you can never do only one thing' is its touchstone.

All technologies and, indeed, all purposive human activities have not only their intended positive results, but also a host of unintended effects, many negative. For energy, such unintended consequences include climate change, acid precipitation and health-damaging air pollution, as well as societal vulnerability to ice storms and terrorist attacks. Even energy efficiency can have some negative impacts; for example, if houses designed to reduce air infiltration don't have adequate ventilation, poor indoor air quality and health problems can be a result. Thus a soft path strategy, even while making difficult choices, keeps as comprehensive a view as possible of context, constraints and a full range of implications, recognizing that there are no simple, all-encompassing solutions.

For all of these reasons, soft paths do not attempt to provide forecasts, that is, estimates of where the society *will* be at some point in the future. Rather, they explore the viability of some particular future scenario – more commonly a set of scenarios – that reflects an emphasis on certain environmental, social and economic considerations. Scenarios permit longer-term analysis, which is critical when dealing with societal and technological change. Typical soft path scenarios look a minimum of 25 and commonly 40 or 50 years into the future. They are not useful for looking just a few years ahead.

Soft path technologies

Over the years, different soft path analysts have formulated the essential characteristics of soft technologies – technologies appropriate to a soft path approach – in various ways. The key points behind the different formulations, however, are the same, so it is appropriate to return to Lovins' now-classic description (Lovins, 1977; italics in original).

- 'They rely on renewable energy flows that are always there, whether we use them or not, such as sun and wind and vegetation: on energy income, not on depletable energy capital.'
- 'They are diverse, so that, as a national treasury runs on many small tax contributions, so national energy supply is an aggregate of very many individually modest contributions, each designed for maximum effectiveness in particular circumstances.'
- 'They are flexible and relatively low technology – which does not mean unsophisticated, but rather, easy to understand and use without esoteric skills; accessible rather than arcane …'
- 'They are matched in *scale* and in geographic distribution to end use needs, taking advantage of the free distribution of most natural energy flows.'
- 'They are matched in *energy quality* to end use needs …'

Some analysts add such terms as *relatively environmentally benign* and *safe-fail* to underline the safety and environmental concerns driving the analysis, or *decentralized* to make that element more explicit. However, the core principles remain as Lovins originally stated them.

The first three characteristics are easy enough to understand, but the last two, and especially the terms *end-use needs* and *energy quality*, require explanation. Much of the planning around energy is concerned with the availability and price of primary energy supplies such as coal, crude oil and natural gas. However, what we really want is not the energy resource for its own sake – having a barrel of crude on the front porch, or a pile of coal in the backyard – but for the *energy services* it provides. We don't want natural gas for our furnace, we want a warm house; we don't want gasoline for the car, we want to be able to haul things and get around. For analytical purposes, almost all *end-use energy needs* can be grouped into just a few categories:

- lower-temperature heat, eg, for warming homes or water;
- higher-temperature heat needed for industrial purposes;
- electricity-specific, as for electric motors, lighting and electronics;
- motive power for transportation.

A fifth end-use for petroleum products is as a direct input to make plastics and other petrochemicals, and these uses require special treatment.

Defining energy 'needs' in terms of the services that are actually required puts energy conservation and energy supply on an even footing when considering the environment, price and other factors. It should be noted that neither energy supply nor energy conservation activities can be undertaken without causing environmental impacts, but those resulting from supply are enormously higher. Moreover, from the early analyses of cost effectiveness through to the present, reducing demand has almost always turned out to be cheaper than increasing supply (Ross and Williams, 1981; Lovins et al, 2004).

Physicists have understood differences in *energy quality* for many years, but it was soft path analysts who introduced this concept into energy policy. Our energy accounting system measures energy (the ability to do work) in units such as the kilowatt-hour, the British thermal unit (Btu), or the joule in the Système International d'Unités (SI). In this sense, a joule is always a joule in that it always performs the same quantity of work. However, from a user's point of view, the kind of work (energy service) that you need is what matters. Different forms of energy, like electricity or solar radiation or natural gas, have different capabilities for delivering different categories of energy services and, hence, different qualities. If we want to use our available energy supplies effectively, we need to match the appropriate quality of energy to the service required and reserve the highest quality energy for the most demanding services.

Using technologies that *match energy quality to end-use needs* has relevance to both efficiency improvements and energy planning. This can be demonstrated by looking at the fact that a large portion of society's end-use needs is for low quality energy in the form of low-temperature heat. (Think about raising room temperatures to comfortable levels, a matter of tens of degrees in most cases.) Using electricity generated thermally (eg, in coal- or gas-fired power plants) – a high-quality form of energy – to provide these services, greatly reduces efficiency in terms of the thermodynamic potential of the fuel.

The significance for energy planning is that conventional forecasts incorporated the requirements for the coal or other fuels used to produce thermally generated electricity. When that high-quality electricity was used for low-temperature heating, forecasts of overall energy demand were effectively inflated because of that inherently wasteful use of resources. This was one reason why energy planners at first regarded the much lower energy use scenarios in soft energy path studies with scepticism. No one had previously explored the impact on primary energy demand that a mismatch of end-use and energy quality could produce, nor the savings to be gained from addressing it (Ross and Williams, 1981).

Results of typical soft energy path studies

In the wake of Lovins' work, some of which he developed in Canada for the then Science Council of Canada, soft energy analyses were undertaken in many (mainly industrialized) countries of the world. In total some 35 other soft path studies have been published, for countries ranging from Denmark to India.

The Canadian soft energy path study was one of the largest and most detailed of these analyses (Bott et al, 1983; Brooks et al, 1983). It had three uniquely Canadian characteristics: first, methodologically it was undertaken as a set of 10 linked provincial studies plus one for the Northern Territories that, when integrated, represented all of Canada. Second, it was built on studies at Statistics Canada that provided a model of the Canadian economy based on energy flows rather than dollar flows. Third, it was funded by federal government agencies that knew, a priori, that they were likely to oppose the recommendations that would emerge.

The more conservative of the two scenarios of the Canadian study concluded the following (Brooks et al, 1983, p241):

> *Under conditions of strong economic growth (an increase of more than 200 per cent in GDP) and moderate population growth (an increase of over 50 per cent), it would be technically feasible and cost-effective to operate the Canadian economy in 2025 with 12 per cent less energy than it requires today, and, over the same 47-year period, to shift from 16 per cent reliance on renewable sources to 77 per cent.*

It is worth noting that the study results for the same scenario, at the interim point of 2000, showed an *increase* in energy use of about 4 per cent. This simply demonstrates how long it takes, as a result of the slow turnover of housing stock, cars, appliances and industrial equipment, for major improvements in energy efficiency to take hold.

The dramatic Canadian results were not atypical for alternative energy studies. For example, a panel of experts from the National Academy of Science in the US created a number of scenarios for 2010, one of which demonstrated that similar lifestyles and economic growth could be provided in the US using almost 20 per cent less energy than was used in the late 1970s (Stobaugh and Yergin, 1983).

And then the 1990s

Energy prices stopped climbing after the mid-1980s and, in the case of crude oil, even dropped back nearly to 1973 levels (a drop caused largely by the energy glut brought about by reduced demand). Prices then remained relatively stable until after 2000, when oil prices in particular started to rise once again. Efficiency improvements continued to gain some ground in North America and Europe. Their scope was enormous, and most made good economic sense even with lower energy prices. Better information and government financial support of various energy efficiency programmes, as well as wider awareness of the multiple benefits of energy efficiency, also played strong roles in this process.

In light of lower-than-anticipated conventional energy prices, the analysts who did the Canadian soft path study had to revisit their earlier scenarios. A shorter, revised Canadian study incorporated oil prices that were roughly half those used previously (Torrie et al, 1988). The earlier conclusion about the viability of a significantly more efficient energy system was barely changed at all. However, the competitiveness and the practicality of most renewable supply options were greatly reduced. With minor exceptions, only wood (for heating) and hydroelectricity remained economically attractive. The other renewable sources had been replaced, mainly by natural gas.

Given that the major soft energy path study done for Canada had 2025 as its end point, perhaps the right question is not 'Are we there yet?' but rather 'Are we going in the right direction?' The answer seems to be 'Yes', but it is a very qualified 'Yes'. There is now an immense range of new and improved technologies and methods to conserve energy. Virtually none of these come close to the 'hair-shirt' lifestyles and economic stagnation that many pundits in the 1970s had viewed as synonymous with energy conservation (and as a few politicians and commentators evidently still do). However, just as in the 1970s, transportation remains by far the most difficult problem. Only with the rocketing upward movement of oil prices in 2007 and 2008 did serious attention return to automobile and truck efficiency, to alternative supply options and to planning for less automobile-dependent communities.

One striking difference between the 1970s and the present in Canada is that, during the earlier period, exported energy was about one-fifth of domestic demand, whereas now it is around four-fifths and moving toward equality. Much of this energy production goes to the US, where there has been little political commitment to energy conservation. Consequently, even if Canada were wholeheartedly to adopt a domestic soft energy approach, there would still be significant negative social and environmental impacts from the high rates of energy production in Canada and the high rates of energy use in the US.

Renewable energy technologies have lagged in Canada, although by the new millennium attention was beginning to turn to wind power, solar heating and other options as part of a growing interest in a 'greener' society. Wood heating, now with more efficient technology, began its modern resurgence in the 1970s. Its use has grown so much that, by 1997, it was contributing twice as much energy as nuclear sources (6 per cent vs 3 per cent). Wood fuel, in some cases as logs but more often as compressed and pelletized pulp, has also made a comeback in northern Europe, Scotland and Austria, where it is as widely used to generate electricity as it is to heat buildings.

Since about 2005, the pace of other forms of renewable energy use has also begun to pick up. Installed wind capacity has grown at about 30 per cent a year in the last few years, and stood at 1876MW by 2007, according to the Canadian Wind Energy Association. Similarly, the solar industry association in this country claims that the Canadian industry has been growing at about 45 per cent a year during this decade. During the same period, however, European countries have done much more to promote renewable energy. The Global Wind Energy Council states that by 2007, there were 56,535MW of installed wind capacity in Europe, with an overall EU target for 2010 of 21 per cent of electricity generated from renewable sources. Discussions about higher targets for 2015 are ongoing, with Germany, Denmark, Spain and the UK leading the way in wind applications.

Overall, while Canada has not exactly been following the soft path that the Canadian study mapped out, increased energy conservation and the curtailment of hard path projects indicate that the country has not been going in the opposite direction, either. It remains to be seen which of a number of sometimes contradictory considerations, such as the public outcry about rising gasoline prices, or, in contrast, the growing awareness of the environmental implications of growing energy demand, will dominate the direction of Canada's energy policy choices over the next few years.

Re-visioning the soft path perspective

Not surprisingly, soft path analysts think that their approach is, if anything, more appropriate now than it was 25 years ago. Since then, concerns about health and environmental problems related to energy have continued to grow, especially those related to avoidable respiratory illnesses and childhood asthma linked to air quality, and greenhouse gas emissions linked to fossil fuel use. It should be mentioned that soft path researchers were among the first to pay attention to climate change. A book was published in 1981 about using soft path approaches to solve the carbon dioxide problem (Krause et al, 1981) and, though not designed with greenhouse gas emissions in mind, even the higher energy use scenarios in the 1988 revision of the soft path study for Canada would allow us to meet our Kyoto commitments (Torrie et al, 1988).

The strength of these early studies was confirmed by a study prepared for the David Suzuki Foundation and the Climate Action Network Canada (Torrie et al, 2002). Their sector-by-sector scenarios showed how readily available, cost-effective, demand-side technologies could cut energy use by so much that Canada would not only exceed its Kyoto commitments, but consumers would save tens of billions of dollars per year. The same is true elsewhere, as examples of 'Factor 4' improvements – that is, reductions of 75 per cent in resource use per unit of output in industrial and commercial activities – demonstrate (von Weizsäcker et al, 1997). More recently in Canada, Ralph Torrie led a project on greenhouse gas emissions for Canada's National Round Table on the Environment and the Economy. This effort, though not based on soft path strategies as such, adopted many soft path recommendations, and a major finding was that, 'with consideration for some key enabling conditions and acknowledgment of certain risks and uncertainties', cuts of 60 to 70 per cent in greenhouse gas emissions by 2050 were 'manageable, and may even provide some unique opportunities' (NRTEE, 2007, pii).

Conclusion

If there is a single conclusion to be drawn about soft energy studies around the world, it is that the need to prioritize energy conservation cannot be overstated. The environmental and social implications of unchecked demand growth are enormous, whether we are talking about habitable cities, habitat loss, the security of supply, or any number of other issues. From a global perspective, the developing world's aspirations for a reasonable level of economic prosperity and well-being will require growth in their energy use and, if this is to occur without crossing further ecological thresholds, it will be imperative to see an equal or greater reduction in energy use in the developed world. Simply substituting renewable for non-renewable sources is not and cannot be the answer by itself. Only major success in reducing demand will put us firmly on the soft path – a conclusion that is as applicable to water as to energy.

Were the original soft path approach and strategies right about everything? Of course not – for a number of reasons. First, the emphasis placed on finding low-tech and easy-to-understand technologies, as well as the aversion to *any* technologies involving large-scale, centralized facilities, was overstated. Advanced solar cell technology, or even a high-efficiency gas furnace, is not really much simpler to understand than nuclear power, though a toppled wind turbine is certainly a lot easier and cheaper to fix than a nuclear plant that is 'down'. And even though the hard and soft paths have some opposite assumptions and approaches, the real world always has elements of both at the same time. Though a similar larger–smaller mix is likely to be true for water, water supply systems are typically simpler even than natural gas, which is the simplest of the modern fuels. However, the emphasis on smaller scale and more local sources remains relevant for water since the weakest link in water supply systems is typically the piping (Brooks and Linton, 2009).

Second, the soft path strategies were too limited in their analysis of what drives change. Comparatively high prices for conventional fuels and rational economic behaviour were presumed to be the main motivators for change in the original studies. Though the right economic signals are essential, it is now apparent that other factors are equally or, in some cases, even more important. For individual consumers, comfort, convenience and safety often matter more than saving money. This can work both for and against the soft path, depending on whether greater energy efficiency can be married with these other desired attributes. Ceiling fans and high efficiency furnaces that are very quiet and improve comfort have strong customer appeal, but so do gas-guzzling SUVs, apparently because they appeal to drivers' sense of safety and security. If anything, this lesson will be more true for water, which must be withdrawn from sources that have social and cultural as well as economic values, and which is desired for a variety of purposes that do not, directly, have utilitarian purposes. Just as with energy, cost effectiveness will be an important driver for changes in water use and water policy, but it will not be the only driver.

Third, some of the political realities that hold back change needed to be more effectively addressed. Governments, both at the political level as well as the bureaucracy, always prefer a situation where there are no (visible) problems to one where they are expected to solve problems. It was therefore not remarkable that the years of energy 'normalcy' were unproductive for soft path initiatives. This tendency towards inertia on energy policy was reinforced in Canada by programme and staff reductions as governments struggled to get deficits under control, and in the US by the election of governments unwilling to support pro-environment interventions for fear they would constrain business. Revenue stability from taxes and royalties on energy resources also matters a great deal to governments, particularly in jurisdictions where traditional energy industries are the mainstay of economic activity. More attention needed to be paid to developing ways to finance the transition away from dependency on those major sources of state revenue and prosperity. As will be shown in Chapter 7, these political characteristics are shared by both energy and water. If anything, political factors have even greater significance for water, where other actors and other forces play a role on both the demand and the supply sides.

Finally, the concept of sustainable development has highlighted the need to consider equity implications of policies alongside economic and environmental matters. For example, more fully incorporating environmental costs would raise most energy prices, and the effect this would have on companies and employees in the energy sector and on particular groups of consumers needs evaluation. Low income is not the only factor that might increase vulnerability. Rural communities are affected to a much greater extent than urban dwellers as the costs of transportation increase. Other factors that could make adaptation to a changing energy situation more burdensome might include age, education level, family situation or even being a recent immigrant. It will be critical to assess these impacts and to ensure that those most at risk are adequately supported. Apart from First Nations communities, where inadequate water treatment and sanitation are a shamefully neglected national problem, equity in availability of water is not a big issue in Canada or in other OECD countries. In contrast, it is a huge issue in many developing countries, and it is linked to issues of race, class and gender. Equity issues with water receive special attention in Chapter 17, which is devoted to water soft path thinking in India, South Africa and the Middle East.

The general soft energy approach and the specific soft energy study for Canada have both proven to have lasting, and indeed growing, value. On the one hand, the Canadian study turned out to be more prescient than even the 18 analysts who worked on it might have expected. On the other hand, both the approach and the study overestimated government's willingness to recognize the value and act on the principles of the soft path. Nowhere is this contradiction better illustrated than in the changing reactions of Canadian energy bureaucrats over the course of the study. In the early days of soft path analysis, the typical response was, 'Yes, you have created a very desirable future for Canada, but do you *really* think it is feasible?' After the study was completed, the response changed: 'Yes, you have shown that this future scenario is feasible, but do you really think it is *desirable*?'

Will the same be true for water?

Notes

1 Portions of the material used in this chapter were previously published as 'Reverse engineering' in a book entitled *Fueling the Future: How the Battle Over Energy is Changing Everything*, edited by Andrew Heintzman and Evan Solomon. We are grateful to House of Anansi Press, Toronto, Ontario, for permission to use this material.

References

Bott, R., Brooks, D. B. and Robinson, J. B. (1983) *Life After Oil: A Renewable Energy Policy for Canada*, Hurtig Publishers, Edmonton, AB

Brooks, D. B. (2003) *Another Path Not Taken: A Methodological Exploration of Water Soft Paths for Canada and Elsewhere*, Report to Environment Canada, Friends of the Earth Canada, Ottawa, ON

Brooks, D. B. and Linton, J. (2009) 'Less is more: Approaching water security and sustainability from the demand side', in J. Jones, T. G. Vardanian and C. Hakopian (eds) *Threats to Global Water Security*, Springer, New York, NY

Brooks, D. B., Robinson J. B. and Torrie, R. D. (1983) *2025: Soft Energy Futures for Canada*, Report to the Department of Energy, Mines & Resources and Environment Canada, vol 1, *National Report*, Friends of the Earth Canada, Ottawa, ON

Krause, F., Bach, W., Lovins, L. H. and Lovins, A. B. (1981) *Least-Cost Energy: Solving the CO_2 Problem*, Brick House Publishing, Andover, MA

Leiss, W. (ed) (1979) *Ecology versus Politics in Canada*, University of Toronto Press, Toronto, ON

Lovins, A. B. (1976) 'Energy strategy: The road not taken', *Foreign Affairs*, vol 55, no 1, pp186–218

Lovins, A. B. (1977) *Soft Energy Paths: Toward a Durable Peace*, Ballinger/Friends of the Earth, Cambridge, MA

Lovins, A. B., Datta, E. K., Bustnes, O.-E., Koomey, J. G. and Glasgow, N. J. (2004) *Winning the Oil Endgame: Innovation for Profits, Jobs, and Security*, Rocky Mountain Institute, Snowmass, CO

National Round Table on the Environment and the Economy (NRTEE) (2007) *Getting to 2050: Canada's Transition to a Low-emission Future*, NRTEE, Ottawa, ON

Ross, M. H. and Williams, R. H. (1981) *Our Energy: Regaining Control*, McGraw-Hill Book Company, New York, NY

Stobaugh, R. and Yergin, D. (1983) *Energy Future: Report of the Energy Project at the Harvard Business School*, Vintage Books, New York, NY

Stone, P. B. (1973) *Did We Save the Earth at Stockholm? The People and Politics in the Conference on the Human Environment*, Earth Island Publishers, London, UK

Torrie, R. D. and Brooks, D. B. with Burt, E., Espejo, M., Gagnon, L. and Holtz, S. (1988) *2025: Soft Energy Futures for Canada – 1988 Update*, Submission to Energy Options Policy Review, Canadian Environmental Network, Ottawa, ON

Torrie, R. D., Parfett, R. and Steenhof, P. (2002) *Kyoto and Beyond: The Low Emissions Path to Innovation and Efficiency*, The David Suzuki Foundation, Vancouver, BC, and Climate Action Network Canada, Ottawa, ON

von Weizsäcker, E. U., Lovins, A. B. and Lovins, L. H. (1997) *Factor Four: Doubling Wealth, Halving Resource Use*, Earthscan, London

Ward, B. (1976) *The Home of Man*, Penguin Books, Harmondsworth, Middlesex, UK

World Commission on Environment and Development (1987) *Our Common Future*, Oxford University Press, Oxford

4
Getting it Right: Misconceptions About the Soft Path

Peter H. Gleick

If I were called in
To construct a religion
I should make use of water.

Philip Larkin

An historical overview

Humanity's experience with water has varied over time. For the purposes of this chapter, it will be helpful to describe this experience in terms of three, more or less distinct, 'water ages'. The First Water Age began when *homo sapiens* lived in simple primitive hunter-gatherer groups or communal societies. During this Age, water was available and simply taken when needed. The natural hydrologic cycle of evaporation, condensation, precipitation and evaporation all worked to purify water, and the rivers, streams, lakes and springs fed by rain were usually safe to drink. If the water was too dirty, early humans got sick and died, but life was pretty short, brutish and basic anyway.

The Second Water Age began when humans started to organize into larger, more formal urban communities and outgrew the limits of local water resources. During this Age, we see the first intentional manipulation of the hydrologic cycle. This activity is found everywhere in the archeological record, even in desert regions. It is no accident that the greatest early civilizations arose on the banks of perennial rivers, such as the Tigris, Euphrates, Indus, Ganges and Nile. Wherever ancient civilizations arose we find traces of irrigation canals, early dams to store or divert water, aqueducts, qanats and acequias that move fresh water tens to hundreds of kilometres with only the force of gravity, and wastewater systems to separate good water from bad. At this same time, we also see the first laws and social structures for managing water. Nearly 4000 years ago, the Code of Hammurabi, an early king of Babylon, laid out the laws governing the society that developed in ancient Mesopotamia. Among them are laws for rational and fair management of irrigation water and the maintenance of water systems, including punishments for water theft and for failure to properly maintain irrigation canals. Some two thousand years later, by the time the Talmud and Sharia were being compiled, respectively, by Jewish and Islamic religious authorities, the rules were well accepted and even extended to cover times of drought and times of war (Hirsch, 1959).

The Second Water Age reached its full bloom in the 19th and 20th centuries, by which time we had truly mastered the natural hydrologic cycle in order to provide society with clean water and learned how to recycle our wastes using chemical, mechanical, biological and institutional systems that mimic and magnify nature. All of our engineered water treatment processes that flocculate, coagulate, precipitate, condense and distill water are mechanical imitations of natural processes. We build massive sand or charcoal or mechanical filters that mimic the purification role played by soils. We run water through reverse osmosis membranes that imitate the ability of cells to separate salt from solution. We flow water past high-intensity ultraviolet lamps that replicate the purification effects of the sun. We grow vats of naturally occurring waste-eating bacteria that take the biological products we excrete and consume them, producing fertilizer, oxygen and energy. All of these artificial interventions are necessary because the population of the planet has outgrown the ability of nature to provide adequate water for our needs and to purify our wastes.

Particularly during the last two centuries, the Second Water Age has also been characterized by massive physical interventions in the natural hydrologic cycle. We built (and still try to build) huge dams to capture water in wet periods to use in dry periods; aqueducts to move water from wet regions to dry regions; and a complex network of pumps, treatment plants, distribution pipelines, wastewater collection systems and waste treatment plants to ensure health and support economic growth.

We are now in the midst of another transition – to a Third Water Age. The second age brought enormous benefits to us, but has ultimately failed to satisfy our needs, while also failing to protect the natural ecosystems on which we all depend. We know that we must do more than just 'more of the same' if we are going to truly address global water problems, including meeting basic human needs for water, living within a fixed resource, protecting natural ecosystems and addressing the challenges of climate change. In short, we need a Soft Path for Water (Wolff and Gleick, 2002; Gleick, 2003).

A new way for a new age

The old water development path – successful as it was in some ways – is increasingly recognized as inadequate for the water challenges that face humanity. We must now find a new path, but the process of defining, developing and implementing an alternative path has not yet been completed. Despite accumulating evidence to the contrary, powerful groups in the water sector continue to believe that we must do more of what we've always done; that is continue to focus on traditional infrastructure and management, but just do it harder. They claim that this approach is still the best way to meet global water needs.

The soft path offers great potential. However, there is, as yet, less than full agreement on the characteristics of the soft path – indeed, as the different chapters in this book reveal, there is still a healthy discussion under way about the definitions, components and implementation of a 'soft path'. But there are things on which we all agree: the adjective 'soft' is a reminder that there are important *non-structural* components of a comprehensive approach to sustainable water management and use, including equitable access to water, proper application and use of economics, incentives for efficient use, social objectives for water quality and delivery reliability, public participation in decision-making and more. Chapter 3 of this book detailed some of the ways in which soft paths differ in principle from hard paths. In addition to these fundamental principles, a soft path would change the way water services companies or agencies would operate in at least five ways:

1   The soft path redirects government agencies, private companies, and individuals to work to meet the water-related *needs* of people and businesses, rather than merely to supply water. For example, people want to be clean or to clean their clothes or produce food and other goods and services using convenient, cost-effective, and socially acceptable means. They don't have an ideological preference (or shouldn't) for how much water is used, and may not care whether water is used at all.

2   The soft path requires that we differentiate between waters of different qualities and match the quality needed with the quality that is available. Higher quality water should be reserved for those uses that *require* higher quality. For example, storm runoff, grey water and reclaimed wastewater are suited for many uses that are currently satisfied with far more expensive potable water. This practice exaggerates the amount of water actually needed and inflates the overall cost of providing it.

3   The soft path requires water agency or company personnel to interact closely with water users and to effectively engage community groups in water management. In contrast, the hard path is governed by an engineering mentality that is accustomed to meeting large-scale generic needs in a top-down way.

4   The soft path recognizes that ecological health and the activities that depend on it (eg, fishing, swimming, tourism, delivery of clean raw water to downstream users) are fundamental, not peripheral. In contrast, the hard path assumes that water left in a river or lake or aquifer is not being used productively.

5   The soft path recognizes the complexity of water economics, including the power of economies of scope and recognizes that investments in decentralized solutions can be just as cost effective as investments in large, centralized options. The hard path looks at projects, revenues and economies of scale. An economy of scope exists when a combined decision-making process would allow specific services to be delivered at lower cost than would result from separate decision-making processes (Wolff and Gleick, 2002). For example, water providers can often reduce the total cost of services by accounting for the interactions that separate agencies cannot account for alone. Thus decisions about water policy might be very different if water providers work with land use planners, flood protection agencies and energy utilities in an integrated, not isolated, way.

What keeps the hard path in place?

The dominance of the hard path in the 20th century, entrenched ways of thinking and entrenched economic interests are barriers to a soft path. In part, this resistance is the result of economic informational issues, but there are also a wide variety of misconceptions and misunderstandings about the soft path. The cumulative effect of these misconceptions is to block alternative perspectives from gaining ground, in favour of the water hard path and supply-side approaches. The remainder of this chapter presents a compilation of the most important misconceptions that are, unfortunately, still active and that hinder far faster adoption of efficiency improvements, technologies and policies needed to shift society onto a water soft path. In the third part of this book, Chapter 12 goes on to identify and suggest remedies for the key institutional barriers that originate, in part, in these misconceptions.

Misconception 1: Efficiency opportunities are small

Traditional water planners and managers often have very little experience with the concept of water use efficiency or with how to estimate the potential for such efficiency improvements.[1] In part, this is because efficiency improvements depend on a different set of actions than water managers usually apply or understand. It is far easier for traditional water planners and managers to evaluate the behaviour of a massive dam or new water supply project than the behaviour of myriad individual water users. Yet study after study shows that the potential for improving the efficiency of use, without diminishing economic or social benefits, is enormous in both urban and agricultural end uses (see, e.g. Gleick et al, 2003; Cooley et al, 2008). Even if such gains in efficiency defer rather than eliminate the need for some water supply project, the savings to the public purse are typically large, as are the benefits to the environment. And, as several studies have shown, there is no shortage of ways to increase the efficiency of water use (Vickers, 1999, 2001; Brandes and Ferguson, 2004; Cooley and Gleick, 2008). As an example of the pervasiveness of this myth, a new briefing paper with recommendations for 'A National Agenda for Drinking Water', prepared in November 2008 for US President-elect Barack Obama by traditional water managers, including the American Water Works Association, Association of Metropolitan Water Agencies, National Association of Water Companies and National Rural Water Association, emphasized the need for new investment in traditional hard path approaches and completely ignored the potential for far less costly, and more effective, efficiency investments (American Water Works Association et al, 2008).

Misconception 2: Water demand is relatively unaffected by market forces

Many water managers work from the fundamental assumption that the price elasticity of demand is effectively zero. Thus, water demand has traditionally been projected – erroneously – to be independent of costs, prices, subsidy considerations and market forces. Because water is an essential and basic good, some argue that the price elasticity of water demand is small. That is the case in some instances, or over short time periods, but even then the price elasticity is certainly not zero. On the other hand, there are numerous examples of water users responding to price increases by significantly changing their behaviour or investing in or inventing devices that reduce water use dramatically without a reduction in the final, water-based service that is desired. A good example of this is the old practice of permitting urban water connections without any meters, and simply charging flat rates (or sometimes even no rates) for unlimited water use. Data from a variety of cities in the south-western US now clearly demonstrate that customers in cities with higher urban water rates reduce their water use, especially outdoor water use, to a greater degree than consumers who get less expensive water (Brandes with Ferguson, 2003; Cooley et al, 2007). In short, the price elasticity of water is not zero, and can be an effective tool for managing demand.

Given the prevalence of a mindset that says that the demand for water is inelastic to price, it is not surprising that most historical estimates of future water demand have greatly overestimated actual demand (Figure 4.1). In places where prices and markets have been used, very substantial effects on water demand have been seen.

Many 'projections' have been made of future water use. Figure 4.1 shows actual global water withdrawals and projections made over the past 40 years. Almost all projections overestimated future water use – often substantially (Gleick, 2000).

Misconception 3: Conserved water is not 'real'

Another result of the difference in 'mindset' between the hard and soft paradigms is the fundamental misunderstanding that efficiency improvements involving non-consumptive water uses are not real.[2] Hard path planners argue

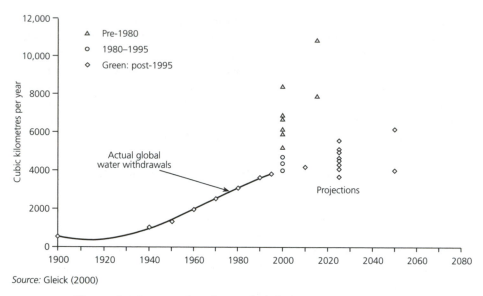

Source: Gleick (2000)

Figure 4.1 *Projected and actual global water withdrawals*

that all efficiency programmes should focus only on improving the efficiency of consumptive uses, in order to save water that can be reallocated to other users. But hard path planners have been confused about non-consumptive uses of water: uses that permit reuse (eg, household uses that go to treatment plants and can be treated and then reused, or excess irrigation that flows to other users). Reducing non-consumptive uses, they argue, offers no advantages, because that wasted water simply satisfies another demand downstream. This is half true, but it also reflects a fundamental failure of hard path practitioners to comprehend the full implications of water use. In particular, improving the efficiency of non-consumptive uses may or may not result in additional water for other users, but it also permits water to be left instream for ecological uses and it saves energy required to capture, treat and deliver water, which in turn helps reduce the emissions of greenhouse gases. All of these are substantial 'co-benefits' accruing to improving efficiency of water use, whether those savings are consumptive or non-consumptive uses. Similarly, every use involves some degradation in the quality of the water that either requires treatment (as in the case of household water) or that makes the water less useful to downstream users (as in the case of agricultural runoff).

Misconception 4: Efficiency improvements are speculative and risky

Even when hard path water planners believe that the technical potential for water efficiency improvements is large, and the water saved is 'real', they also tend to believe that relying on efficiency improvements is risky. Traditional water planners are happy to base water policy on assumptions about the probability *a* that there will be *b* people in the future using *c* amounts of water per person requiring *d* new reservoirs and treatment plants. Yet the same planners have historically rejected as speculation that economic or technical strategy *w* will lead to the installation of *x* high-efficiency toilets and shower-heads that each save *y* cubic metres of water capable in total of eliminating the need for *z* new reservoirs and treatment plants. Hard path water planners argue that our well-being and economic health rely on proven approaches rather than speculative (in their minds) policies that may not work.

Decentralized efforts to curb demand may be unreliable. Left entirely alone, water customers may fail to notice that efficient water use devices are no longer operating efficiently, or may fail to continue their initially water-conscious and efficient behaviour. On the other hand, aggregate water use patterns – such as seasonal and daily variations – are so predictable and reliable that water planners use them routinely. One wonders if rigorous statistical analysis would find that conservation is any less reliable than, for example, surface water supply in areas that experience periodic droughts. Furthermore, there are answers and solutions to these problems, including training, public education and ongoing feedback to customers from the water supplier. Just as centralized water systems are unreliable when they are improperly designed, operated or maintained, decentralized systems may be unreliable unless water users are able to integrate them into day-to-day behaviour, or are offered incentives for continuing to be efficient. Moreover, it is possible to implement conservation and efficiency programmes that operate completely independently of human behaviour – leak reduction programmes and technology replacement efforts are two examples.

Misconception 5: Efficiency improvements are not cost effective

Large centralized water facilities were historically cheaper – within a somewhat narrow accounting methodology – than decentralized investments in efficiency. But this is changing now and the belief that efficiency improvements are more expensive than new or expanded centralized water supply is incorrect in most circumstances. In part, the change has come about because of a growing realization that traditional economic costs of supply-side projects are consistently underestimated (see Box 4.1) and have often failed to account for many environmental and social costs. Both of these factors result in water infrastructure costing society far more than expected (and believed) through environmental damages, impacts on human health, and other externalities. Dams and reservoirs and other capital intensive projects routinely end up costing two, three or even more times their originally projected capital costs, and new facilities are many times more expensive than the first ones built in a region or watershed.

Another reason for the belief that efficiency improvements are too expensive is that hard path water planners usually compare the cost of efficiency

---

BOX 4.1 PERENNIAL COST OVERRUNS ON THE HARD PATH

For major water infrastructure projects, international data show that cost overruns are the rule rather than the exception. World Bank statistics on dam construction projects over the last four decades suggest that construction cost overruns averaged 30 per cent on the 70 hydropower projects funded by the Bank since the 1960s. Another World Bank study found that three-quarters of the 80 hydro projects completed in the 1970s and 1980s had costs in excess of their budgets, and almost one-third of the projects studied had actual costs that exceeded estimates by 50 per cent or more (World Commission on Dams, 2000).

There are many reasons for cost overruns, including delays, design errors, poor quality construction or corruption of project advocates and managers. For example, the Chixoy Dam in Guatemala was delayed for nine years by the collapse of some poorly designed tunnels. Its final cost of $1.2 billion was more than five times its initial cost estimate. The Yacyreta Dam on the Parana River between Argentina and Paraguay became known as a 'monument to corruption' as the cost of the project increased to $8 billion from an original estimate of $1.6 billion.

Cost overruns are not restricted to projects in less developed countries. Dam projects in Canada and the US have experienced similar overruns, in some cases, as with Tocks Island Dam on the Delaware River in Pennsylvania and New Jersey, so great as to have the project cancelled.

Sources: World Commission on Dams (2000), International Rivers Network (2001)

Improvements without accounting for secondary benefits. Without accounting for the avoided energy expense for water heating, for example, low-flow toilets and showerheads are the only residential investments that are cost effective compared with most water-supply augmentation proposals. After accounting for the associated energy benefits, however, a far wider range of solutions are seen to be cost effective, such as clothes- and dishwashers, even if new water supply could be obtained for free (Gleick et al, 2003).

There are other secondary benefits as well that are rarely evaluated in traditional 'hard path' assessments, but that make efficiency improvements even more attractive (Dziegielewski, 1999; Brooks, 2006):

- Reductions in *peak water system loads*. Peak loads determine the size of capital facilities required, hence capital costs. Lower peak loads mean that existing capital facilities can serve more customers, avoiding or reducing the expense of these facilities.
- Reductions in *peak energy demands*. Reduction of peak energy demand caused by less water pumping, treatment or heating will allow energy utilities to serve more customers with existing capital facilities, and thereby avoid or reduce capital expenses that are ultimately paid by energy purchasers.
- Reductions in *wastewater treatment expenses*, both operational and for expansion of existing sewers or treatment facilities.
- Reductions in *environmental damage* from water withdrawals or wastewater discharges in environmentally sensitive locations.

- Increases in *employment*. Investments in large, centralized capital facilities increase employment during construction, but use relatively little labour once construction is complete.
- Reductions in *costs resulting from disruptions to water supply systems after accidents and natural disasters*. Evidence is strong that the weakest link in most water supply systems is the distribution pipes and, the less water needed to be delivered, the lower the damages (Brooks and Linton, 2009).

Another advantage of the soft path is the shorter lead times required to put in place decentralized and small-scale responses. For example, in Santa Barbara, California, a severe drought in the late 1970s stimulated local residents to support the construction of a large desalination plant, as well as a pipeline to connect it to the centralized state water project. When the very high economic costs of those 'hard path' options were passed on to consumers, reductions in demand occurred so quickly that the hard path options became unnecessary (though they were built anyway). If effective pricing programmes, education and community planning had been done first, the expense of these facilities could have been long delayed, and perhaps completely avoided. As Lovins noted for the energy industry, the industrial dynamics of the soft path are very different from the hard path: the technical risks are smaller, and the dollars invested are far more diversified, which reduces financial risk.

Misconception 6: Demand management is too complicated

Traditional water agencies are usually dominated by engineering experts who know how to design and build large structures that can serve a million people. But these same experts are unfamiliar with methods for designing and implementing efficiency programmes that reach a million individual customers. It is not surprising that working with individual customers and coordinating among many customers seems too complicated to engineers. These tasks *are* complicated, but no more so than engineering projects. They just require different professional skills and training. A growing number of water agencies now have water conservation departments and professional societies are adding water conservation experts and groups. Better water management will also be aided by advances in information processing, water use monitoring and more efficient end-use devices and practices, but these gains will only be fully realized if water agencies make more of a commitment to this 'human' side of demand management.

Conclusions

Acting alone, none of the misconceptions and misunderstandings identified above would pose a serious block to a shift from a hard to a soft path for water. Each of them can be refuted with better information, better management approaches and closer attention to broader changes in society. However, taken together, and coupled with what has been called a 'masculine' tendency towards engineering approaches (Zwarteveen, 2008), these misconceptions create a myth in favour of a continued push for large-scale, capital-intensive supply systems for urban water supply and for commercial irrigation – in effect, in favour of water hard paths. In contrast to misconceptions and misunderstandings, myths cannot be refuted, at least not easily or quickly; rather, they infuse thinking and constrain the range of options that are considered feasible. The tasks confronting soft path analysts are to chip away at those misconceptions, to challenge the misunderstandings and to remove the institutional barriers until the myth of hard path effectiveness, and even hard path efficiency, is no longer so persuasive.

Notes

1 A gain in water efficiency means that the savings in water are cost effective compared with the alternative of supplying the water. Short-term gains in efficiency compare water savings only with the delivery costs for additional water, which implies excess capacity in the supply system; long-term gains also include the capital costs (and other costs) of building new water supply infrastructure. In societies that are growing in either population or income, the appropriate comparisons are based on long-term efficiency.
2 Consumptive uses of water are those that prevent that water from being reused. These include evaporative loss from bodies of water, evapotranspiration from plants, contamination that cannot be removed by treatment or discharge to a salt sink such as the ocean or to a deep aquifer.

References

American Water Works Association, Association of Metropolitan Water Agencies, National Association of Water Companies, and National Rural Water Association (2008) *A National Agenda for Drinking Water*; available at www.awwa.org/files/GovtPublicAffairs/PDF/Transition.pdf

Brandes, O. M. with Ferguson, K. (2003) *Flushing the Future: Examining Urban Water Use in Canada*, The POLIS Project in Ecological Governance, University of Victoria, Victoria, BC

Brandes, O. M. and Ferguson, K. (2004) *The Future in Every Drop: The Benefits, Barriers and Practice of Urban Water Demand Management in Canada*, The POLIS Project in Ecological Governance, University of Victoria, Victoria, BC

Brooks, D. B. (2006) 'An operational definition of water demand management', *International Journal of Water Resources Development*, vol 22, no 4, pp521–528

Brooks, D. B. and Linton, J. (2009) 'Less is more: Approaching water security and sustainability from the demand side', in J. A. Jones, T. G. Vardanian and C. Hakopian (eds) *Threats to Global Water Security*, Springer, New York, NY

Cooley, H. T. and Gleick, P. H. (2008) 'Urban water-use efficiencies: Lessons from United States' cities', in P. H. Gleick (ed) *The World's Water 2008–2009*, Island Press, Washington, DC

Cooley, H., Christian-Smith, J. and Gleick, P. H. (2008) *More with Less: The Potential for Agricultural Water Conservation and Efficiency in California*, The Pacific Institute, Oakland, CA

Cooley, H., Hutchens-Cabibi, T., Cohen, M., Gleick, P. H. and Heberger, M. (2007) *Hidden Oasis: Water Conservation and Efficiency in Las Vegas*, A Report of the Pacific Institute for Studies in Development, Environment, and Security, Oakland, CA

Dziegielewski, B. (1999) 'Management of water demand: Unresolved issues', *Water Resources Update*, no 114, pp1–7

Gleick, P. H. (2000) 'The changing water paradigm: A look at twenty-first century water resources development', *Water International*, vol 25, no 1, pp127–138

Gleick, P. H. (2003) 'Global freshwater resources: Soft path solutions for the 21st century', *Science*, vol 302, no 5650, pp1524–1528

Gleick, P. H., Haasz, D., Henges-Jeck, C., Srinivasan, V., Wolff, G., Kao Cushing, K. and Mann, A. (2003) *Waste Not, Want Not: The Potential for Urban Water Conservation in California*, The Pacific Institute, Oakland, CA

Hirsch, A. M. (1959) 'Water legislation in the Middle East', *The American Journal of Comparative Law*, vol 8, no 2, pp168–186

International River Network (2001) *When the Rivers Run Dry – The World Bank, Dams and the Quest for Reparations*; available at http://internationalrivers.org/en/latin-america/mesoamerica/chixoy-dam-guatemala/when-rivers-run-dry

Lovins, A. B. (1977) *Soft Energy Paths: Toward a Durable Peace*, Harper Colophon Books

Vickers, A. L. (1999) 'The future of water conservation: Challenges ahead', *Water Resources Update*, no 114, pp49–51

Vickers, A. L. (2001) *Handbook of Water Use and Conservation*, WaterPlow Press, Amherst, MA

Wolff, G. and Gleick, P. H. (2002) 'The soft path for water', in P. H. Gleick et al (eds) *The World's Water: Biennial Report on Freshwater Resources, 2002–2003*, Island Press, Washington DC

World Commission on Dams (2000) *Dams and Development: A New Framework for Decision-Making: The Report of the World Commission on Dams*, available at www.dams.org/report/wcd_overview.htm

Zwarteveen, M. (2008) 'Men, masculinities and water powers in irrigation', *Water Alternatives*, vol 1, no 1, pp111–130

5
Practising Ecological Governance: The Case for the Soft Path for Water

Oliver M. Brandes

> *We are all downstream*
>
> *Ecologist* motto

The era of 'limitless' water supply is ending. In much of the Western developed world, water scarcity remains primarily a *social dilemma* – a problem that requires attention to the social contexts that shape decision-making, attitudes and behaviour. It will not be addressed by technical solutions alone. The social nature of water scarcity highlights the reality that the crisis is substantially of our own making, and is really a crisis of governance (Global Water Partnership (GWP), 2000a; UNWWDR, 2003; Wolfe and Brooks, 2003; UNWWDR, 2006; Conca, 2006; Bakker, 2007). However, this lesson is still being learned. The old approach of 'man over nature' and a cultural assumption that focuses on building larger physical infrastructure to increase supply remains stubbornly entrenched. Society's collective myth of abundance is fuelled by existing power structures and past habits that disconnect nature from individuals and communities.

Many current decision makers and proponents of sustainable development actually limit our collective potential to address these challenges. Sustainable development, as it is currently applied maintains current approaches, emphasizing conventional ideas of development with, at best, only minor 'environmental' reforms tacked on.[1] Driven by the tenets of neoclassical economics, the status quo is reinforced by beliefs that advances in technology and market mechanisms will more or less automatically solve key problems. It diverts attention from what is needed to address the real water crisis looming before us because it pays little or no attention to issues of power relations and processes of decision-making. To address the crisis of governance requires profound change – change that entails new forms of management and institutions governing natural resources generally and water specifically. The same old decision-making structures and institutions that got us here are not going to help get us 'beyond here'.

Conservation and water efficiency do not *just happen*. Changing use habits and balancing demands with availability are functions of the institutions and decision-making processes in which water management and planning (and indeed any resource management) are embedded. Current management approaches that favour technologies and practices that emphasize continued extraction from the environment must be challenged.

The purpose of this chapter is to introduce *ecological governance* and place this concept in the context of water management, with particular emphasis on the potential role that the soft path can play in the transformation needed to cope with the water challenges outlined in the opening chapters. Changing how we think about water scarcity *starts us on the soft path*, but fundamentally changing the power structures and collective decision-making processes – and the inevitable wider ecological and societal implications of reducing water use – *begins moving us to a system of governing ecologically.*

It is exactly this transformative potential that may lead to what Gleick (in Chapter 4) calls 'the third age of water management', and to broader changes throughout our economic and social systems for the benefit of our environment and our long-term prosperity.

Introducing ecological governance

Governance, in simple terms, is the process of arriving at collective intentions and realizing those intentions through individual action. It addresses the questions of *who* decides, *what* limits those decisions and *how* decisions are made. Ultimately, it also inevitably involves holding those who make the decisions to account. The Commission on Global Governance (1995) provides a helpful definition:

> *The sum of the many ways individuals and institutions, public and private, manage their common affairs. It is a continuing process through which conflict or diverse interest may be accommodated and co-operative action may be taken. It includes formal institutions and regimes empowered to enforce compliance, as well as informal arrangements that people and institutions either have agreed to or perceive to be in their interests.*

Government is not the same as governance, nor are all decisions that affect our lives made by government bodies or through regulatory processes. Corporations, non-governmental organizations (NGOs), business associations and community groups also make critical decisions. Dynamic and evolving over time, this concept of governance inevitably includes the institutions, practices, laws and regulations and even customs through which a society makes those decisions, as well as the norms and practices that ultimately guide individual action. Institutions of governance mediate the relationships among citizens, the economy and the environment, and embody the collective power of citizens to direct the future.

Ecological governance extends this concept. It focuses on those aspects of institutional reform that enable and embed ecologically sustainable solutions as the priority. Ecological governance is not a mere 'add-on'. Rather, it incorporates the environment in all levels of decision-making, and treats the environment as central to our lives and our well-being. It recognizes biophysical limits and starts by recognizing the economy as a subset of the ecosystem. Practices such as 'triple bottom line' (ecological, economic and social) accounting are increasingly adopted as guides to action. The key principles of ecological governance are summarized in Box 5.1.

Natural systems have extensive feedback loops. They have the freedom to evolve over time, to grow, to change. Governance, if it is to become ecological and resilient, must mimic nature in this way. Feedback loops must be cultivated to promote change and adjustment in the face of new priorities and new information in an ever-changing world. What is required is adaptive management, as well as adaptive governance, that houses and is guided by decision-making systems designed to embed precaution, robust in the face of expected *and* unexpected shocks, resilient in the face of surprise and responsive to the particularities of place. For example, ecological governance seeks to replace the uni-directional path of resource throughput and ever-accumulating waste with cascading systems that provide inputs for the next process down the line. 'Extraction' becomes merely the first step in a process that resembles what occurs in natural systems.

The following attributes help clarify the ecological governance concept by contrasting it with more traditional perspectives on governance and its applications:

- ecological governance evolves in place and avoids 'one size fits all' solutions;
- ecological governance recognizes problems as messy and complex, eschewing neat and tidy models that are adopted from elsewhere;
- ecological governance is about whole system change, addressing complex issues such as the functioning of markets, entire cities and communities, the education process, the development of law and policy, values and consumer preferences and the role of government in planning and management; individual sectors, industries or specific practices must be addressed within this larger context; and
- ecological governance treats sustainability more as a journey than a destination;

BOX 5.1 ECOLOGICAL GOVERNANCE IN A NUTSHELL

To maintain *ecosystem services*, the *inherent uncertainty* of our current activities that undermine ecosystem integrity must be addressed through *prevention and precaution* that can, in
turn, ensure our economy and politics are rooted in a *sustainable consumption*.

In seeking to 'develop sustainability', ecological governance is guided by the following
four concepts, which are not exhaustive but together provide an idea of what needs to be
'developed':

- recognizing decision-making processes (including economic calculations) of government,
  business and the public as embedded within in the dynamics and values of the ecosystem
  of which our social structures are just a part;
- taking uncertainty seriously so that future consequences are reflected in flexible processes
  that extend decision-making beyond the electoral cycle, calculations beyond short-term
  returns to investment and personal values beyond isolated consumer preferences;
- experimenting with new approaches to regulation, resource management regimes and
  jurisdictional designs that can inculcate ecological thinking into decision-making; and,
- facilitating explicit socio-political choices at the macroeconomic level to 'shift' demand
  curves rather than just move along them.

Sources: Brandes et al (2005, p11) and Brandes et al (2007, p295).

- ecological governance recognizes a huge social component to this process –
  asking how do 'we' make collective decisions. It places great importance on
  creating the space and capacity to enliven the role of non-government
  actors – civil society, businesses, NGOs and community groups – and to
  giving them real 'power' to influence (and act on) decisions.

'Practising' ecological governance is radical because it requires engaging
society to create systemic reforms to go well beyond sustainable development
and instead emphasize *developing* sustainability (M'Gonigle, 1989). It means
actively seeking opportunities to disconnect economic growth from consuming
and metabolizing our natural capital, and instead reconnecting resource use to
its effects on human and environmental interactions. Many traditional cultures
included ecological and social considerations in their decisions, but those
integrated approaches became less common in the so-called modern world
(M'Gonigle, 2000). Taken to its full conclusion, ecological governance not
only *re-embeds* ecology in our governance systems, but also the very nature of
governance structures and processes 'become' ecological.

Taking uncertainty seriously – resilience and the praxis of ecological governance

To govern ecologically, society must begin by taking uncertainty and complexity seriously. We must untangle current approaches in law, policy and
regulation that are framed by an underlying assumption of certainty – a belief
that everything is knowable, and, once known, can be managed.

A number of strategies and tactics can be used to better account for certain types of uncertainties. For example, including monitoring and feedback to detect, correct and adjust decisions as an integral part of planning processes helps build adaptive capacity. Recognizing the role of uncertainty, especially in the context of the interaction between social and ecological systems, firmly entrenches the importance of adaptive management (Gunderson and Holling 2002).

Learning by doing becomes critical in a world where we don't have all the answers and recognize that we *can't* have all the answers. In a world of 'unknown unknowns', we must constantly be learning from our actions and making adjustments and changes to what we are doing and how we are doing it. However, a commitment to ecological governance requires us to go further. It requires a focus not just on managing risk, but on developing strategies aimed at risk *reduction*. New forms of regulations that require a prior justification procedure are examples of the institutional arrangements that would embed such risk reduction strategies (M'Gonigle et al, 1994). In the water management context this would mean government could not approve building new water supply infrastructure until they have justified (prior justification) why water efficiency and conservation are not viable options.

Accepting that we need to take precaution and uncertainty seriously – especially when dealing with natural systems and the environment, where surprise is so routine that it is almost unsurprising – emphasizes *resilience* as an important emerging concept. The resilience concept not only informs current approaches to the study of ecological systems (see, eg, Resilience Alliance, 2008) but also underpins appraisal of human interactions with the environment and the nature and character of governance, especially in the context of resource extraction and management.

A system's resilience is defined by its ability to cope with, adapt to and, ideally benefit from, surprises and unexpected change. Recognition of the need to address these kinds of threshold effects shifts the emphasis of policy, planning and management from controlling change to building the capacity to tolerate and adapt to it – all the while building in buffers and precautions that recognize the inevitable uncertainty inherent in complex systems (Holling, 1973; Gunderson and Holling, 2002; Folke, 2006; Walker and Salt, 2006).

Thomas Homer-Dixon (2006) and Jared Diamond (2005), in their landmark books, articulate this need for effective social feedback mechanisms. They make the case that sustainable structures of power must be able to absorb and respond to negative feedback. They emphasize that linear systems of power ignore or suppress such signals and are prone to collapse. Interactive systems that listen to – indeed seek – such feedback are better able to adapt. They demonstrate that some past societies have learned this lesson by, in essence, 'deciding to fail or succeed'.

The soft path, sustainability, power and the potential for change

Ecological governance as outlined previously simply cannot be about just one sector, or specific industries or practices. However, because water policy is so critical to culture and well-being around the world, it represents a crucial focal point for transformation towards any system of ecological governance as well as a critical point of leverage for stimulating change. For example, Sachs (2002) suggests that water has the potential to be the single most important 'weapon of mass salvation'. Naiman et al (1995, p1) stress the primacy of water in their ambitious research agenda – *The Freshwater Imperative* – emphasizing that 'understanding the ability of freshwater ecosystems to respond to human-generated pressures and their limitations in adopting to such challenges has become vital to long term societal stability'. As a management and planning tool, the soft path forces individuals and communities to make explicit choices about the future and the trade-offs involved and the potential consequences of those decisions. By placing priority on achieving the core principles of the soft path – water as service, aligning quality to use, sustaining ecological function and embracing visioning and backcasting for planning purposes – the evolution of existing institutional arrangements into those that fit within environmental limits and ecological processes can begin.

Although the soft path can only be part of a much broader effort to change values and instil a collective water ethic (or indeed an environmental ethic), more than any other part of water planning, it does require the articulation of a desired end-goal that fits an ecological 'truth'. This is the starting point, and by engaging individuals and communities to articulate this goal, soft path analysis opens the possibility of the real changes need to achieve it. Perspectives on risk or priorities that displace ecological function as primary are inevitably challenged when uncovering a potential path – via the backcasting methodology – that connects today's activities to the desired future. For example, the desirability of using rainwater or recycled water to wash clothes or flush toilets increases when weighed against alternatives in a finite water world.

The current supply-driven approach to water resource management does not question the limits of the underlying ecological systems that must endlessly be tapped to fulfil ever increasing human demands for water. The emphasis remains the manipulation of, and extraction from, the environment to ensure a constant access to new supplies with little attention to issues of governance (except to reinforce those institutions and processes that maintain the status quo) or to influencing individual or collective action. In this configuration water management, and by extension the broader social system, remains rigid and provides only sporadic feedback. Even if there is less water per sprinkler, installing more sprinklers in an ever-growing field is simply no long-term answer. It is ultimately not intensity, but scale and impact in the ecological sense that matter.

The soft path brings the biophysical reality of ecological constraints to the forefront and, importantly, engages individuals and communities to be part of the solution. It includes critical players such as civil society, Aboriginal people, professional associations, business and industry, academia and often communities themselves. This diversity of 'professional' and 'personal' engagement brings differing and, often, new forms of knowledge, and even new ways of knowing, to the task of addressing the socio-ecological problems that water management inevitably raises. Its strength is commonly revealed in the technological choices made. For example water saving appliances and rainwater harvesting may be favoured over new infrastructure such as dams and reservoirs. Such widening of governance challenges traditional approaches to both decision-making and management but is increasingly recognized as a global priority (GWP, 2000a; Rogers and Hall, 2003; Conca, 2006; Bakker, 2007).

This kind of direct engagement represents the only way to create lasting change and creates the valuable feedback loops that build resilience and the ability to adapt to social and environmental changes. Conservation and resilience of both natural and the social systems is *the* ultimate goal if sustainability is to have meaning.

Thinking like a watershed – experiments and new forms of governance

Implementing the soft path approach highlights socio-ecological connections and forces communities to consider the watershed context within which they exist. Watersheds are integrators of the landscape. Rivers and streams reflect not only conditions on the land, but also in riparian systems as well as in stream activities. Yet, no current governance model integrates management of terrestrial resources (forests, range, urban development, agriculture, mining, oil and gas, etc.) with water-based management (water extraction, source protection, waste disposal, changes in and about a stream, gravel extraction, ground and surface water, etc.) or atmospheric carbon as a coherent ecological system. Increasingly, broad recognition is emerging that healthy water and watersheds are critical to maintaining ecosystems – and are the foundation of prosperous communities.

Rebalancing the ecological through a focus on watershed function can be seen as part of the much larger debate about the future of government regulations and their role in managing and governing water. Professional water managers around the world recognize the value and critical importance of watersheds as the frame of reference (GWP, 2000b). Yet as a governing entity, the watershed has only recently begun to draw attention (as with Chapter 10 in this book).

This watershed focus for governance fits comfortably with the emerging field of 'democratic experimentalism' and offers solutions on how policy and practice can be made more responsive to innovation while promoting the resilience essential in complex and integrated systems. Karkkainen (2002, p998) describes some of the specific elements that this kind of governance evolution involves: 'innovative regulatory strategies that seek to combine local deliberative experimentations with central coordination and rolling improvement in performance standards.'

This experimental governance approach helps institutions to adjust and to adaptively manage persistent problems that limit sustainability (Dorf and Sabel, 1998). And when applied at the watershed scale – emphasizing the principle of subsidiarity and reconciling it to a relevant ecological scale – solutions are facilitated that meet local needs and are culturally relevant. Examples of this approach are increasingly apparent, with the French water parliament system housed within the context of the European Union's Water Framework Directive embodying such an approach (see Chapter 16 for additional detail). This 'new' governance shifts the focus from centralized control to facilitation of local action by devolving authority to local management authorities operating on the watershed scale. These 'water parliaments' develop plans tailored to local conditions and more formal government provides direction and objectives scaled from the supranational through the national all the way to the local (da Motta et al, 2004).

Travelling the (soft) path to sustainability

Ecological governance addresses the way individual and collective decisions are made within watersheds and more broadly within the ecosystem that supports all life. As water management moves along the spectrum introduced in Chapter 1 from its traditional supply orientation through demand management and towards the long-term integrated and comprehensive approach articulated by the soft path, people and communities start to interact differently with the landscape and change their relationship to water, and indeed to each other. The emphasis moves from managing the natural landscape in response to unsustainable human demands to reshaping human governance to fit within ecological limits (Brandes et al, 2007).

In the increasingly discredited world of the supply-side paradigm – where physical infrastructure and not the ecosystem or the actual water available limits supply – little attention is paid to individual human behaviour or processes of decision-making. But as limits are faced and scarcity emerges, the ways by which human habits and past practices adapt to this changing world become critical.

If governance and society are to become 'ecological', we must reconnect humans to their natural world. Changing institutions can only go so far in eliminating incentives and practices that embed unsustainability; for real change to occur, values must change as well. Water is a critical part of this task as it touches on the ecological, the social and the economic in such tangible ways. We all have a relationship to water – and so we all must be implicated in creating the changes that rebalance our place in the broader ecosystem and water cycle that governs us as living creatures.

To begin moving down this path towards a sustainable water management paradigm, we must be experimental and allow new processes and regimes to take root in unexpected ways. These soft path experiments are the focus of the final section of this book and are the space where the potential of the soft path begins to be revealed, not only as a concept and philosophy, but as a practice that can result in meaningful impacts on the ground or, to be precise, more water in our streams, rivers and lakes.

Note

1 The idea of sustainable development had been discussed almost from the beginning of economics as a discipline. However, just as with Reverend Malthus' gloomy prediction of human starvation (because population growth was geometric whereas growth of agricultural output was only arithmetic), the advance of technology kept overcoming physical and resource barriers, permitting several centuries of economic growth (Barnett and Morse, 1963). In the 1960s and 1970s, some analytically based calls for more attention to our physical and biological environment, and for a shift away from single-minded devotion to economic growth began to appear, as with Barbara Ward's work on the modern city (1976), the work of the American Academy of Arts and Sciences on a no-growth society (1973), or with Daly's work on steady state economics (1977), but they were mainly treated as futurism or, worse yet, eco-dreaming. Modern resurrection of the concept did not really come until wide dissemination of the Brundtland report (World Commission, 1987). Though the Brundtland report proposed only a very modest alternative to the prospect of further unsustainable development, the concept itself was radical. Notably, it inverted the acknowledged concern about the effects of our economy on the environment with its conclusion that it is the environment that is affecting our economy. In recent years, 'sustainable development' has been adopted as a principle by so many organizations that show no evidence of putting it into practice that some people have discounted its substantive value. Many actors, especially those entrenched in existing positions of power, do not see any reasons at all to change their conceptual and ideological orientations – resulting in a business-as-usual interpretation and continued or 'sustained' economic growth at the national level and 'sustained' monetary profits in business at the organizational level (Soderbaum, 2008). For this reason, we refer in this book to *sustainability* rather than *sustainable development*. However, analytical work over the past two decades shows that the original concept is both sound and operational (Daly and Cobb, 1989; Victor, 2008), and also that it is equally if differently applicable in developed and in developing countries (Commission on Developing Countries, 1992; Hall and Hanson, 1992).

References

American Academy of Arts and Sciences (1973) *Daedalus*, vol 102, no 4, entire issue
Bakker, K. (ed) (2007) *Eau Canada: The Future of Canada's Water*, UBC Press, Vancouver, BC
Barnett, H. J. and Morse, C. (1963) *Scarcity and Growth: The Economics of Natural Resource Availability*, The Johns Hopkins Press for Resources for the Future, Baltimore, MD
Brandes, O. M., Brooks, D. B., and M'Gonigle, M. (2007) 'Moving water conservation to centre stage', in K. Bakker (ed) *Eau Canada: The Future of Canada's Water*, UBC

Press, Vancouver, BC

Brandes, O. M., Ferguson, K., M'Gonigle, M. and Sandborn, C. (2005) *At a Watershed: Ecological Governance and Sustainable Water Management in Canada.* POLIS Project on Ecological Governance, University of Victoria, Victoria, BC

Commission on Developing Countries and Global Change (1992) *For Earth's Sake,* International Development Research Centre, Ottawa, ON

Commission on Global Governance (1995) *Our Global Neighbourhood,* Oxford University Press, Oxford

Conca, K. (2006) *Governing Water – Contentious Transnational Politics and Global Institution Building,* MIT Press, Cambridge, MA

Daly, H. E. (1977) *Steady-State Growth,* W. H. Freeman and Company, San Francisco, CA

Daly, H. E. and Cobb, J. B. (1989) *For the Common Good: Redirecting the Economy Toward the Community, the Environment and a Sustainable Future,* Beacon Press, Boston, MA

Diamond, J. (2005) *Collapse: How Societies Choose to Fail or Succeed,* Viking Penguin Group, Toronto, ON

Dorf, M. and Sabel, C. F. (1998) 'A constitution of democratic experimentalism', *Columbia Law Review,* vol 98, no 2, pp267–473

Folke, C. (2006) 'Resilience: The emergence of a perspective for social–ecological systems analysis', *Global Environmental Change,* vol 16, no 3, pp253–267

Global Water Partnership (2000a) *Towards Water Security: A Framework for Action,* Report prepared for presentation at the second World Water Forum, Stockholm, Sweden

Global Water Partnership (GWP) (2000b) *Integrated Water Resource Management,* Stockholm, Sweden

Gunderson, L. H. and Holling, C. S. (eds) (2002) *Panarchy,* Island Press, Washington, DC

Hall, J. D. and Hanson, A. J. (1992) *A New Kind of Sharing,* International Development Research Centre, Ottawa, ON

Holling, C. S. (1973) 'Resilience and stability of ecological systems', *Annual Review of Ecology and Systematics,* vol 4, pp1–23

Homer-Dixon, T. (2006) *The Upside of Down: Catastrophe, Creativity and the Renewal of Civilization,* Vintage Canada, Toronto, ON

Karkkainan, B. (2002) 'Collaborative ecosystem governance: Scale, complexity, and dynamism', *Virginia Environmental Law Journal,* vol 21, pp189–243

M'Gonigle, M. (1989) 'Developing sustainability: A native/environmental prescription for third-level government', *BC Studies,* issue 84, pp65–99

M'Gonigle, M. (2000) 'A new naturalism: Is there a (radical) "truth" beyond the postmodern abyss?', *Ecotheology,* issue 8, pp8–39

M'Gonigle, M., Jamieson, T. L., McAllister, M. K. and Peterman, R. M. (1994) 'Taking uncertainty seriously: From permissive regulation to preventive design in environmental decision-making', *Osgood Hall Law Journal,* vol 32, no 1, pp99–169

da Motta, R. S., Thomas, A., Hazin, L. S., Feres, J. G., Nauges, C. and Hazin, A. S. (2004) *Economic Instruments for Water Management: The Cases of France, Mexico and Brazil,* Edward Elgar, Northampton, MA

Naiman, R., Magnuson, J., McKnight, D. and Stanford, J. (1995) *The Freshwater Imperative: A Research Agenda,* Island Press, Washington, DC

Resilience Alliance (2008) Website www.resallaince.org/1.php. Accessed 19 December 2008

Rogers, P. and Hall, A. W. (2003) *Effective Water Governance*. TEC Background Papers, No. 7, Global Water Partnership, Stockholm, Sweden

Sachs, J. (2002) 'Weapons of mass salvation', *The Economist*, 24 October, pp101–102; available at www.unmillenniumproject.org/documents/Economist_oct24_2002.pdf

Soderbaum, P. (2008) *Understanding Sustainability Economics: Towards Pluralism in Economics*. Earthscan, London

UNWWDR (2003) *Water for People, Water for Life*, United Nations World Water Development Report 1, Paris, France; available at www.unesco.org/water/wwap/wwdr/indes.shtml

UNWWDR (2006) *Water a Shared Responsibility for People*, United Nations World Water Development Report 2, Paris, France; available at www.unesco.org/water/wwap/wwdr/wwdr2/

Victor, P. (2008) *Managing Without Growth: Slower by Design, not Disaster*, Edward Elgar Publishing, Cheltenham, UK

Walker, B. and Salt, D. (2006) *Resilience Thinking*, Island Press, Washington, DC

Ward, B. (1976) *The Home of Man*, Penguin Books, Harmondsworth, Middlesex, UK

Wolfe, S. E., and Brooks, D. B. (2003) 'Water scarcity: an alternative view and its implications for policy and capacity building', *Natural Resources Forum*, vol 26, no 2, pp99–107

World Commission on Environment and Development (1987) *Our Common Future*, (Brundtland Report) Oxford University Press, Oxford

6
Water Policy: Changing Course for the Soft Path

Susan Holtz

In times of change, learners inherit the Earth, while the learned find themselves beautifully equipped to deal with a world that no longer exists.

Eric Hoffer

Introduction

This chapter deals with water soft path policy primarily in the context of the Canadian water soft path work. Most of the themes and observations will also have general relevance elsewhere in the world. However, as the American saying goes, 'All politics is local,' and so too are policy issues, which cannot really be separated from their political setting if they are to be considered in any detail. A worldwide survey of water soft path policy would be a book in itself if it closely described policy issues country by country. Consequently, in this Canada-focused discussion, readers are urged to take what they find useful, but to recognize that some circumstances, institutions and barriers will be quite different in other places.

Two broad factors influence the development of strong national (and regional) differences in the approach to water policy: the first is the economic and political structure coupled with the level of development in a country; and second is the historic, perceived and actual water abundance or availability. Canada is a relatively wealthy developed country, ranking high on such measures as the UNDP Human Development Index, and perceptions are that it is also rich in its freshwater resources. As will be discussed further in Chapters

15, 16 and 17, the first of these factors goes far toward determining which people and which institutions are involved in water policy discussion and change. The second factor, water abundance, affects what the substantive policy questions and controversies are likely to be about.

Policy by default – the first challenge for the water soft path in Canada

Public policy is generally described as the overall direction taken on issues in a specific area of government action. It might seem, therefore, that policy options would, as a matter of course, be debated in public forums, and that politicians and political parties would be the main actors in setting policy. In the real world that often is not the case.

Policy is, indeed, direction-creating decisions that affect broad areas of public affairs but policy choices are not always framed as such. When situations seem to be normal and well in hand, many corporate, bureaucratic or administrative decisions about public matters proceed without any real political attention or debate. However, such routine decisions can shape public options for decades, effectively creating policy. Policy can also be determined when a key level of government consciously avoids taking any action on an issue, notably by *not* developing a new framework for making decisions, when there are clear reasons to rethink priorities and alternatives. Such a policy gap most often occurs when effective action would stir strong political controversy. Canada's 20-year failure to formulate a climate change plan is a case in point (Paehlke, 2008).

Both sorts of circumstances – unchallenged routine decisions and political policy gaps – can be described as *policy-making by default*. In Canada, this is the basic obstacle that water soft path advocates must surmount, and it has two main sources:

- First, water use in Canada has little profile as a public issue. For most community and regional water utilities, routine bureaucratic decision-making predominates (Maas, 2003; Furlong with Bakker, 2007). However, business-as-usual decisions to construct large-scale water infrastructure can dictate water management priorities for years to come. And policy change at this level can be *more* difficult because a soft path approach does not reject but builds on modern water management practice. In particular, the soft path incorporates the advances in safe water supply and sanitation that have dominated the delivery of urban water services in the developed world for the last century. And the recent emphasis on demand management by some water utilities is also an essential part of a water soft path. As a result, the current model may not appear to be dramatically different from the soft path approach, which makes it that much more difficult to attract the attention, knowledge and commitment needed for the soft path's full implementation.

- Second, in Canada there has generally been a conspicuous policy gap related to management of fresh water supplies. Despite sporadic attention to various water issues, senior levels of government generally have not followed up on recommendations for a comprehensive water policy that would involve long-term planning and ongoing action for the sustainable use of freshwater resources (Brandes et al, 2007). In this kind of policy vacuum, a large part of the problem for soft path ideas is their lack of visibility as a clear alternative policy choice. Without ever being actively rejected, water soft path thinking could simply be sidelined indefinitely.

What, then, needs to happen in water management practice today in order to adopt a soft path policy? First, there must be a clear understanding of why things need to change and of how things can be done differently. This latter question entails identifying the ways various actors and their respective institutions must shift direction. It also involves building awareness of the new tools and other actions that the soft path employs to achieve its objective of limiting water use. Finally, it would be useful to pick out the most critical barriers that must be addressed in order to concentrate on efforts to overcome them. (Barriers are discussed in more detail in Chapters 4 and 12.) The following sections of this chapter discuss each of these topics in turn.

The goal is key

The single most important characteristic of a water soft path approach is that it is about ecological sustainability as a new, additional, and explicit goal for water management. Unlike traditional water planning, the soft path takes into account the water requirements for *in situ* functions of the natural resource. This new perspective acknowledges the vital importance of maintaining ecological 'services' such as nutrient cycling and aquatic habitat, as well as aesthetic values and on-site human uses such as swimming and boating, hydroelectric power production, and commercial fishing and shipping. Even in a relatively water-rich country, the capacity of the resource to sustain these functions can be compromised *before* water shortages for agriculture, industry and domestic use become acute. At some point, therefore, water withdrawals and diversion will need to be limited. This fact drives the water soft path.

The Canadian studies presented in this book indicate that, especially in seasonal low-flow periods, shortfalls of replenishable water throughout much of southern Canada are much closer at hand than most people appreciate (e.g. Schindler and Donahue, 2006). Of course, in many other parts of the world, such shortfalls are already a reality. As we will show in Chapters 16 and 17, a number of chronically water-short places such as Australia and the Middle East have already started to use water planning to address ecological requirements. Controversies arising from differing social, economic or political values concerning water allocation may justify the use of a soft path approach to rethink current policies.

The goal of traditional business-as-usual water planning is to provide the infrastructure to tap, treat and distribute water so that people have a safe, adequate supply for all their perceived needs. Demand management as a distinct approach recognizes that reducing demand through improving efficiency and encouraging modest changes in behaviour is usually much cheaper than adding the next increment to the local water supply and infrastructure. The bottom line here is about economic efficiency. Unlike a water soft path, neither a business-as-usual nor a demand management focus highlights actual limits – on the resource, on human uses of it, or on new water infrastructure – as critical to water planning.

Policy that limits use

The water soft path is based on a vision of sustainable water management that explicitly takes such limits into account. As their pragmatic first objective, water soft path strategies in Canada propose that no additional supply infrastructure be constructed until some future date that is at least 20 to 30 years hence. Communities and water managers thus have a reasonable planning period to reach a target intended to approximate the limits needed to achieve ecological goals and sustainable human use. Further analysis is of course needed to determine what limits on water use will be required after the end point of the original strategy. Better ecological data and methodologies are now becoming available to reduce guesswork in setting sustainability objectives for the longer term (Postel and Richter, 2003), but the detailed water use data needed to complement ecological information are not yet widely available.

A truly sustainable approach to water management over time must drastically reshape the human activities that affect water demand. Given Canada's growing population, limiting the infrastructure needed to make water available will mean that per capita domestic use must fall. Businesses, public institutions, industry and agriculture will all need to reduce their requirements as well.

The required changes will certainly have some demanding implications, including adjustments to expectations, habits and budgets. The many actions and programmes needed to bring about sustainable water use will also require political initiative. Most importantly, in order to respond to the challenges creatively rather than with resistance, most sectors of water users, along with bureaucrats and elected officials, will need to understand and support the policy goal of sustainability for water management. Such a near consensus will only come about if it is preceded by, among other things, excellent public information and well-designed public consultation, transparent decision-making, regular feedback about water use, fairness in water allocation mechanisms and pricing, and economically sustainable means of maintaining the water infrastructure. Successful soft path implementation will therefore mean negotiating some complex public issues and furthering many new institutional developments. The general thrust of these institutional changes must be toward greater and more effective public involvement.

Repositioning water management decisions

Probably the most significant institutional reform that will need to be taken concerns the relationship between water management and land use planning. Water planning currently follows from decisions about land use and economic development: plan a new subdivision or industrial park, and municipal engineers will see that sufficient water is available. But if construction of new water infrastructure is to be avoided, water issues must sometimes override other matters – perhaps a proposed subdivision or industrial park of that size really cannot be built in that watershed. Water management must, in some formal and official way, be integrated with land use and economic planning.

As a result, planning departments will need to address wider issues and employ different kinds of information and techniques than they have used in the past. Municipal, provincial and federal governments will also require redefined or additional positions and programmes to enhance supporting activities in environment, economic development and water management agencies.

Initiatives at each level of government

The findings from Canadian water soft path studies carried out at different scales (specifically, at the scale of the municipality, watershed and province) indicate that, although there are many initiatives that senior levels of government must undertake, much of the critical action is at the municipal or community level. This is because the defining decisions for moving toward or away from a water soft path depend very much on variables such as the rate of local or regional population growth, regional economic development, especially in agriculture and resource extraction, and the timing of upcoming decisions about new municipal water infrastructure. Consequently, trying to define a successful national water soft path policy would be rather like stitching together all the pieces of a patchwork quilt (i.e., the sum of all the disparate municipal policies across the country), rather than creating a grand design for the whole country at once.

Taking Canada as an example, there are policy changes that need to be made at every political level:

• Municipal/regional governments, including local watershed authorities such as those in Ontario, are the central actors in water policy development. They must change their land use planning mandates to incorporate a water conservation focus and adjust their budgets and staffing accordingly. As discussed in the section about implementation tools, local water utilities, which are responsible for planning and building infrastructure, must develop scenarios, targets and implementation strategies based on sustainability. Municipalities will need to develop and implement conservation and demand management programmes that incorporate both incentives and new municipal bylaws that impose tough mandatory measures as well as universal water metering and volume-based pricing for both freshwater deliveries and wastewater disposal (Brandes and Ferguson, 2004; Furlong with Bakker, 2008).

- Provincial governments have the main responsibility both to assess the state of the resource as well as to protect it. They will need to review their policies on permitting or licensing well drilling and water takings, introduce stronger measures to protect source water and aquatic habitat and develop their knowledge base and enforcement capabilities. Provincial governments could also consider innovative ways to provide leadership, such as setting up a water commissioner's office or similar agency to coordinate water-related planning, as Manitoba and Alberta have done. They could develop appropriate guidelines for water rates based on marginal, full-cost pricing, or even mandate that a public utilities board approve water utility pricing, with legislative direction to consider fairness, cost recovery and conservation.

- Senior levels of government, both federal and provincial, have a potential role to play in setting standards or guidelines for water efficiency, or use, in areas such as new residential and commercial construction and water-using appliances (similar to what has already been done with the Energy Star Program in Canada and the US).

- The federal government should apply the water soft path approach to planning and operations in areas under its jurisdiction: in Canada, this includes water on First Nation reserves, in the North, and in national parks and other federal lands. As part of its role as a major funder of technology development and environmental science and research, the federal government should designate resources to support the water soft path. It should add to its scientific and environmental enforcement capacities, addressing gaps in the knowledge and protection of freshwater and wetland habitat, ecology and the water resource base. It will be especially important to anticipate the effects of a changing climate in these efforts.

Other countries, of course, have differing jurisdictional responsibilities for different levels of government. However, the kinds of tasks and duties described here will need to be undertaken by the relevant agency with the appropriate authority wherever a soft path approach is used. In some places, community or non-government groups may play a significant role in these various activities. New organizations, sometimes provisional and ad hoc, or else newly created official agencies, may need to take on some of these actions, particularly in cases where important segments of the population lack political power (either because they are women, or immigrants, or poor, or for any other reason), and the context may well be more about a struggle for equality in society than about water issues alone (e.g. Biswas et al, 2008). A longer-term issue for senior or national levels of government is that at some point – sooner rather than later in parts of the world with significant and chronic water shortages – many departments and agencies will have to take notice of the questions raised by the intersection of water policy with policies on energy, the environment, economic development, trade, food and agriculture (Brooks et al, 2007). The water soft path embraces an ecological perspective wherein water is vitally important; but so also are pollution problems or protecting other ecosystem components such as intact forest habitats. These considerations, along with socio-economic goals such as food or energy security, or rural or regional development, have the potential to create sharp conflicts with water soft path-derived limitations on water use. In particular, there are important policy questions related to what is often referred to as 'virtual water', or, more accurately, 'incorporated water' – that is, the water which usually leaves a watershed permanently when it is incorporated in agricultural or manufactured products that are sold elsewhere (Allan, 1998, 2001). Does it make sense to use a great deal of water for irrigation to produce vegetables year round, where there is fertile soil and a warm but dry climate, and to use fossil fuel energy to transport them to places with a less salubrious regime for agriculture – or not? Even with an overarching environmental perspective, there are numerous and complex trade-offs in almost every instance if a number of social goals are considered simultaneously. Substantial analysis will be needed to clarify just what the implications and trade-offs are, in many cases, but that is only a first step. Decisions about such issues are inherently political, and much will depend upon the quality of the debate and the process.

Implementing water soft path policy

Before reviewing the tools that are needed, it is useful to consider whether all the decision-makers involved have to understand and label what they're doing as 'the water soft path' in order to make progress. Actually, they don't, certainly not right away. Water soft paths can be developed and implemented in stages. As noted earlier, precisely because soft paths build on today's water management concerns, it is possible for water utilities to move from traditional business-as-usual planning to a focus on demand management, and from there, increasingly understanding the need for limits, to design and implement a water soft path. The crucial step is to make sure that the right people in the right places have the knowledge and commitment to advance beyond conventional thinking and practice.

Analysts have identified what are often referred to as four principles that characterize the soft path as a policy option distinct from, and more radical than, demand management (see Chapter 1). One of these – the emphasis on ecological goals and related limits – has already been described as the soft path's defining difference as a policy. The other three 'principles', however, are really special tools for achieving this goal. They are the foundation for actually developing and implementing a water soft path.

Backcasting a planning tool designed to get to a different future, one based on deliberately chosen ecological and other goals. It is also a vehicle for public engagement in developing a shared vision for a community's future, and for creating the public and political support for changes needed to make that vision a reality.

The remaining principles, numbers 1 and 3 in our list – respectively, treating water as a service and matching water quality to water needs – are actually innovative concepts for rethinking, and thereby reducing, traditional water demands through redesign: of appliances, buildings, industrial processes and even landscapes or agricultural crops. However, these principles are not the only tools needed. Though they are the distinctive features of a soft path approach, the policy challenge is to bring these principles – this new goal, and the tools for planning and redesign – into practical use. As noted earlier, the first step is just to understand their application in water management. After that comes the complex task of identifying and developing ways to address the different motivating factors, barriers and potential incentives to bring about change for each sector of water users. In many places there are excellent individual programmes that have already been developed (Vickers, 2002). Detailing all these efforts is too large a task for this chapter, but they include categories such as information and education campaigns, pricing and economic incentives, and new bylaws and regulatory initiatives.

Overcoming the critical barriers

Making any change that shifts policy direction is rarely easy. The discussion of barriers, in Chapter 12 of this book, as well as the difficulties described in the chapters on initiatives in other countries and regions, demonstrates – if anyone had any doubts – that for any number of reasons, real progress will not be quickly achieved. However, to bring about a water soft path in Canada, three areas stand out as needing exceptionally creative, determined effort.

First, metering with realistic water pricing is both fundamental to the success of a water soft path and, at the same time, probably the hardest part of the process to sell (Brandes and Ferguson, 2004). In the absence of policies requiring water metering and full-cost accounting and pricing, there is simply no business rationale for farmers, institutions or commercial and industrial customers to invest in redesigning their operations for radical reductions in water use. There is, similarly, no clear basis on which municipalities or water utilities can analyse the costs and benefits of introducing demand management programmes, nor for domestic users to participate in them. Complicating matters is resistance by the public, and often by politicians, to any increase in water rates. At the same time, the rhetoric of activist campaigns for water as a human right, and against privatizing water treatment, may encourage an attitude of entitlement toward water use and hostility to putting any price on it – making matters worse.

Informed and committed leadership will obviously be needed to implement water prices based on real costs. Certainly, water-pricing reforms will (justifiably) find more support if they are designed from the start to ensure that any subsequent hardships are fairly apportioned, and that assistance for the poor to cope with the new situation is available. In places where pricing reforms are already going forward, such as those countries that have signed onto the European Water Framework Directive (see Chapter 16), paying attention to fairness in both process and outcomes will be just as essential.

Second, belief and motivation are underrated as factors that hamper application of the soft path approach. Even with water prices that signal otherwise, the widespread assumption that water is abundant in Canada (or any other country or region that hasn't experienced severe shortages) is still likely to persist for some time. This is especially the case in urban areas where water simply flows from the tap, and people don't have to personally deal with where it comes from or goes to. Sophisticated social marketing programmes can be highly effective in getting individuals to change their behaviour for social goals like water conservation. But getting politicians to alter institutional structures and policy frameworks usually requires a perception that there is a serious public crisis. Information programmes about the state of water resources and the implications of current use patterns must be innovative and compelling in order to reach the public and encourage officials to support institutional change.

Finally, there is the challenge of inadequate and poor quality data. As the Canadian water soft path studies make crystal clear, limited monitoring and data for both the resource base and water use allow only a sketchy picture at best of the present situation. This lack of information not only complicates water soft path planning, it also hinders the development of any public sense of urgency about water issues. A revival of a commitment to state-of-the-environment reporting could help motivate agencies to improve their performance by publicly spotlighting the need for more monitoring and better data.

The good news

The implementation of changes similar to the ones that are important for water soft paths is by no means unprecedented in other policy areas. In many countries, the oil price shocks of the 1970s resulted in the creation of new agencies dedicated to energy conservation and efficiency at all levels of government (Holtz and Brooks, 2003). New analyses, policies and programmes followed, as did the formation of many new businesses that specialized in energy saving technologies and techniques. Despite the subsequent weakening of the drivers for those changes – high energy prices and energy security worries – many of the achievements of that period still survive today.

Although there is no water crisis in Canada comparable to the 1970s upheaval in energy prices and supply, increasing awareness about environmental sustainability is creating a political window of opportunity. There is a discernable growth in demand for practical changes such as greener building construction, alternative transportation options, and local organic food. Links with other environmental issues, such as the impact of climate change on agriculture and food security, the need to protect source water, and the detection of pharmaceuticals and endocrine-disrupting contaminants in treated drinking water, could provide a springboard to broaden water-related reforms into water soft path policies. The challenge, therefore, is to link water use to the broader range of ecological issues, about which people are passionately concerned, and which many now realize as requiring a longer-term perspective for planning, political initiatives and personal responsibility. This can be done – the widespread success of domestic recycling programmes comes to mind – but the acceptance that there is a real threat to society as a whole is always the prerequisite condition. The second condition is the confidence that the threat can be defeated. As evidence in this book attests, the water soft path is not an easy road, but with determination, inventiveness and perhaps some luck, it can be taken.

References

Allan, J. A. (1998) 'Virtual water: A strategic resource: Global solutions to regional deficits', *Groundwater*, vol 36, no. 4, pp546–557

Allan, J. A. (2001) *The Middle East Water Question: Hydropolitics and the Global Economy.* I. B. Tauris, London

Biswas, A. K., Rached, E. and Tortajada, C. (eds) (2008) *Water as a Human Right for the Middle East and North Africa*, Routledge, Milton Park, UK

Brandes, O. M. and Ferguson, K. (2004) *The Future in Every Drop: The Benefits, Barriers, and Practice of Urban Water Demand Management in Canada*, POLIS Project on Ecological Governance, University of Victoria, Victoria, BC

Brandes, O. M., Brooks, D. B. and M'Gonigle, M. (2007) 'Moving water conservation to centre stage', in K. Bakker (ed) *Eau Canada: The Future of Canada's Water*, UBC Press, Vancouver, BC

Brooks, D. B., Thomson, L. and El Fattal, L. (2007) 'Water demand management in the Middle East and North Africa: Observations from the IDRC forums and lessons for the future', *Water International*, vol 32, no 3, pp193–204

Furlong, K. with Bakker, K. (2007) *Achieving Water Conservation: Strategies for Good Governance*, Program on Water Governance, University of British Columbia, Vancouver, BC

Furlong, K. with Bakker, K. (2008) *Water Governance in Transition: Utility Restructuring and Water Efficiency in Ontario*, Program on Water Governance, University of British Columbia, Vancouver, BC

Holtz, S. and Brooks, D. B. (2003) 'Reverse engineering – soft energy paths', in A. Heintzman and E. Solomon, *Fueling the Future: How the Battle for Energy is Changing Everything*, House of Anansi, Toronto, ON

Maas, T. (2003) *What the Experts Think: Understanding Urban Water Demand Management in Canada*, POLIS Project on Ecological Governance, University of Victoria, Victoria, BC

Paehlke, R. C. (2008) *Some Like It Cold: Ambivalent North – Strong and Free*, Between the Lines, Downsview, ON, Canada

Postel, S. and Richter, B. (2003) *Rivers for Life: Managing Water for People and Nature*, Island Press, Washington, DC

Schindler, D. W. and Donahue, W. F. (2006) 'An impending water crisis in Canada's Western prairie provinces', *Proceedings of the National Academy of Sciences*, Washington, DC

Vickers, A. (2002) *A Handbook of Water Use Conservation*, WaterPlow Press, Amherst, MA

Part II
Water Soft Paths as Analytical Method

7
Getting Quantitative: The Canadian Water Soft Path Studies

David B. Brooks and Susan Holtz

If you go to the hardware store looking for a drill, chances are what you really want is not a drill but a hole. And then there's a reason you want the hole. If you ask enough layers of 'Why?' ... You typically get to the root of the problem.

Amory B. Lovins

As indicated in Chapter 1, all soft paths incorporate a vision, analysis and tools.[1] This chapter will focus on the analysis, as it was used in the Canadian case studies of the application of water soft paths to specific geographical, ecological and jurisdictional settings. Much of the material presented applies to all forms of soft path analysis, but we will of course focus primarily on the application to water. The section following this introduction explores the nature of soft paths analytics. Because the analytics were first developed for energy, the third section compares energy and water for analytical purposes. And then, because soft paths must start from, but go beyond, resource efficiency, the fourth section compares demand management and soft paths, again from the perspective of analysis. The fifth section identifies qualifications that limit soft path analysis. The final section offers a brief summary of the Canadian studies – to our knowledge the first such studies anywhere in the world. The Annex to the book provides a step-by-step summary of the methodology for water soft path analysis.

Nature of soft path analytics

The four core principles of water soft path studies were introduced in Chapter 1. Here we can begin by indicating just how those principles lead to an analytical approach that differs from more conventional approaches. Though it is typically convenient to break the process into additional steps, they can all be resolved into the four key ones, and all four must be present for a true soft path analysis.

1   Instead of accepting projections of human water demand as 'needs' that must be met, soft paths treat most water requirements as a means to an end – as, for example, growing food, cooling machines or removing wastes. Drinking water is an obvious and important exception, but not a large one. Beyond the 50 litres per person/day needed for an adequate lifestyle, and for which water is a final good, there are alternative ways to satisfy demands that now require water. Water for cooling – the largest industrial use – is more typical as it can be accomplished in many ways. Therefore, instead of looking for additional supplies of water, soft paths look for additional ways to economize on water use through demand management and to conserve water through changes in habits and practices, as well as by limiting water-intensive economic growth patterns.

2   Instead of developing new sources or conveyance plans, and then looking at ways to mitigate environmental and social effects, soft paths treat environmental and social goals as *a priori* constraints that cannot be violated except as a last resort. For water, the bedrock environmental goals are: to keep freshwater withdrawals within the bounds of renewable water availability, to avoid significant inter-basin transfers and to keep waste-water releases within the ability of ecological capacity to maintain healthy ecosystems. It is not so easy to generalize about social goals (nor to measure whether or not they have been achieved), but they would have strong elements of economic equity, public participation and cultural preservation.

3   Instead of focusing entirely on the quantity of water delivered, soft paths also take account of water quality. For both ecological and economic reasons, it is almost as important to conserve the quality of a resource as to conserve its quantity. High-quality resources can be used for many purposes; low-quality resources for only a few. Happily, we need relatively small quantities of high-quality (and high-cost) resources, such as potable water, but there are huge demands for resources of lower quality (and lower cost) water – most importantly for irrigation, which accounts for 70–80 per cent of global water use.

4   Instead of projecting forward to demonstrate so-called water 'requirements' and then figuring out how to satisfy them, water soft paths start by defining a sustainable future. Then, working backwards ('backcasting'), the analysis identifies environmentally, economically, socially and politi-

cally feasible 'soft paths' – typically there is more than just one – that will serve to link that desired future with the present situation. It is at this stage that appropriate policies and programmes to bring about the desired changes must be defined, along with the transition technologies used.

In many ways, the last principle is the most important. Appropriate policies in water soft path thinking are dependent on context. One has to start the backcasting process by designing a water regime that is socially equitable and ecologically sustainable, as well as economically efficient, but this always takes place in a particular community or region, with its own ecological, economic and cultural realities. *Soft path policies are less a set of technologies than a socio-political process for choosing, from a range of technical, social and economic options, specific ones that can move society toward a desired future state.* Analytically, a soft path is thus more reliant on political and social science than it is on a mechanistic application of technical and biophysical information, though all the water sciences, ranging from elementary school descriptions of the water cycle to complex investigations of endocrine disrupters, define the range within which the social sciences must operate.

Energy and water: many similarities; some differences

Water and energy exhibit many similarities, particularly as physical materials. Both, of course, follow the same natural laws, as with the conservation of matter and entropy gain. More importantly for present purposes, there are also parallels in the ways in which they have come to be developed as resources for human use (Brooks with Rose, 2003; Linton, 2009). The gradual shift from simple, to combined, to highly complex technologies, and from individual, to local, to centralized systems, has typified these two key resources for human development. However, as illustrated by Lovins' now classic descriptions of soft technologies (1976, 1977), the shift has proceeded much further for energy than it has for water. For instance, a much larger share of energy than of water comes from nonrenewable sources. With the exception of fossil (enclosed) aquifers, which can be depleted just as oil fields can be, most water is taken from renewable sources. Unfortunately, in some cases, so much water is drawn from lakes, rivers or renewable aquifers that, though renewable under natural conditions, the sources become depleted from excessive extraction. For another example, water supply technologies are still mainly a matter of pipes and pumps and, with the partial exceptions of desalination and of wastewater treatment, are nowhere near the scale or the complexity of many energy supply technologies.

One physical difference between energy and water must be highlighted. With energy, most waste flows 'disappear' after use. Of course, they do not really disappear but emerge as exhaust gases, waste heat or radiation. All have environmental impacts, but, with the exception of opportunities to recover waste heat, they are of little economic interest. This is not the case with water.

For the most part water remains in, or returns to, a liquid state after use. It then either flows back into the hydrological cycle (as in runoff from fields) or is contained in lakes or tanks and moved through ditches or pipes to an outflow, with or without treatment. All of these wastewater flows require management (which is not to imply that they always get it), and most permit recycling or reuse.

Though water and energy may share many characteristics as physical substances, they are less analogous in their social and economic characteristics. For example, because water is of principal interest in one form and state – fluid water – whereas energy appears and is delivered in a variety of forms and states, differentiation of the market is much less common for water. Thus, we have oil companies, gas companies, coal companies and electrical utilities, among others but, except for the separation of agencies dealing with irrigation water from those dealing with potable water in many countries, we just have water utilities, a few private, most public, but all with more or less the same goals.

Other key differences can be listed as follows:

- Unlike energy pricing, there is no global or even national reference unit pricing for water. Moreover, economics plays a less significant role for water than for energy as a driver for decisions about pricing. Bottled drinking water to one side, water prices are typically so far below actual costs that they are barely considered by water users and suppliers. Further, no one would think that oil or gas or coal could (or should!) be extracted from natural sources without paying a royalty, but in most places water can be withdrawn at no cost other than pumping. Consequently, though one can make 'least cost' arguments for saving water on analytical grounds, it is more difficult to make those arguments politically persuasive because the costs are hidden.

- Compared with energy, where federal and provincial initiatives dominate, and where private, national and multinational corporations operate with ease, there is a much greater role for municipalities and regional governments, and for their public water utilities, in implementing water policies and programmes. Though some large water management corporations have begun to operate on the international scene in recent years, they have experienced nothing even close to the success of international energy firms (Gleick et al, 2003).

- The strong opposition to energy mega-projects, and notably to nuclear generating facilities, has no comparable 'hot button' environmental issue for freshwater use (in contrast to water pollution issues). The closest analogy involves opposition to the construction of large dams. It is more commonly at the local or regional level that water issues can become hot, as indicated by reports from many communities around the world (Dinar and Loehman, 1995). Few of these issues reach the national stage, and only a tiny fraction – the Narmada project in India and Three Gorges in China are examples – become *causes célèbres*. Consequently, also absent from debates about water is the political energy that supported renewable energy and conservation as alternatives to energy mega-projects.

• Finally, it is a tenet of soft energy path analysis that no one wants a litre of petrol or a battery with stored electric power for itself. Rather, people want the services that the petrol or the electricity can provide. This is not the case for water, which has inherent value – a fact that lovers around the world have never thought to question. Placid lakes are beautiful; tumbling waterfalls are dramatic; springs can have religious importance. In this sense, an analogy can be made between the sun and water, but not between energy and water. We are beginning to have tools for putting the value of ecosystem services on an analytical basis (Postel and Richter, 2003; Millennium Ecosystem Assessment, 2005; Katz, 2006). However, there will always be some inestimable gap that reflects the value that water has for human beings on aesthetic, religious or cultural grounds.

Despite this wide range of socio-economic differences, water and energy exhibit one striking similarity in their development patterns. In the early years of industrial development, growth in the use of water and energy tracked growth of the economy fairly closely. In recent years, decoupling of energy use and economic growth has been evident, and now statistical evidence indicates that water is following the same pattern. As Wolff and Gleick (2002) have shown, water use in absolute, not just per capita, terms is declining in the US. A Task Force created by the International Joint Commission to review water uses in the Great Lakes basin has concluded 'that the consumptive use "problem" has been consistently and significantly overstated for the past three decades' (IJC, 2002, p83). Though the decoupling is most pronounced in industrial countries, they also find that the pattern is global. Almost all recent forecasts of water use are significantly lower than older ones (Gleick, 2003). The reasons for reduced water use are highly varied, and more often than not involve industrial restructuring around the world rather than conservation per se.

Finally, it is worth noting that low-income and other disadvantaged people commonly suffer more from inadequate water supply and poor water quality than from insufficient energy. Except in extreme climatic areas, for both immediate needs and long-term survival, water is *the* essential resource.

First demand management; then soft paths

Gleick (1998) suggests that soft path thinking requires a paradigm shift because it moves away from a central focus on economic efficiency to give equal standing to equity and ecology, and because it brings behaviour change and institutional change into the analysis. Conventional demand management techniques then become an important component of a soft path, but they neither go so far in changing water uses as do soft paths nor do they incorporate such other elements as wide public consultation in backcasting and policy development.

Demand management options have been known for years in Canada (Brooks and Peters, 1988; Tate, 1990), but, with water prices kept artificially low, little incentive has existed for widespread adoption. Even today, demand management is seen by managers, in many Canadian water utilities, mainly as a short-term measure (Brandes and Ferguson, 2004; Furlong and Bakker, 2008). In some countries, water utilities do not even consider it part of their mandate to urge consumers to conserve water. However, once demand management is recognized as incorporating a wide range of activities – saving water quality as well as quantity and adjusting use from peak to off-peak hours – it is a very powerful tool and one that is generally consistent with environmental and social goals (Brooks, 2006).

Quantitative studies of demand management measures show that, in many cases, reducing demand is already our best 'source' of water (Brandes and Ferguson, 2004). A detailed study for California (Gleick et al, 2003) demonstrates that total urban water use could be cut by 30 per cent using off-the-shelf technologies that are cost effective and that can be implemented in less time than any new supply project. A follow-up study added agricultural and rural uses of water, and adopted the same population, housing and economic projections, as did the official California Water Plan; it concluded (Gleick et al, 2005, p1):

> Under a High Efficiency scenario, total human use of water in California could decline by as much as 20 per cent while still satisfying a growing population, maintaining a healthy agricultural sector, and supporting a vibrant economy.

Water soft paths accept the importance of greater water efficiency, but go further by incorporating conservation measures, including changes in water use habits, water management institutions, and economic and demographic growth rates and patterns (Gleick, 1998; Brooks, 2005). But is the change indicated in Chapter 1 from asking 'How' to asking 'Why' so very different? Are soft paths not just a more extensive form of demand management? Though some soft path measures are indeed used in demand management programmes today, conceptually and practically, there are differences. For example, installation of more efficient sprinklers is a demand management approach whereas replacing lawns with some form of xeriscaping is a soft path approach. The latter clarifies what the underlying goal actually is, in this case, attractive landscaping, and addresses it in an alternative, not just a more efficient, manner. Lawns and xeriscape planting are not so different, which is why the latter has been absorbed into the demand management toolkit, but it is really a soft path approach.

Soft path measures are also different from water use efficiency at the theoretical level. Everyone who took Introductory Economics can remember those curves for supply and demand. Another of those basic diagrams shows the production possibilities curve, which illustrates how to achieve efficiency in

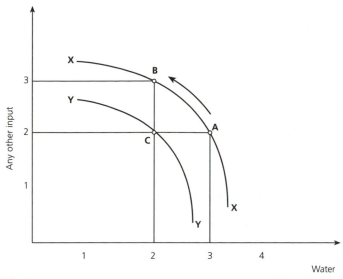

Source: David Brooks

Figure 7.1 *Production possibilities graph*

resource management by adjusting the proportions of inputs used in production. In the typical textbook description using just two inputs (see Figure 7.1), demand management entails a shift along that curve to a position that is less dependent on one natural resource, water in our case, and more dependent on another input, for example, energy. Soft paths entail a shift of the whole curve so that every position on the curve is less dependent on water for the same amount of the other input.

A production possibilities curve (or surface, depending upon the number of variables) can be used to illustrate the relationship between the two inputs that are used in some region to produce some output. Every point on the curves in Figure 7.1 is efficient because each represents the best possible combination of the two inputs; points inside the curve are possible but inefficient (less productive) whereas points outside the curve are impossible to attain. (The point of maximum profitability cannot be determined until the costs of the two inputs are known, but that discussion is beyond the scope needed for present purposes.) The production possibilities graph shows that water can be saved by moving from Point A to Point B along Curve XX, while still maintaining efficient production of the output, but only by using more of the other input. It also shows that if, because of technological or managerial improvements, the whole curve shifts to the left, as to Curve YY, the same output can be produced efficiently at point C with less use of water and no increase in use of the other output. The shift from Point A to Point B illustrates a demand management measure; the shift to Point C illustrates a soft path action.

Finally, there are political and social differences stemming from the soft path insistence on ecological sustainability and on its use of backcasting, both of which involve human values and choices, and which are usually held constant when identifying demand management options. Soft path approaches create winners and losers, and that means politics in the narrowest, almost pejorative, sense. Sometimes the answer to a potential opportunity for economic growth – a new golf course or subdivision – will be: 'No. That is not how we choose to use our limited water resources.' Good for the natural environment and for those who want free-flowing water, but not so good for workers in a community with 20 per cent unemployment. Big choices are never easy, but water soft paths provide a better framework for making them than does demand management alone.

Limitations of water soft path analysis

Soft path studies are data intensive, and the potential for good results is limited by the absence, in all but a few jurisdictions, of adequate time series and cross-sectional data on water use. Because of their focus on the demand side, water soft path analyses need at least basic information on water use by region and by sector. Ideally each sector should be further broken down according to major end-uses (as with cooling water, washing water, incorporation into product) and by major users (as with single family houses, small apartments, large apartments) at least on a sample basis. The absence of more than rough and partial data precludes detailed analysis of alternative water use options, to say nothing of water non-use options. This lack of detailed data also precludes analysis as detailed as is generally possible with energy use. Though an earlier study in Canada, testing the feasibility of water soft path analysis, did conclude that available data were sufficient for at least preliminary work (Brooks et al, 2004), data limitations force us to admit that, though research results are probably accurate, they are by no means precise.

Two other limitations of water soft path analysis are inherent in the method. First is the absence of statistical tables that relate changes in economic scale and structure to changes in water use for the economy as a whole. The Canadian study of soft energy paths undertaken by Friends of the Earth Canada in the early 1980s (Bott et al,1983) had the enormous advantage of building upon materials balance and input–output tables that described the Canadian economy in terms of energy flows rather than dollars (Gault et al, 1987). This allowed the analysts to compare energy use in detail. For example, to save energy we could postulate a shift of freight from road to rail and, at the same time, allow for related changes in the necessary increase in capital investment in railroads (and energy use associated with that investment) as well as a parallel decrease for roadways. The water soft path study described below did not have the benefit of water-based input–output tables nor, so far as we know, do such tables exist anywhere in the world. Therefore, analysis has to focus on just the most water-intensive sectors and assume that everything else will respond without major interactions between sectors. For example, the process of pulping wood to make paper can be accomplished using different technologies; some of these are more water intensive, but economize on energy, whereas others are more energy intensive but economize on water. If we were to suggest shifting new plants to the latter approach, we could show major water savings at the pulp mill level, but we would have ignored a probable increase in water use in the energy sector. In this sense, water soft path studies may overstate potential gains. However, effects related to the scale of the whole economy and shifts in economic structure probably overwhelm any such overstatement. The 'Scenario Builder' model described in Chapter 8 is a partial substitute for the absence of a full input–output model with water as the 'currency'.

Use of the energy-based input–output tables also permitted the Canadian soft energy study to analyse structural change in the economy. Shifts in the industrial structure away from natural resources and toward services resulted in significant reductions in total energy use. It is very likely that the same pattern would be found with water use. The absence of the ability to make analyses of this kind for water probably leads to more conservative results than would otherwise be the case.

Second, because soft path analyses look inward at a particular society, they are also limited in dealing with water that is exported from the area under study – exported perhaps as bulk or bottled water but more importantly embedded in products. Although actual exports of water are very limited – even the apparently large volumes of water moving in bottles as soft drinks, beer, wine and water itself are small in national or regional terms – the far more difficult area involves what has come to be called 'virtual water' (Allan, 2001; Schendel et al, 2007). Virtual water is a concept that emerged from the School of Oriental and African Studies at the University of London in the 1990s to replace the less expressive term 'embedded water' (Allan, 2003). It reflects the volume of water that is incorporated into products throughout the production cycle including, to take the example of insulated electrical wire, the water to grow the wrapping fibre and to mine the copper as well as that to produce the cloth and manufacture the wire.[2] Soft path analytics offer no way to show the impact of options for conservation of any water, whether direct or virtual, once it crosses the border of the region under study. About all one can do is to treat such water as totally consumed; it disappears not just from the community but also from the ecosystem. Virtual water is a minor consideration with most industrial products, but a major one for metals, beverages and a few other sectors, and an enormous one for agricultural crops. For countries in which water is scarce, the export of products with high volumes of virtual water can – indeed, should – become a political issue (Allan, 2003). However, for purposes of soft path analysis, the problem is one of accounting, not of politics. Still, it is worth noting that, given Canada's international specialization in primary metals and agriculture, it is highly likely that Canada exports far more virtual water than it imports.

Finally, one limitation of existing water soft path studies is self-imposed, a result of limited time and limited resources. Most soft path visioning, analysis and planning to now has focused on urban and peri-urban areas and on selected industrial sectors. Rather less effort has been devoted to rural areas and to commercial agriculture. There is no intellectual barrier to the application of water soft paths to these areas, but application must take account of critical differences between water use in urban and rural areas, or at least between urban and agricultural areas. In urban areas, institutional change for water generally affects a critical but small portion of people's lives and incomes. Land use decisions are generally made with only passing reference to water use, and the balance between water for urban uses and water for ecosystem services tends to be complementary. In rural areas, water availability and livelihoods are almost the same thing; land use decisions are often directly coupled to water use decisions; and there can be serious competition between water for rural (mainly agricultural; in some cases mining) water use and water for ecosystem services. As a result of these differences, water soft paths in rural areas must be carefully considered and certainly introduced more cautiously, and the whole approach must be linked to rural development policies, with particular emphasis on agriculture. This is a very important distinction since we have already seen that the urban–rural 'divide' has played an important role in policy debates on questions involving such issues as land use planning, the environment or animal welfare.

Application of water soft path analysis in Canada

There is as yet only limited experience with water soft path analysis; even less experience with its application in policy; and none at all as a way to promote water security over the long term. Though there is a modest body of published material, the only study that incorporates all elements of soft path analysis and applies it to specific jurisdictions with specific geographies, economies and ecologies was undertaken by Friends of the Earth Canada in conjunction with research teams at three Canadian universities. The main part of the study consisted of three case studies (described in Chapters 9, 10 and 11), each at a different scale and each undertaken by a different research team.

In addition, a number of supplemental studies were undertaken to provide additional examples of ways in which soft path analysis could be used. Several of these supplemental studies were used as part of the three case studies – for example, those that examined water saving options in the pulp and paper industry and in the transportation equipment industry; the results appear in the appropriate chapters below. Other supplemental studies had a cross-cutting nature and were therefore not incorporated into specific case study results. Selected examples of these studies are summarized below. Though not incorporated in the case studies, they serve to show ways in which soft path approaches can add to the overall water savings, and therefore indicate that our quantitative results are conservative compared with what could actually be achieved.

- *Urban scale*, undertaken by The POLIS Project for Ecological Governance, University of Victoria, Victoria, British Columbia.
- *Watershed scale*, undertaken by The Arthur Irving Academy for the Environment, Acadia University, Wolfville, Nova Scotia.
- *Provincial scale*, undertaken by the Department of Resource and Environmental Studies, University of Waterloo, Waterloo, Ontario.

For each scale, the study developed three scenarios for water use over the next 30 or 40 years. A Business-as-Usual scenario (really a projection) was compared with the reductions in water use that could flow from policies under (a) an efficiency-oriented, demand management scenario and (b) under a soft path scenario. The three scenarios all use the same 'official' expectations of economic and population growth, although modest changes in economic structure are included. As gaps in information were identified, the three core studies were supplemented by additional (mainly secondary) research on specific sectors or uses of water. Chapters 8, 9 and 10 present, respectively, the research results for the three case studies.

A summary of the Canadian study, with short articles on each of the three case studies, was published in the July 2007 issue of *Alternatives Journal* (vol 33, no 4); complete study history and results appear on a CD-ROM entitled *Lexicon of Water Soft Path Knowledge*, Vol. 1 (2007), available from Friends of the Earth Canada.

Supplemental studies

In addition to the three regional case studies, a number of supplemental studies were undertaken to provide complementary information. These studies varied widely, ranging from sector-specific reviews of demand management opportunities in some water-intensive industries, through analyses of institutional barriers that impede wider adaptation of water saving practices and technologies, to the effects of human diets on water. A quintessentially Canadian study analysed water use in ice rinks. Selected results from these supplemental studies provide a good indication of the range of considerations that can be brought to bear on a water soft path study. Results for some of the supplementary studies appear in one or another of the three regional chapters to follow. The studies of institutional barriers to implementation of water soft path policies and of the potential for 'greener' buildings and urban design were deemed important enough to appear, respectively, as Chapters 12 and 14. Some of the studies that cut across sectors or regions are summarized here:

- *Water use in human diets*: The study of variations in the water used to supply different human diets illustrates a change that is largely a matter of personal preference and is thus entirely a soft path choice. This study focused exclusively on the water required directly and indirectly for food production. It compared three diets standardized to include the same number of calories and the same protein content. One diet reflected typical eating habits in Canada; the second excluded all red meat but allowed poultry and fish; the third diet was ovo-lacto vegetarian. Calculations based on data contained in tables of water requirements in Canada for each food type showed that the three diets occur in the expected order – meat-based diets require the most water and vegetarian diets the least – but that: (a) the different diets differ by factors of two or three, not ten as has been reported in some studies; and (b) there is a large overlap between the three diets – irrigated vegetables can require more water than range-fed animals. Therefore, selection of low-meat diets generally *can* reduce water use in agriculture, but selection of foods and specific methods of production for different products within each diet is as important as the type of diet.

- *Water use at ice rinks*: Investigation of water use at ice rinks illustrates the effect of potential water savings for activities that are desired by the community and that are individually rather small but that can be important for water-constrained communities. A typical year-round ice rink needs 1100–1200 cubic metres of water each year to build and maintain the ice surface. Assuming 20 per cent of Ontario's rinks operate all year and 80 per cent operate for six months per year, total provincial water use is about 0.5 million cubic metres per year. This volume can be reduced by a variety of techniques, including using purified water, which makes harder ice, flushing toilets with melt water and otherwise recycling the scrapings from the ice surface, and by forgoing ice-based recreation in the summer. A shift in rink use involving less hockey and more curling – a possibility as the population ages – would reduce water use further.

- *Water use at golf courses*: Golf courses form a contrast to ice rinks because water use is much higher and, in many cases, involves heavy use of pesticides and fertilizers – typically four to six times the rate applied on agricultural fields (Environment Canada, 2005). There are over 600 golf courses in Ontario, most of them on the urban fringe. As one example of local impact, a 2003 study of the Long Point region showed that golf courses accounted for over one-quarter of commercial water use (Dryden-Cripton, 2005). Unfortunately, the managers of golf courses are notably reluctant to release information about their water use. Several groups have established guidelines for ways to reduce water use and water contamination, but they are voluntary and there is no published information on monitoring of results. A major opportunity exists to replace fresh water for irrigation with treated wastewater, but this approach has been adopted at only a few golf courses in Canada.

Conclusions

Taking the full soft path approach requires some elements of compromise in analysis. Nevertheless, experience in Canada shows that soft path analysis for water is feasible. More specifically, we believe that our analytical methods have shown that:

1 Despite statistical difficulties that were evident from the start and, despite analytical methods that stray from the conventional, water soft path analysis is indeed feasible and distinct from cost-effectiveness analysis.
2 Potential savings can be demonstrated that go well beyond those available with demand management and that also take direct account of such issues as ecological protection and climate change. Equity in water availability was not included as an objective of the Canadian study, but it could have been.
3 Results can be obtained that are not merely impressive in themselves, but suggestive of potential for stronger studies, with even more impressive results, regarding the potential for saving water while simultaneously providing for economic development and ecological protection.

The upshot of these qualified general conclusions is that, for now, and probably for some time in the future, research results from water soft path analyses should be seen as suggestive and indicative, but far from definitive. Certainly, no jurisdiction should feel constrained to look for new water supplies until it has, first, adopted and enforced water demand management options and, second, undertaken an alternative plan based on a fully developed backcasting exercise incorporating water soft path options.

The strength of water soft paths is their ability to identify and respond to the potential for redesigning living patterns and specific economic activities, as well as structural shifts in whole economies, such as those required to adjust to climate and geopolitical change. However, those strengths can also be considered a weakness. Soft paths cannot boast, as can most demand management strategies, that they are win–win options. Soft paths imply changes in socioeconomic, political and perhaps even cultural relationships and they will necessarily be contentious. If the analysis stimulates discussion about those relationships, it may be as much as one can hope for from the long-term scenarios that are presented.

Notes

1 This chapter is an expanded version of the paper submitted for publication to *Water International*. We are grateful to Taylor & Francis for permission to use this material.
2 There is a sizeable literature on virtual water. For an introduction to the subject, see the web site: www.wateryear2003.org/en/ev.php-URL_ID=5868&URL_DO= DO_TOPIC&URL_SECTION=201.html

References

Allan, J. A. (2001) *The Middle East Water Question: Hydropolitics and the Global Economy*, I. B. Tauris, London
Allan, J. A. (2003) 'Virtual water – the water, food, and trade nexus: Useful concept or misleading metaphor?' *Water International*, vol 28, no 1, pp4–11
Bott, R., Brooks, D. and Robinson, J. (1983) *Life After Oil: A Renewable Energy Policy for Canada*, Hurtig Publishers, Edmonton, AB

Brandes, O. M. and Ferguson, K. (2004) *The Future in Every Drop: The Benefits, Barriers, and Practice of Urban Water Demand Management in Canada*, The POLIS Project on Ecological Governance at the University of Victoria, Victoria, BC

Brandes, O. M., Maas, T., Mjolsness, A. and Reynolds, E. (2007), 'A soft path for water case study – the town of Oliver, British Columbia', *Lexicon of Water Soft Path Knowledge*, vol 1 (CD-ROM), Friends of the Earth Canada, Ottawa, ON

Brooks, D. B. (2005) 'Beyond greater efficiency: The concept of water soft paths', *Canadian Water Resources Journal*, vol 30, no 1, pp83–92

Brooks, D. B. (2006) 'An operational definition of water demand management', *International Journal of Water Resources Development*, vol 22, no 4, pp521–528

Brooks, D. B. and Peters, R. (1988) *Water: The Potential for Demand Management in Canada*, Science Council of Canada, Ottawa, ON

Brooks, D. B., with de Loë, R., Patrick, R. and Rose, G. (2004) *Water Soft Paths: Can the Concept be Applied in Ontario?* Friends of the Earth Canada, Ottawa, ON

Brooks, D. B. with Rose, R. (2003) *Another Path Not Taken: A Methodological Exploration of Water Soft Paths for Canada and Elsewhere*, Revised Report, Friends of the Earth Canada, Ottawa, ON

Dinar, A. and Loehman, E. T. (eds) (1995) *Water Quantity/Quality Management and Conflict Resolution*, Praeger Publishers, Westport, CN

Dryden-Cripton, S. (2005) *Big Creek Watershed Characterisation Report*, Guelph Water Management Group, University of Guelph, Guelph, ON

Environment Canada (2005) *Sustainable Communities Environmental Project*, Manitoba Golf Superintendents Association (MGSA), www.pnr-rpn.ec.gc.ca/community/ecoaction/fp-pt/page.asp?lang=en&id=MB-13126, accessed July 2005

Furlong, K. and Bakker, K. (2008) *Water Governance in Transition: Utility Restructuring and Water Efficiency in Ontario*, UBC Program on Water Governance, Vancouver, BC

Gault, F. D., Hamilton, K. E., Hoffman, R. B. and McInnis, B. C. (1987) 'The design approach to socio-economic modelling', *Futures*, vol 19, no 1, pp3–25

Gleick, P. H. (1998) 'The changing water paradigm: A look at twenty-first century water resources development', *Water International*, vol 25, no 1, pp127–138

Gleick, P. H. (2003) 'Global freshwater resources: Soft path solutions for the 21st century', *Science*, 14 November

Gleick, P. H., Haasz, D., Henges-Jeck, C., Srinivasan, V., Wolff, G., Cushing, K. K. and Mann, A. (2003) *Waste Not, Want Not: The Potential for Urban Water Conservation in California*, Pacific Institute for Studies in Development, Environment, and Security, Oakland, CA

Gleick, P. H., Cooley. H. and Groves, D. (2005) *California Water 2030: An Efficient Future*, Pacific Institute for Studies in Development, Environment, and Security, Oakland, CA

International Joint Commission (IJC) (2002) *Protection of the Waters of the Great Lakes: Three Year Review*, International Joint Commission, Ottawa, ON

Katz, D. (2006) 'Going with the flow: Preserving and restoring instream water allocations', in P. H. Gleick (ed) *The World's Water: 2006–2007*, Island Press, Washington, DC

Linton, J. (2009) *What is Water? The History and Crisis of a Modern Abstraction*, UBC Press, Vancouver, BC

Lovins, A. B. (1976) 'Energy strategy: The road not taken', *Foreign Affairs*, vol 55, no 1, pp186–218

Lovins, A. B. (1977) *Soft Energy Paths: Toward a Durable Peace*, Ballinger/Friends of the Earth, Cambridge, MA

Millennium Ecosystem Assessment (2005) *Ecosystems and Human Well-Being: Current State and Trends*, vol 1, chap 7: Freshwater Ecosystem Services, World Resources Institute, Washington, DC

Postel, S. and Richter, B. (2003) *Rivers for Life: Managing Water for People and Nature*, Island Press, Washington, DC

Schendel, E. K., Macdonald, J. R., Schreier, H. and Lavkulich, L. M. (2007), 'Virtual water: A framework for comparative regional resource assessment', *Journal of Environmental Assessment Policy and Management*, vol 9, no 3, pp341–355

Tate, D. M. (1990) *Water Demand Management in Canada: A State-of-the-Art Review*, Social Science Series 23, Inland Waters Directorate, Environment Canada, Ottawa, ON

Wolff, G. and Gleick, P. H. (2002) 'The soft path for water', in P. H. Gleick et al (eds) *The World's Water: Biennial Report on Freshwater Resources, 2002–2003*, Island Press, Washington, DC

8
Turning Principles into Practice: The WSP Scenario Builder

Carol Maas and Tony Maas

The best way to predict the future is to invent it.

Alan Kay

Introduction

This book – and all of the work that came before it – takes on the task of building up the soft path for water from broad concept and principles to a planning process. Yet, at the end of the day, the success of the soft path approach is likely to be judged, in large part, on how much water is saved – or better, on how much is left in place to sustain the health and productivity of freshwater ecosystems. Therefore, part of that approach must focus on the analytics of using less water, which means some attention must be paid to numbers.

This is the first of our 'numbers' chapters. But the chapter is not just about finding numbers to support our case or perspective. It is about developing a Decision Support Tool – the Water Soft Path (WSP) Scenario Builder – to generate the right type of numbers, in a usable format, to reflect the conceptual basis and the principles of the soft path approach.

WSP Scenario Builder

The origin of the WSP Scenario Builder is the soft path 'graph' (Figure 8.1). This illustrative graph is intended to show how the soft path approach is conceptually different from conventional water supply and water efficiency planning. The WSP Scenario Builder was born out of an effort to generate quantitative information that would reflect what is shown in the illustration.

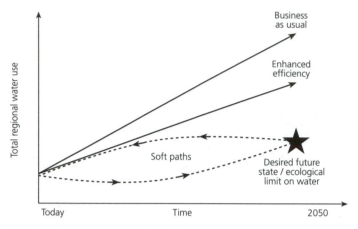

Source: Oliver M. Brandes and David B. Brooks (see Figure 1.1)

Figure 8.1 *WSP conceptual graph*

The tool began as a crude spreadsheet developed in a graduate school course and was later refined into a more functional version to support the urban and to some degree the watershed case studies that follow in this book. A complete description of the backcasting framework, which is the backbone of the Scenario Builder, was developed and published by Brandes and Maas in 2007. Since then, the tool has evolved into what it is today: a sophisticated, spreadsheet-based model of urban water use, and, as a bonus, of the connections among water use, energy demand and greenhouse gas emissions.

The WSP Scenario Builder is a tool designed for a specific purpose, from a particular perspective. Other tools exist to support activities such as water supply planning, water footprinting and water efficiency planning. Each is intended to answer a particular question. How much water do we need (water supply planning)? How much water are we using (water footprinting)? Or how can we affordably use less water (water efficiency planning)?

Each of these tools is also set within a particular view of the world. Most neglect ecological limits to human water use. Most are based on the assumption that past political, economic and social trends will determine future conditions. And most rely on a benefit–cost framework to determine what is feasible in terms of developing new supply, or what water efficiency measures are economically efficient under existing conditions.

The WSP Scenario Builder fits with and complements (rather than replaces) most of these tools. It takes an important step toward developing detailed conservation audits or water efficiency plans by engaging urban communities in 'What if?' discussions about possible futures for water use – before asking what is economically feasible. It sets aside analysis of both the economic costs and benefits associated with implementing the measures, and also the operating and capital cost savings that result from reductions in water use, to maintain a clear focus on *ecologically* sustainable water use.

Most importantly, the WSP Scenario Builder is set within a worldview that recognizes that ecological limits to human water use *do* exist – and one that strives to constrain human water demand within those limits. It seeks then not to answer 'what is economical', but rather to demonstrate 'what is possible'. More formally stated, the WSP Scenario Builder, and the planning process it supports, establish a coarse scale reflection of what 'could be' with respect to the scale and intensity of socio-economic development in a particular place without undermining the health and productivity of local freshwater ecosystems. It is *future seeking* rather than *trend modelling*. And the future it seeks is an ecologically sustainable one.

Scenario-based planning and backcasting

Future seeking is inherent to the scenario-based planning that is central to the soft path approach. Many futures are possible and all depend, at least in part, on decisions we make today.

Approaches to studying the future rarely claim the ability to predict in detail. Rather, future studies usually focus on assessing various possible futures and the conditions that make them probable (Makropolous et al, 2008). The goal is to understand trajectories of development and the implications of decisions taken in the present on realizing that future.

Scenario-based planning entails developing descriptions of *possible* futures – narratives or stories of how the future might unfold. In developing scenarios, analysts describe a logical sequence of events that follow from some set of stated assumptions (Mitchell, 2002). Backcasting is one of many established concepts in the literature related to future studies that can be used to develop scenarios (Robinson, 1982, 2003; Swart et al, 2004). The approach focuses on how a desirable future might be created, not on what futures are likely to occur. The process works by first establishing a desired future state – in our case, one that reflects the ideal of sustainable water use – and then working backwards to determine what policies and what technological and behavioural changes are required to connect the desired future to the present.

Supporting the scenarios – how the WSP Scenario Builder works

The WSP Scenario Builder facilitates a systematic approach, illustrated in Figure 8.2, to determining the potential for water savings through application of efficiency and conservation measures. The tool works on the basis of integration – on determining the *macro impact* of integrating different packages *of micro measures* (ie, policies, programmes and technologies) on total water use. It accomplishes this by:

*   disaggregating total water demand of an urban or watershed community into its component elements (uses);

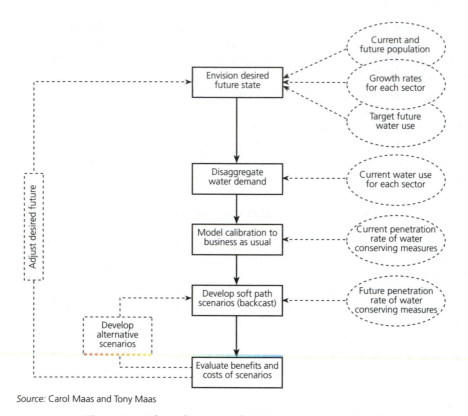

Source: Carol Maas and Tony Maas

Figure 8.2 *Flow diagram of WSP Scenario Builder logic*

- treating each of those elements with water efficiency and conservation measures using four water sectors: Residential, ICI (Industrial, Commercial and Institutional), Agricultural and Non-Revenue;[1]
- then re-aggregating to determine the macro impact of the various micro measures on total water use.

By iterating through this process, the analyst (or planning team) can refine the micro measures to arrive at a package showing total water use that reflects desired future conditions. It sounds simple, but as with most complex socio-ecological problems, the devil is in the details – those details, and the devils within, are described below.

Desired future state

The first step in the backcasting process – and in developing the resulting scenarios – is to define a desired future state for water use. This begins by deciding how far into the future to look; or in the parlance of the WSP Scenario Builder, selecting a *design year*. Variables such as current and future population and estimated growth in the various water sectors, are used to define the context of the design year.

The selected design year must be 20–50 years in the future. This long view is critical for a number of reasons. First, philosophically, any effort aimed at developing a sustainable society requires thinking in terms of intergenerational equity – to meet the needs and aspirations of present generations without compromising the opportunities for future generations to do the same. Second, and more pragmatically, the design year should be set far enough into the future to allow sufficient time to observe the full impact of proposed technological, social and policy shifts associated with scenarios. Transformational change of the type envisioned by the soft path approach can take decades to be fully realized. Third, no magic wand exists to change instantly all inefficient toilets into low-flow ones; even with incentives, rates of replacement of existing stock will be slow. Finally, taking a short view – looking only 5–10 years into the future – is also likely to direct attention away from non-technological measures, such as education, social marketing and policy changes, that often take significant time to stimulate behavioural change and to result in water use reduction. Indeed, taking a short view may prematurely write off the soft path approach or a particular scenario before the full impact can be realized.

The future that is put forward should be one that is desired broadly by the urban or watershed community that will influence, and be influenced by, actions taken to realize it. Ideally, it will have been developed in consultation with the community. A future vision is more likely to have influence if it is a shared vision. Therefore, visioning processes strive for participation by a broad range of community interests and actors. That said, the process of establishing this future state should not be viewed as a bargaining process to arrive at consensus around a lowest common denominator. It must be imaginative rather than simply a projection of the status quo. And it must incorporate the best available science on local hydrological carrying capacity, with allowance for unpredicted changes in that carrying capacity (as with those stemming from climate change).

For some communities or individuals, this visioning step may prove to be the most difficult part of the soft path approach. In some cases, dense or jargon-laden scientific and engineering studies may challenge non-technical participants to engage effectively in decision-making. More often, an absence of studies and other information will challenge *all* participants. This difficulty in defining a reasonable target future for water use should not prevent or dissuade practitioners from pursuing a soft path for water. Rather, an adaptive approach should be adopted – working from an initial desired future that can be refined over time (using the Scenario Builder) as new information on water demand, local hydrological conditions, and climate change impacts becomes available.

To get started, a goal of maintaining, at a minimum, current watershed health is probably a reasonable desired future state. This goal – often referred to as *no new water* – has been used in several soft path studies to date. Essentially, no new water means capping water takings at existing volumes and rates so as to exert no additional pressure on the watershed ecosystem from higher rates of water use.

Disaggregating demand

By disaggregating water demand into its component elements, the WSP Scenario Builder digs deep into the details of a community's water use. It exposes the intricacies of who uses water, how much and for what purposes. Reviewing these intricacies exposes a wealth of opportunities to apply water efficiency and conservation measures.

The Scenario Builder takes a step-wise approach to disaggregating water demand – first into sectors, onward into sub-sectors, and finally, where possible, to end-uses (see Figure 8.3). Using an urban centre as an example, *sectors* would include residential, ICI, agricultural and non-revenue water. *Sub-sectors* under the residential sector would include single and multi-family and indoor and outdoor water use. Finally, *end-uses* in the residential indoor sub-sector would include showers, toilets, washing machines, etc.

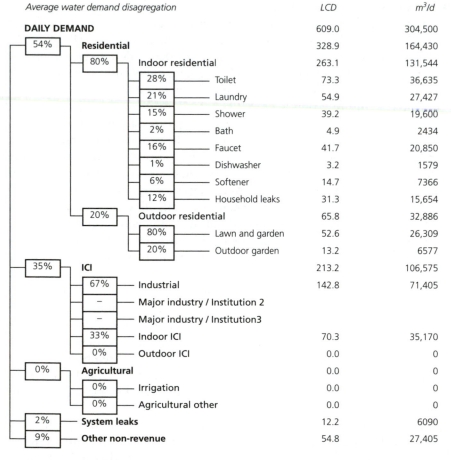

Average water demand disaggregation				LCD	m³/d
DAILY DEMAND				609.0	304,500
54%	**Residential**			328.9	164,430
	80%	Indoor residential		263.1	131,544
		28%	Toilet	73.3	36,635
		21%	Laundry	54.9	27,427
		15%	Shower	39.2	19,600
		2%	Bath	4.9	2434
		16%	Faucet	41.7	20,850
		1%	Dishwasher	3.2	1579
		6%	Softener	14.7	7366
		12%	Household leaks	31.3	15,654
	20%	Outdoor residential		65.8	32,886
		80%	Lawn and garden	52.6	26,309
		20%	Outdoor garden	13.2	6577
35%	ICI			213.2	106,575
	67%	Industrial		142.8	71,405
	–	Major industry / Institution 2			
	–	Major industry / Institution3			
	33%	Indoor ICI		70.3	35,170
	0%	Outdoor ICI		0.0	0
0%	**Agricultural**			0.0	0
	0%	Irrigation		0.0	0
	0%	Agricultural other		0.0	0
2%	**System leaks**			12.2	6090
9%	**Other non-revenue**			54.8	27,405

Note: LCD = litres per capita-day
Source: Carol Maas and Tony Maas

Figure 8.3 *The disaggregation process in the Scenario Builder*

Whenever possible this disaggregation should be based on current information. However, given the paucity of empirical data on water use, particularly at the scale of end-use, it is often necessary to adopt benchmarks from other sources. Sources may include case studies or water management plans, conversations with water management practitioners or nationally or regionally averaged compilations, such as that provided by Environment Canada (2008) or the American Water Works Association (Mayer et al, 1999).

Model calibration to business as usual

The goal of any water conservation plan or soft path strategy is to increase the uptake (penetration rate) of water conserving practices (measures) and decrease the prevalence of water-intensive practices. To understand the behavioural, technological and policy changes required to realize a desired future state, a reasonable depiction of *existing* water use patterns must first be established. This depiction – often referred to in scenario-based planning as the 'business as usual' (BAU) case – is, quite simply, a forward extrapolation of current water use patterns based on population and economic growth projections.

The BAU scenario provides a benchmark against which to compare all additional scenarios, but it is more than that. For modellers it represents an opportunity to 'calibrate' – a critical though often overlooked step in developing an understanding of current community water use. Calibration provides an opportunity to question, challenge and better understand assumptions of penetration rates for the BAU scenario, and to refine those assumptions to arrive at values that represent, as closely as possible, the actual prevalence or absence of water conserving practices in today's society. Figure 8.4 illustrates the model's ability to estimate and adjust penetration rates for each measure until the prevalence of water saving fixtures and practices reflects the disaggregated per capita water use assumptions entered into the Scenario Builder. For example, Figure 8.3 demonstrates that the end-use assumptions applied to the total per capita water demand of 609 litres per capita-day (LCD) would result in a toilet end-use estimated at 73.3LCD. The WSP Scenario Builder, with input by the practitioner, 'calibrates' the BAU penetration rates for each possible type of toilet currently in use in the community to equate to the specified average of 73.3LCD for toilets (Figure 8.4). This is an important step. To assess accurately, for example, the conservation potential associated with wider penetration of water-efficient toilets, the analyst must first have a realistic estimate of the current number of water-wasting toilets.

Through a process of calibration and recalibration, *assumptions* of water use and penetration rates are replaced with *empirical data*, which essentially means that the BAU becomes less speculation and more reality. In this way, the BAU resolves uncertainties related to input assumptions and the WSP Scenario Builder evolves toward a working model that more accurately represents a society's water use.

Toilet		1 old toilet	2 6 L toilet	2 dual flush toilet
	MEAS			
	L/flush	16.5	6.0	3.8
−	Flush/c/d	5.05	5.05	5.05
	LCD	83.3	30.3	19.2
BAU 73.3	PENET	82%	14%	3%
SCEN 1 50.0	PENET	43%	32%	15%
SCEN 2 40.0	PENET	24%	50%	16%

Laundry		1 old machine toilet	2 new machine	3 energy / star
	MEAS			
	L/load	200.0	130.1	93.3
0.3	Loads/c/d	0.30	0.30	0.30
	LCD	60.0	39.0	28.0
BAU 54.9	PENET	78%	17%	5%
SCEN 1 40.0	PENET	28%	40%	23%
SCEN 2 30.0	PENET	7%	33%	36%

Source: Carol Maas and Tony Maas

Figure 8.4 *Residential sector sheet illustrating the suite of measures, and the penetration rates for each scenario*

Soft path scenarios

With a desired future state established and BAU conditions determined, the work of building alternative scenarios begins. At this point the disaggregated water demand – the intricate details of water use – is subjected to 'treatments'. These treatments come in the form of a combination of water efficiency and conservation measures and penetration rates. The Scenario Builder lays out the required community uptake of various measures necessary to realize its desired future.

The many measures available have the potential to reduce or even eliminate water use across the full range of end-uses. Penetration rates are quantitative measures of the uptake of a given measure into use by society over some period of time. They are strongly influenced by policies and programmes such as water pricing, rebates, education and social marketing, and bylaws and regulations. The policy context must be considered as alternative scenarios are developed because it directly affects the penetration of behavioural change and technology into use. For example, an aggressive toilet rebate programme or an increase in water price will result in a high degree of low-flow toilet penetration. Figure 8.4 illustrates two alternative scenarios in addition to business as usual. Looking closely at the penetration rates, one can see in numbers the shift toward water saving fixtures and alternative sources of water (i.e. in alternative scenarios, a shift toward higher penetration rates for water saving fixtures, and lower penetration rates for water-wasting technologies and practices).

The WSP Scenario Builder's strength lies in its capacity to explore a multitude of 'what if' scenarios by experimenting with various combinations of measures and penetration rates to determine the impact of particular packages of technologies or practices on future water use. For example, one community may choose to focus on residential and ICI rebate programmes as its primary mechanism for water conservation. Another community might choose to implement policies that encourage rainwater harvesting, grey-water reuse and xeriscaping to reduce future water use. Both scenarios could ultimately lead to the same end but through different means.

If, after selecting a suite of measures and penetration rates, the resulting future water use exceeds the threshold identified in the community visioning process, efficiency and conservation measures must be revisited, increasing the application and penetration of water saving measures in an iterative manner until the desired future state is reached. As the community begins to understand in more explicit terms the extent to which water efficiency and conservation must be employed, it may decide that the desired future water state itself should be adjusted. This is the essence of the iterative visioning and backcasting process using the WSP Scenario Builder as a tool to support decision-making.

Additional model features

The WSP Scenario Builder is not only a model to estimate water savings. It was designed to foster ongoing compilation and comparison of research findings. The WSP Scenario Builder has also been adapted to capture not only the ecological benefits derived from water savings but to help practitioners understand the implications of water use for climate change.

Toward a learning model of society's water use

'Garbage in = garbage out' is a modeller's way of saying that if input data is limited or of poor quality, model outputs will probably be wrong. This is as true for models of chemical or biological processes as it is for models of human society. For this reason, scenarios developed with inaccurate, incomplete or unsubstantiated input data can, at best, be considered as demonstrative. As water efficiency and conservation programmes expand and mature, we can probably expect more data, and more reliable data. The WSP Scenario Builder is designed to deal with this new information. It is a learning tool that is adaptable to new knowledge.

The many references used to develop current assumptions are documented in a comprehensive database – the 'back end' of the model. This database, and all other model assumptions, should be made transparent in order to encourage users to examine the relevance of each assumption for the community. This storehouse for logging and managing new information can be expanded or modified as new and better data are generated. As this happens, the model, and the practitioner(s) working with the model, learn more and more about a society's water use.

The WSP Scenario Builder can also be used to help to decide what data to collect first, and what to leave for later. The process of disaggregating water use and experimenting with penetration rates can provide both the direction and impetus for a monitoring programme that ultimately increases the depth of water conservation knowledge. Used in this way, the tool can help design monitoring programmes that make sense, not just accumulate data.

Capturing connectedness – the water–energy–climate nexus

The flow of water – whether through forest or river ecosystems or through human built environments – creates complex interconnections among people, places and issues. This connectedness is often viewed as a major challenge in addressing environmental issues – but it also provides opportunities. For water soft paths, those opportunities lie in the interconnections among water, energy and climate change.

The reduction in water use that is the backbone of the soft path approach also provides co-benefits of energy conservation and greenhouse gas mitigation. Pumping, treating, distributing and heating water takes energy; so too does collecting and treating the resulting wastewater. Therefore, reducing water use results in reduced energy use; depending on the source of that energy, also reduces greenhouse gas emissions to varying degrees. These interconnections are integrated into the WSP Scenario Builder, which enables it to quantify savings in energy and reductions in greenhouse gas emissions possible through water efficiency and conservation.

Conclusion

Historically, the practice of water efficiency and conservation in North America has paid minimal attention to technical detail and quantitative metrics. As a result, generalized assumptions of water end-uses and impacts of water efficiency and conservation measures have been used to assess the potential for conservation. Unless these assumptions are challenged with quantitative data, water efficiency and conservation programming and public awareness of how to best conserve water will be informed more by social perceptions than by actual experience.

The soft path approach to water is a paradigm shift for water management. As with any change in operating paradigm, it is unrealistic to expect communities, researchers and water practitioners to embrace a change in practice without effective support tools. The WSP Scenario Builder is a tool designed to bring life to the concepts of the soft path approach with hard numbers from 'on the ground' experience. It provides a link between the broad concepts of the soft path and the detailed water conservation planning that is necessary for communities and ecosystems alike to realize the benefits purported by the soft path for water.

Notes

1 Non-revenue water is defined as the difference between the total water production and the total billed water use. A portion of non-revenue water stems from leaks and other system losses.

References

Brandes, O. and Maas, T. (2007) 'Urban water soft path: Back of the envelope backcasting framework', http://poliswaterproject.org/publications/papers

Environment Canada (2008) 'Water use in the home', www.ec.gc.ca/water/images/effic/a6f7e/htm, accessed 20 October 2008

Makropolous, C. K., Memon, F. A., Shirley-Smith, C. and Butler, D. (2008) 'Futures: An exploration of scenarios for sustainable urban water management', *Water Policy*, vol 10, no 4, pp345–373

Mayer, P., DeOreo, W. B., Optiz, E. M., Kiefer, J. C., Davis, W. Y., Dziegielewski, B. and Nelson, J. O. (1999) *Residential End Uses of Water*, AWWA Resource Foundation. Denver, CO

Mitchell, B. (2002) *Resource and Environmental Management*, 2nd Edition, Prentice Hall, Harlow, UK, p64

Robinson, J. (1982) 'Energy backcasting: A proposed method of policy analysis', *Energy Policy*, vol 10, no 4, pp337–344

Robinson, J. (2003) 'Future subjunctive: Backcasting as social learning', *Futures*, vol 35, no 8, pp839–856

Swart, R. J., Raskin, P. and Robinson, J. (2004) 'The problem of the future: Sustainability science and scenario analysis', *Global Environmental Change*, vol 14, no 2, pp137–146

9
Thinking Beyond Pipes and Pumps: Water Soft Paths at the Urban Scale

Oliver M. Brandes and Tony Maas

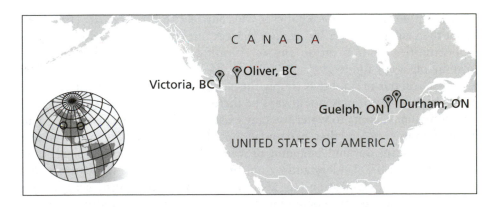

The trouble with water – and there is trouble with water – is that they aren't making any more of it

Marq de Villiers (2000)

Introduction

Water, as we all know, is the stuff of life. The constant cycling of fresh water from sky to land, through lakes, wetlands and rivers and onward to the sea is critical to the health of aquatic and terrestrial ecosystems – to all living creatures – including us humans.

In the urban context, water takes on a totally different character. The urban water cycle flushes our toilets, waters the lawn (and yes, sometimes even driveways and sidewalks (pavements)), washes our clothes, keeps things (including us) clean and quenches our thirst. In our homes and in our towns and cities, water is critical, most certainly, but almost always taken for granted. Inevitably, the urban reality influences society's very perception of, and the fundamental relationship with, water and the ecosystems it supports.

While the benefits to society of our historical approach to water management are obvious – safe, reliable drinking water and sanitation – the cultural implications are less so. Culturally, urban water infrastructure has a 'distancing' effect to the extent that few people associate fresh water in lakes and rivers with the potable water delivered to their homes. The networks of infrastructure through which this transformation takes place have become a basis for urban life, but are also an integral component of culturally driven social and economic development in contemporary urban settlements (Kaika and Swyngedouw, 2000).

The pumps, pipes and treatment facilities that comprise municipal and community water systems transform water from its 'natural' state to a potable form and, in so doing, distort urban culture's relationship with nature. Water thus becomes 'de-naturalized' – removed of all ecological and spiritual connection and, instead, becomes situated almost entirely within a convenience and utilitarian context.

In urban culture, reverence for the stuff of life is often reduced to a focus on what it *does* for *us*, not what it *is*. This entirely anthropocentric context is what then entrenches the status quo, charges our endless thirst and limits the opportunities for innovation and re-visioning of societies' potential for a sustainable water future.

Water in our urban life is simply flushed and forgotten – at least until we begin to hear that it may not always be there for the taking, that yes, even in *our* community, limits to water use may exist. It is this very recognition – that natural limits exist, and that water might not always just be there for the taking – that reawakens our understanding of water's broader role on our planet and in all forms of life. Understanding not only the importance of water in the endless march of civilization, but also as the lifeblood of healthy ecosystems, and therefore prosperous communities, opens the potential to unleash the soft path as both a governing philosophy and as a practical management approach for water in modern society.

A crisis of governance – thinking beyond the pumps and pipes

Urban water management has always been a challenging endeavour; in the context of 21st-century mass urbanization, it is increasingly so. The 20th-century tradition of finding, securing, storing and using more water to meet urban demand is faced today with real, physical limitations (both quality and quantity), the financial costs of moving water from ever more remote locations to urban centres, and significant social concern over the ecological consequences of endlessly increasing water use.

Today, the urban water challenge has shifted from a technical problem to a governance issue. Indeed, the 2003 United Nations World Water Development Report's oft-quoted phrase says it all: 'The water crisis is essentially a crisis of governance.' Many of the problems, and indeed the solutions needed to address them, relate much more to social and institutional factors than to a lack of basic scientific understanding or adequate technology (Kreutzwiser and de Loë, 2004). To begin addressing these social and institutional factors, the soft path seeks to develop a fundamentally different kind of urban water infrastructure – one that looks beyond pipes and pumps to the infrastructure of efficiency and conservation (Brandes et al, 2006).

The diversity of water uses in the urban sphere is often seen as a central challenge of sustainable water management. But where some see these diverse points of use as an intractable water management challenge, the soft path practitioner views the multiplicity as opportunity. It is the *very diversity* of water uses in the urban context that provides the wealth of opportunities to use less water, either through more efficient practices or outright conservation. Saving water is the opportunity, but the potential for societal transformation is much more.

Redefining infrastructure

As a first, and critical, step the soft path recognizes a fundamentally different concept of infrastructure. This different kind of infrastructure includes, for example: decentralized technologies, such as low-flow appliances and plumbing fixtures; programmes that emphasize changing behaviour and the development of a lasting water conservation ethic; and practices that put water use in the larger ecological context, such as using drought-resistant local plants and appropriate 'greenery' (or attractive rock gardens!) in our yards (gardens), public parks and spaces as a clear substitute to the manicured, water-hungry, urban lawn.

This new concept of appropriate infrastructure is not intended to *replace* the existing stock of built, supply-side infrastructure; to the contrary, it is meant to *complement and enhance* what is already in the ground. In fact, it is in the urban context, much more than in the other sectors or scales we have studied, that the soft path approach is so dependent on this legacy of built infrastructure, which has been the foundation of the water services we rely on for our quality of life and urban development.

The initial focus on water efficiency is sometimes called a demand management approach. Economic and legal measures are used to promote the uptake and technological innovation aimed at increasing water-use productivity. Options to maximize urban water use productivity abound: drip irrigation, low-flow faucets (taps), showers and toilets, and the latest 'Energy' and 'Water Star' appliances are readily available. So are legal tools such as building code changes, water use bylaws and economic approaches such as rebates, incentives and pricing strategies that better reflect the actual cost of water supply and wastewater treatment. These steps, however, are merely the beginning.

From managing demand to changing the nature of demand

The momentum behind efforts to improve water efficiency is building in communities all around the globe. Some, especially in parched, water-scarce regions have been engaged in promoting efficiency and conservation for decades. Even in Canada, one of the world's relatively water rich nations, a growing number of municipalities are developing increasingly sophisticated programmes to improve water productivity and reduce per capita water use. Most are doing so primarily to delay spending on major capital projects – pipelines, diversions, dams and reservoirs, new water and wastewater treatment facilities – or to make better use of existing allocations available for (potable) consumption. These significant efforts toward maximizing the efficiency of the existing hard infrastructure are the critical first steps towards water sustainability.

A few early innovators are going further and are setting the foundation for a longer-term, more integrated approach to urban water management by also seeking to establish the cultural shift associated with soft path thinking. These communities are beginning the journey down the soft path to the broader goal of sustainability by working to manage individuals', industries' and whole communities' demands on the available supply of water by *changing the fundamental nature* of these demands. (Part III of this book introduces some specific communities and regions that are making this shift reality.)

Changing the nature of our water demands is a slow and sometimes tedious process. It requires transformative modification of our behaviour and practice and can only be achieved through a range of foundational initiatives including:

- education and community-based social marketing;
- source substitution;
- altering current modes of urban development to design communities with the water cycle and conservation as the priority; and, most importantly,
- changes in the framework of decision-making.

In tangible terms, these solutions include innovative building technologies, such as green roofs, permeable surfaces, the use of recycled grey water and/or harvested rainwater for toilet flushing and laundry, and a transition to smaller, more compact communities that rely on native, drought-resistant landscaping to reduce outdoor irrigation. In essence, soft paths advocate a new paradigm for urban (re-)design – one that focuses on conservation, and that relies on water-centric design as *the* guiding principle. In this way, water management and community design become fused – changes in practices and in human demands become embedded in the landscape and in the local culture. Land and water management are treated as one holistic endeavour.

Committing to 'no new water' – going forward by looking backwards

The first step towards this transformative goal is to make sure that we know where we are trying to go and, critically, to have the destination in mind before we set off. In planning terminology, this means establishing a vision of a desired and sustainable future regime of water use that reflects ecologically and socially acceptable limits on water withdrawals and discharges of wastewater, within the assimilative capacity of the local ecosystem.

In the case study below, the vision of 'no new water' is the objective we have set for the 'invented' generic urban centre used to explore the potential of the soft path approach. What this means is that all future water demand resulting from growth in water use by households, industry, agricultural operations, etc. will be constrained within the capacity of existing municipal water infrastructure.[1]

Setting such a limit establishes the water constraints within which an urban centre must function and begins the process of reframing current beliefs about available water options as well as the nature of water management, governance and decision-making. Our vision of 'no new water' is defined as being limited by the existing built infrastructure. Its objective is to reframe current water management towards a focus on improved water efficiency and conservation efforts to offset increased demand (rather than on increased supply). This approach will ensure that the urban influence on the local water budget remains constant at today's levels and begins the incremental process that will transform the urban environment so that it can achieve a sustainable relationship with the watershed within which it exists.

Case study – A 'generic' urban centre

No community in Canada – where our comprehensive soft path study was conducted – has yet undertaken and implemented a complete water soft path approach. However, as is outlined in the next section of this book, a few communities have taken the first steps in this process. The experience and characteristics of a number of communities, including actual water use, anticipated growth and development considerations, were used to develop the case study explored below. Communities involved in the study included: in BC, the Town of Oliver in the Okanagan Basin, Victoria and the Capital Regional District; in Ontario, the Region of Durham and the City of Guelph. This case study is a proxy, associated with mid-sized Canadian urban centres, and has been designed to be 'generic' so that it has relevance and is replicable across urban regions in Canada, and indeed, much of North America and the developed world.[2]

This 'invented' urban centre is a municipality with a base population of 200,000 in 2005 that is anticipated to increase to a population of 300,000 in 2050. To establish our starting point for the case study we calculate current total water use (ie, for a population of 200,000) using the most recent published aggregate average per capita urban use in Canada (Environment Canada, 2004). Chapter 8 by Maas and Maas introduced the technical and contextual aspects of the tools used to perform the analytical analyses that follow.

Three distinct scenarios

Three distinct future scenarios are used to explore the potential of the soft path in this urban case study: *Business as Usual (BAU), Demand Management (DM)* and *Soft Path (SP)*. Each scenario integrates a range of micro measures (technologies and practices) into bundles to determine the macro effect on overall water use. The first two are *projections* – extrapolations based on certain assumptions of types of water saving measures employed and penetration of those technologies or practices into common usage.

The *Soft Path* scenario makes use of the backcasting approach to chart a future with an objective of 'no new water' until, at least, 2050 – and, as the scenario unfolds, we begin to see how transformative this process can be.

The *Business as Usual* scenario simply extrapolates current water use patterns forward based on population and economic growth projections. This scenario is the status quo or baseline to which all other scenarios are compared to demonstrate the water savings possible through conservation and efficiency. In this BAU scenario, only limited (generally existing) water conservation and efficiency measures and initiatives are included.

Our *Demand Management* scenario demonstrates the significant potential of committing to a demand management approach that incorporates readily available technologies and practices. In our invented urban example, this scenario results in water savings of approximately 24 per cent, or approximately 16,000,000 cubic metres per year by 2050 (as compared to the business as usual case). The water savings associated with this scenario are realized primarily through increased indoor efficiency: low-flow and dual flush toilets, efficient showers and faucets (taps) and water saving clothes washers.

The *Soft Path* scenario, by employing more aggressive measures in a more comprehensive package, yields water savings of almost 44 per cent, or just under 30,000,000 cubic metres of water per year compared to the BAU case. This is a significant amount of water savings and would mean approximately 7,000,000 cubic metres *less* water being used in 2050 than in 2006, based on a current water use of approximately 45,000,000 cubic metres per year or 622 litres per capita daily use – the Canadian average (Environment Canada, 2004). Thus a population growth of almost 75 per cent – a near doubling of the population – can be offset through conservation and efficiency.

The *Soft Path* scenario extends the initial water savings developed in the *Demand Management* scenario using an incremental approach to create a potentially transformative impact. The *Soft Path* scenario starts by incorporating commonly available efficiency-based measures such as: low-flow toilets and showerheads, water efficient clothes- and dishwashers, and policies such as

Table 9.1 *Summary of water use in various soft path scenarios for a generic urban region in 2050*

Water use sectors	Business as usual		Demand management		Soft path	
	Total water use*	Daily water use**	Total water use*	Daily water use**	Total water use*	Daily water use**
Total	**68,109**	**622**	**51,891**	**474**	**38,379**	**350**
Residential	35,416	323	24,740	226	17,631	161
Res. indoor	17,708	162	9,688	88	6,263	57
Res. outdoor	17,708	162	15,052	137	11,368	104
Institutional and commercial	12,940	118	8,489	78	3,720	34
Industrial	10,897	100	9,807	90	8,173	75
Non-revenue	8,854	81	8,854	81	8,854	81

Note: assumes a base population of 200,000 in 2005 and 300,000 in 2050.
* all data in 1000s of cubic metres per year
** litres per capita per day
Source: Brandes and Maas (2007b)

building code changes, lawn watering bylaws, some education and basic economic incentives such as volume-based pricing systems. In order to achieve the desired future of 'no new water', it goes significantly further, by also including more advanced technologies and practices, for example, composting toilets and waterless urinals (in some specific cases); xeriscaping; widespread water reuse, recycling and rainwater harvesting. These more aggressive measures require changes to individual behaviour and perceptions, laws and regulations and, in some cases, water management institutions themselves. It is in this more comprehensive package that the transformative potential of the soft path becomes most apparent as it emphasizes that it is the *ends* (a reduction in water use) not the *means* (specific technologies or infrastructure) that really matter. The results of this case study are clearly illustrated in Table 9.1 and Figure 9.1.

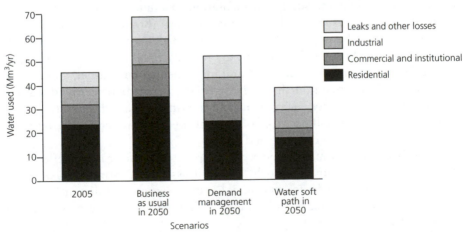

Source: Brandes and Maas (2007b)

Figure 9.1 *Graphical illustration of water use in three soft path scenarios*

A future different from the past

What this technical analysis set out to do was to demonstrate that a commitment to 'no new water' – at least until 2050 – is not only conceptually possible, but also readily achievable. The scenarios that we have put forward have illustrated that our premise – that a community can grow without expanding its local water footprint – is achievable and applicable in a wide array of circumstances.

In setting out these scenarios, we demonstrate that multiple possible paths lie before us – not all of which lead to a sustainable future – and that deciding which to take is fundamentally a governance challenge. Business as usual – over the long term – brings with it significant financial and ecological costs. Demand management demonstrates the existence of a significant potential for reduced water use by implementing readily available technologies. However, this approach delays, but does not avoid, the construction of that inevitable dam or diversion, and does not fundamentally change the context of the dialogue about society's role in water management, and its relationship with water.

The urban application of the soft path *begins* by maximizing the use of existing 'hard' urban water infrastructure – the dams and reservoirs, treatment facilities, pumps and pipes – but then goes much further. Soft paths look beyond simple efficiency and beyond the traditional context of decisions about when to add more pipes, tap the next watershed or build larger pumps – they look at the means, as well as the ends.

The *Soft Path* scenario shows that a dramatically different – and potentially ecologically sustainable – solution is possible. It is only through this scenario that a broader transformative change can take place – so that, in the end, the culture of conservation becomes embedded in urban society.

This is what the soft path is fundamentally about – moving conservation from being an adjunct to supply augmentation to a much more important role as the foundation of sustainable water management (Brandes et al, 2007a).

At its core, the *Soft Path* scenario outlined here, and the soft path approach, more broadly, is not a means to 'buy time' until the next mega-project is needed or can be financed and implemented but, rather, a blueprint that shows how to establish a new 'social' infrastructure of education programmes, community engagement and the financial and human resources needed to liberate the full potential of innovation and water conservation from a reliance on large-scale concrete and steel.

This is the transformation society so desperately needs if it is to effectively adapt to a rapidly changing world and address the daunting challenges of increasing infrastructure deficits, social disconnection and distancing from nature, and the mounting tide of ecological degradation caused by our urban water systems and lifestyles.

The soft path analysis outlined in this discussion is concrete proof that we do not need to elevate 'trend to destiny' – our past urban water use patterns and habits need not dictate our future – because, as the opening quotation so succinctly states: *they really aren't making any more of it.* Of course, the real potential of the approach can only be known when applied on the ground – in our communities. That is the critical next step – and the focus of Part III of this volume.

Notes

1 For the purposes of our study the limit of no new water is only a proxy for a more elaborate desired future condition that could (and should) be developed through public engagement at the local level.
2 For additional details on the various scenarios and the water conservation calculations that drive the urban soft path analysis see Brandes and Maas (2007b) and the detailed case study for the Town of Oliver: Brandes et al (2007b) (available at www.poliswaterproject.org).

References

Brandes, O. M. and Maas, T. (2007a) 'Community paths – investigating BC's urban water use', *Alternatives Journal,* vol 33, no 4, p14

Brandes, O. M. and Maas, T. (2007b) 'Urban water soft path "back of the envelope" backcasting framework', POLIS Working Paper Series, The POLIS Project on Ecological Governance, University of Victoria, Victoria, BC

Brandes, O. M., Maas, T. and Reynolds, E. (2006) *Thinking Beyond Pumps and Pipes: Top 10 Ways to Save Water AND Money,* The POLIS Project on Ecological Governance, University of Victoria, Victoria, BC

Brandes, O. M., Brooks, D. B. and M'Gonigle, M. (2007a) 'Moving water conservation to centre stage', in K. Bakker (ed) *Eau Canada: The Future of Canada's Water,* UBC Press, Vancouver, BC

Brandes, O. M., Maas, T., Mjolsness, A. and Reynolds, E. (2007b) 'A new path to water sustainability for the Town of Oliver, BC – soft path case study', POLIS Working Paper Series, The POLIS Project on Ecological Governance, University of Victoria, Victoria, BC

Environment Canada (2004) *Municipal Water Use 2001 Statistics,* Government of Canada, www.ec.gc.ca/Water/en/info/pubs/sss/e_mun2001.pdf

Kaika, M. and Swyngedouw, E. (2000) 'Fetishizing the modern city: The phantasmagoria of Urban Technological Networks', *International Journal of Urban and Regional Planning,* vol 24, no 1, pp120–138

Kreutzwiser, R. D. and de Loë, R. C. (2004) 'Water security: From exports to contamination to local water supplies', in B. Mitchell (ed) *Resource and Environmental Management in Canada: Addressing Conflict and Uncertainty,* Oxford University Press, Toronto, ON

United Nations (2003) *Water for People Water for Life,* The United Nations World Water Development Report, UNESCO – World Water Assessment Program, Paris

de Villiers, M. (2000) *Water,* Stoddart Publishing, Toronto, ON

10
Focusing on Geographic Boundaries: Water Soft Paths at the Watershed Scale

Lisa Isaacman and Graham R. Daborn

Skirting the sunbright uplands stretches a riband of meadow,
Shorn of the labouring grass, bulwarked well from the sea,
Fenced on its seaward border with long clay dikes from
*   the turbid*
Surge and flow of the tides vexing the Westmoreland shores.
          'Tantramar Revisited' by Charles G. D. Roberts

Introduction

From ecological and integrated management perspectives, the watershed (or catchment basin) may be one of the most suitable and effective scales for the application of water soft path analyses. On the one hand, the watershed is a basic ecological unit, within which the fundamental processes of the hydrological cycle operate. On the other, human water use reflects social,

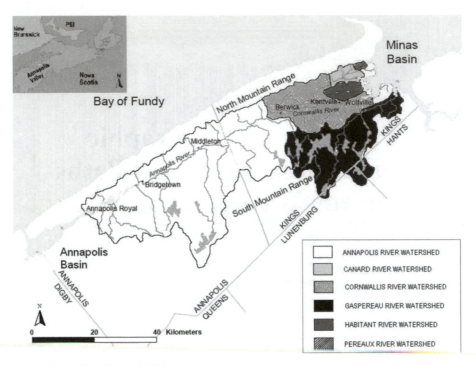

Source: Adapted from Timmer (2003)

Figure 10.1 *Watersheds of the Annapolis Valley, Nova Scotia*

economic and political influences that are often incompatible with natural phenomena. This raises the question of whether a management system based on a WSP approach can actually be carried out on a watershed basis.

The Annapolis Valley illustrates many of the water issues found in rural, agricultural areas of Eastern Canada. The Valley is approximately 100km long and actually contains six watersheds that together drain almost 2600km² into the Annapolis and Minas Basins (Figure 10.1). The Valley contains the largest and most productive farmland area in Nova Scotia (Trescott, 1968) and, although mainly rural, is experiencing rapid residential growth at its eastern end. Most of the >82,000 residents now rely on groundwater because surface waters have become overused and contaminated and about 60 per cent of homes are on individual wells (Timmer, 2003).

Superficially, water supply seems adequate, with more than 1100mm per year of precipitation, mostly as snow in winter, and rain in spring and fall. The Valley's rivers, however, are short, and deliver much of their surface water into nearby estuaries within 2–3 days. Summers are dry and warm and, with the area's larger lakes serving as reservoirs for hydroelectric power generation, there is little capacity available to store water for irrigation. In recent years, summer droughts and shifts in agriculture – from grains to vegetables and soft fruits that require larger quantities of higher quality water – have led to the increasing use of groundwater (AGRA, 2000). Other stressors on the Valley's water balance include growth in residential and tourism/recreation (eg, golf courses) demand, contamination of surface waters and more frequent droughts (Isaacman and Daborn, 2007).

The Valley has experienced frequent dry periods over the past few years. Moreover, periods of water scarcity are expected to become increasingly common occurrences in the Valley in the future as a result of climate change, especially during the summer, when water demand is highest. Several of the Valley's freshwater systems already appear to be overexploited, or are near their sustainable limits. Higher demand and fluctuations in precipitation and temperature will amplify the prevalence and severity of overexploitation in the Valley, posing threats to ecological and economic systems, especially agriculture.

Based on the WSP principles and methodology outlined in Brandes and Brooks (2006), a case study was undertaken, utilizing the Annapolis Valley as the model, to explore and demonstrate the potential for applying WSP analysis at a watershed scale by:

- developing and comparing alternative scenarios for achieving sustainable water use in the Annapolis Valley by 2030;
- exploring the opportunities and barriers to applying WSP at a watershed scale in Nova Scotia; and
- promoting the WSP methodology by involving local managers and stakeholders in the exploration of demand management options.

Methodology

This study represents an aggregated regional-scale analysis of the Annapolis Valley as a whole. Although the Annapolis Valley was selected as a model for a watershed scale soft path study due to its distinct geographical, ecological, socio-economic and political characteristics, specific freshwater supply and demand conditions are variable by watershed, sub-watershed and individual aquifer and river system throughout the region.

Raw data on water supply and demand, and background information on demographic and socio-economic trends, were compiled from federal, provincial and municipal databases, academic and NGO research and consultants' reports. Supply and demand approximations were based on our analyses of raw data sources; gaps were filled by applying educated assumptions or parameters from studies elsewhere. The data were then used to calculate:

- current surface and groundwater supply and availability for withdrawal;
- current freshwater use (demand) by each sector; and
- minimum water requirements for maintaining the ecological functions of the Valley's watercourses.

Several stakeholder meetings were held to identify and assess data quality and explore future options. Each potential option was analysed to identify those that would be most appropriate (ecologically, socially and politically) and effective (achieve the most savings) for the region.

Through quantitative analysis (backcasting) of water availability, and the potential of different management options to minimize water use, the study developed and investigated three possible scenarios for future water use through 2030:

1 *Business as Usual* scenario (BAU), which assumes that present socio-economic and water use trends would continue;
2 *Demand Management* scenario, which aims to maintain water demand at current levels (ie, avoiding the need to develop new water supplies); and
3 *Water Soft Path* (WSP) scenario, which aims to maintain the same water services into the future, with no more than 50 per cent of the current water demand.

Through this exercise, several potential political and socio-economic opportunities and barriers to WSPs in the Valley were identified and used to assess the general practicality of implementing a WSP approach at a watershed level.

Detailed study methods, results and WSP plans are published in Isaacman and Daborn (2007).

Findings

Current (circa 2004) conditions
Total annual water supply (from both surface and groundwater) to the Valley averages 1500 million cubic metres (Mm^3), with less than 10 per cent arriving during the summer (June–August). Assuming that 75 per cent of surface and 50 per cent of groundwater must remain unused to maintain ecosystem services (based on provincial and federal objectives; Nova Scotia Department of Environment, 2006; J. C. Leadbetter, Fisheries and Oceans Canada, personal Communication, 2006), almost $496Mm^3$ is available for ecologically sustainable withdrawal (Table 10.1).

Total annual water use is estimated at $25Mm^3$, approximately 50 per cent of which occurs during the summer. Agriculture (crop and livestock produc-

Table 10.1 *Mean surface and groundwater base supply, ecological requirements and availability (Mm^3)*

| | Surface | | Groundwater |
	Annual	Summer	
Surface discharge/groundwater recharge	1389	143	113
Ecological requirements	949	91	56
Availability for withdrawal	440	52	56

Source: Isaacman and Daborn (2007)

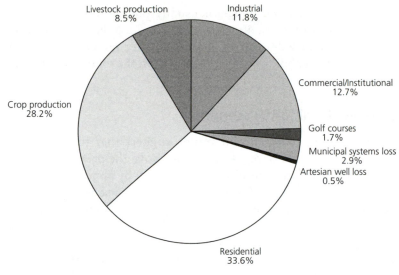

Source: Isaacman and Daborn (2007)

Figure 10.2 *Annual water withdrawal by sector*

tion) is the largest annual water user with over 36 per cent of total withdrawals, with the residential sector a close second (33.6 per cent) (Figure 10.2). In the summer, agriculture and golf courses together take almost two-thirds of total withdrawals (mostly from surface water) (Figure 10.3). Groundwater, which is the primary source for residential, commercial and industrial sectors, accounts for 71 per cent and 43 per cent of annual and summer withdrawals, respectively.

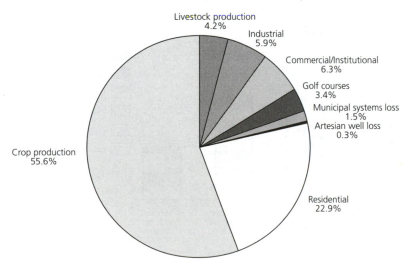

Source: Isaacman and Daborn (2007)

Figure 10.3 *Summer water withdrawal by sector*

Although the current water budget is usually balanced on an annual basis, withdrawals in 12 of the last 40 years have exceeded the summer availability (resulting in temporary drawdown of groundwater reserves), and in three of those years, annual withdrawals were greater than the total recharge (Isaacman and Daborn, 2007).

Business-as-Usual (BAU) scenario

When projected to 2030, current trends suggest that total annual water withdrawal could rise by about 45 per cent above the present level, to about 36Mm^3. Summer withdrawals alone would grow by almost 80 per cent. The highest growth (more than 100 per cent) in water use is expected for crop production, because of expected shifts in practice from grains, fruits and livestock to vegetables. Lower increases (7–35 per cent) are predicted for most other sectors. These forecasts indicate that, under BAU conditions, annual surface water availability will be inadequate to meet annual demand at least once in 12 years, but *nearly every second year* (44 per cent of the time) *during the summer*. Groundwater availability will fail to meet annual demand two years in five. Under BAU, future water use levels would exceed ecological thresholds during dry periods, thus risking potentially long-term damage to species, ecosystems and the local economy.

Pursuing the WSP

Results from backcasting analyses demonstrate that substantial water use reductions (Demand Management and WSP goals) can be achieved by 2030 using currently available and practical measures (Figure 10.4).

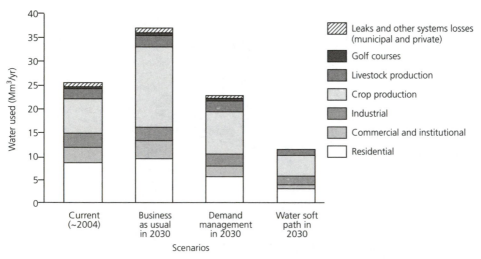

Source: Isaacman and Daborn (2007)

Figure 10.4 *Annual water demand by sector in the Annapolis Valley under BAU, Demand Management and WSP scenarios*

Demand Management scenario

Under the Demand Management scenario, using readily available water conservation methods, annual withdrawal could be limited to roughly $22Mm^3$, an overall reduction of 40 per cent over the year, and a 48 per cent reduction in summer compared to BAU. Thus, adopting demand management measures may be sufficient to restrict water demand to current volumes without significantly affecting social or economic activities in the Annapolis Valley. Despite this reduction, the region could still continue to experience periods with insufficient availability under this scenario, especially given climate change forecasts that suggest precipitation will become higher in the fall, winter and spring, but lower during the critical growing season. In addition to policy and regulatory changes, improved monitoring and enforcement, financial/technical support and education programmes, achieving this scenario involves the moderate adoption of currently existing technologies and practices to improve the efficiency of water use (standard demand management measures) such as the following:

- repairing leaks (especially municipal water mains);
- capping artesian wells;
- drip/trickle irrigation or high-efficiency sprinklers;
- high-efficiency technologies (eg, low-flow toilets and fixtures; water-conserving cooling/heating systems etc.); and
- water-conserving practices (eg, crop, golf course and lawn irrigation; industrial/agricultural procedures);

WSP scenario

A WSP scenario could result in the reduction of annual demand to almost $12Mm^3$ (only one-third of the BAU scenario), which is 55 per cent and 54 per cent below current annual and summer demand, respectively. To achieve this level, the region would require the widespread adoption of Demand Management scenario measures, as well as the significant uptake of one or more of the following soft path measures by each sector, to reduce overall water extraction needs:

- implementation of a strong conservation ethic and other changes to water use policies, behaviours, habits and attitudes;
- changes in population, economic and agricultural activities and growth patterns, where needed;
- maximizing benefits from extracted water through water and wastewater recycling and reuse;
- full exploitation of renewable low impact sources such as rainwater and surface runoff; and
- waterless technologies and practices (eg, toilets, cooling systems, industrial cleaning).

Table 10.2 *Considerations for selecting appropriate sector-specific reduction measures*

Consideration	Description
Effectiveness	Individual or cumulative water savings potential
Local suitability	Is it feasible given the local natural conditions, economic and population composition and needs, and technical capacity?
Value/importance of water use	What is the local economic and/or social value of the water use activity? Does the water provide a worthwhile service, is that volume necessary to provide the service, or does it create an unnecessary wastage of water?
Community and institutional support/ resistance	How willing would the community/sectors and local governments be to adopt this option? To what extent has the measure currently been adopted in the region? What types of policies and programmes (eg, education, enforcement, incentives) may be needed to facilitate the implementation of this action?

Source: Isaacman and Daborn (2007)

Water reductions may be more feasible, desirable and necessary in some sectors than others. Thus, the sectors and end-uses with the most potential for water savings were identified and targeted. A holistic approach needs to be taken to achieve a sustainable water use society, and thus strategies were developed to address inefficiencies in all sectors. It is also important to 'share the conservation burden' equitably; failing this it might be quite difficult to convince users to support conservation in their own efforts if other sectors are allowed to continue to use water irresponsibly.

Key considerations that were used for determining critical sectors and end-uses, and for selecting locally appropriate sector-specific measures are outlined in Table 10.2. Each sector-specific measure was assigned a potential water savings value based on the best available information. Where possible, potential water savings were based on values suggested in publications or by experts. However, in the cases where values were either extremely case specific or not available, the researcher assumed conservative water savings goals based on an assessment of available information. Assuming that not every measure is appropriate to be adopted by all the users in each sector, each measure was also assigned a minimum user adoption target (goal).

These outcomes demonstrate that, by adopting a soft path approach, the Valley could sustain continued population and economic growth, while withdrawing significantly less water than at present. Through the reduction of water extraction needs, the likelihood of insufficient supply to meet both human and ecological needs in the region is much reduced when compared to the BAU and Demand Management scenarios. Moreover, through the changes in water use needs, the economic, social and political structure of the region would become more resilient and better equipped to manage periods of water scarcity.

Barriers and opportunities to watershed level WSP planning in the Annapolis Valley (and other regions)

In most provinces, including Nova Scotia, the bulk of resource management authority lies at the provincial level rather than at the watershed level. The ability to undertake effective local/regional level conservation strategies therefore depends on strong, complementary policy and regulatory capacity in the provincial bureaucracy. The present institutional/managerial arrangement also limits the capacity for integrated watershed management, especially in areas containing diverse political jurisdictions and stakeholder groups. Although several municipal and provincial policies, regulations, land-use planning strategies and environmental programmes in Nova Scotia have addressed water quality concerns, water *demand management* has generally received much less attention (Smith, 2004; Willcocks-Musselman, 2005).

From a local perspective, although concerns are often raised regarding local availability of surface water during times of drought, the general perception of abundant groundwater supplies in the Annapolis Valley has resulted in low public awareness of issues related to water over-exploitation and conservation (AGRA, 2000; Smith, 2004; Willcocks-Musselman, 2005). As a result, managers have tended to focus on short-term supply management solutions, such as expanding groundwater use and developing irrigation systems, to address water scarcity concerns.

Moreover, as with most jurisdictions in Canada, users may withdraw water for little or no cost. Public utilities charge a nominal fee for their water compared to its value or the cost of providing it, and unserviced users, accounting for 70 per cent of total water use in the Valley, pay nothing for the water they use. As a result, there is little or no financial incentive for most users to conserve water.

Most of these existing and potential constraints could be addressed through provincial and local level policy and institutional reform (such as education, incentive programmes and increased stakeholder involvement in the planning process). It is interesting to note, however, that, even without these initiatives, water managers, and users in the Annapolis Valley and across Canada, are becoming increasingly aware of the limits on freshwater availability and of the value and importance of demand and watershed scale management. This positive change in awareness and attitude, and increasing level of interest, suggest that there is a real opportunity for viable, government-supported, watershed scale WSP efforts, and policy/institutional reform, to be implemented in the Valley and elsewhere in the province.

However, another major challenge to the application of a WSP approach at the watershed scale is the requirement for diverse and accurate hydrological data. In comparison with most watersheds in Canada, the Annapolis Valley has been relatively well studied. Recent geophysical surveys have produced, for the first time, a reasonable water budget for the Annapolis Valley, including an estimate of the size of the groundwater aquifers, their recharge rates, etc. Full metering of residential water use is available in many of the region's towns, but the vast majority of withdrawals by rural dwellers and the agriculture sector are from private wells or surface waters that continue to go unrecorded. It needs to be emphasized that the collection of adequate water use data will be a critical element in the development of a WSP model for a sustainable future.

Conclusion

This study illustrates that, while the Demand Management model may be a more effective approach than Business as Usual, it cannot, on its own, ensure future ecological and human water security, even in a relatively well-watered region of Canada such as the Annapolis Valley. In contrast, the WSP scenario illustrates that use of soft path strategies that reduce social and economic reliance on the withdrawal of 'new' freshwater from natural systems can reduce the strain such regions put on these ecosystems and lessen the impacts caused by periods of water scarcity.

Even though the research suggests that the WSP approach would be highly practical, effective and ecologically sustainable, the currently weak political and socio-economic climate has not encouraged the implementation of watershed scale water soft path planning in Eastern Canada. However, with strong social and political support and commitment, these challenges could be overcome to ensure an ecologically and socio-economically prosperous water future.

References

AGRA Earth and Environmental Limited (2000) *Water Resources Needs of the Agricultural Industry in the Annapolis Valley, Nova Scotia*, Report prepared for the Growers Water Group, Horticulture Nova Scotia, Halifax, NS

Brandes, O. M. and Brooks, D. B. (2006) *The Soft Path for Water in a Nutshell*, revised edition, Friends of the Earth Canada, Ottawa, ON and POLIS Project on Ecological Governance, University of Victoria, Victoria, BC

Isaacman, L. and Daborn, G. (2007) 'A water soft path for the Annapolis Valley, Nova Scotia: A case study of sustainable freshwater management at a watershed-scale', in *Lexicon of Water Soft Path Knowledge*, vol 1 (CD-ROM), Friends of the Earth Canada, Ottawa, ON

Nova Scotia Department of Environment and Labour (2006) 'Groundwater management', www.gov.ns.ca/enla/water/groundwater/groundwatermagmt.asp, accessed 26 September 2006

Smith, M. (2004) 'Groundwater supply and demand issues in Kings County, Nova Scotia', MES Thesis, Dalhousie University, Halifax, NS

Timmer, D. (2003) 'Source water protection in the Annapolis Valley, Nova Scotia: Local capacity in a watershed context', MA Thesis, University of Guelph, Guelph, ON

Trescott, P. C. (1968) *Groundwater Resources and Hydrogeology of the Annapolis–Cornwallis Valley, Nova Scotia*, Nova Scotia Department of Mines, Halifax, NS

Willcocks-Musselman, R. (2005) 'An assessment of local-level capacity for integrated water management in Kings County, Nova Scotia', MES Thesis, Dalhousie University, Halifax, NS

11
Focusing on Political Boundaries: Water Soft Paths at the Provincial Scale

Paul Kay and Elizabeth Hendriks

Now, here, you see, it takes all the running you can do, to keep in the same place. If you want to get somewhere else, you must run at least twice as fast as that!
Lewis Carroll, *Through the Looking-Glass and What Alice Found There*

Among the triumvirate of spatial scales studied in the original Canadian soft path project, that of the province recommends itself for primarily policy reasons. Constitutionally, the provinces have jurisdiction over the uses of most of the water within their boundaries. The federal government reserves to itself jurisdiction over a limited variety of waters, leaving to the provinces authority for water under their resources acts. Thus, policy for sustainable water futures should be a provincial responsibility.

The name 'Ontario' is thought to derive from a word in the Iroquoian language, suggesting 'beautiful (or sparkling) water (or lake)' or 'large body of water' (Ontario, 2008). This etymology evokes the vast streams, rivers, lakes and wetlands in the Province of Ontario, an image still powerfully at play in the collective perception of Ontarians and Canadians. The geographic, population and economic size of Ontario suggest it provides a useful lens to better grasp the policy implications of the soft path concept and operation.

Ontario has almost 12.3 million people (39 per cent of the national population), over 50 per cent of the nation's manufacturing sales and over 20 per cent of national agricultural production (all data for 2003 from Statistics Canada, 2007). Unlike the other studies reported in this book, industrial activity is a very important component of the total water budget. Ontario has a great deal of surface water (a quarter of a million lakes and 'countless' rivers). Looks are deceiving, however, as the distribution of population and water does not coincide. More than 80 per cent of the province's population, and thus most of its agricultural and industrial activity, is concentrated in the Great Lakes–St Lawrence River Basin (GLSLRB); the very size of the Great Lakes fosters a vision of unlimited water. Yet the sparsely populated northern part of the province contains a considerable amount of the province's water supply, which flows into Hudson Bay, away from the population concentration. Volumetrically, the water in the Great Lakes is mostly fossil endowment from the Pleistocene ice age. Projections of population growth of at least 30 per cent by 2030, with accompanying economic growth, imply the demands on water will increase beyond renewable water supply in southern Ontario.

Ontario may already be in a state of 'running as fast as it can to stay in the same place', certainly with regard to energy and increasingly with regard to water in the south. To run twice as fast, the usual approach in water management is oriented to supply-side solutions, such as pipelines from the Great Lakes. These approaches, however, represent enormous financial investments, may be politically thwarted by international agreement not to engage in inter-basin water transfers, and do not include explicit consideration of the impact of energy costs to pump and transfer water on already strained energy supplies. The water soft approach, however, may allow Ontario to slow its pace but still get 'some place', that is, to a desired future that is sustainable. The specific question posed by the provincial-scale study of the water soft path approach was: can we imagine Ontario, in 2031, coping with population and economic growth but with no new water?

Overview of Ontario water situation at the millennium

As our focus was provincial in scale, we looked for existing water use summaries according to major sectors. The Great Lakes Commission (GLC) maintains one such data repository for the GLSLRB (Ratliff, 2005, Table 1; these data are not, it should be noted, for the entire province). The data were assembled by the Science and Information Branch of the Ontario Ministry of

Natural Resources, from a variety of sources in the Ontario Ministry of Environment, Environment Canada and Statistics Canada. Since well over 80 per cent of Ontario's population and economic activity is within the GLSLRB, these data capture much – but not all – of the water use in the province. Hydroelectric power generation withdraws the most water of any of the sectors studied, but consumes practically none of it. Power production draws 108.3 thousand million cubic metres (Mm^3) of water per year, about 95 per cent of which is for hydroelectric generation. There is essentially no consumption in this mode. In fossil-fuel and nuclear energy production, water is used for cooling and some is lost by evaporation, although less than the 1 per cent loss reported in the GLC (especially as no loss is reported for the fossil-fuel power sector). The three major sectors considered in this chapter – agriculture ($55.6Mm^3/yr$), municipal ($439.2Mm^3/yr$) and industry ($465.6Mm^3/yr$) – ranked in that order from lowest to highest water consumption. However, the definitions provided suggest that there may be double counting between the categories 'domestic' and 'public supply' and between 'public supply' and 'industry'. In our work, we identified the municipal sector as comprising residential, commercial, institutional and public space uses; this category also includes system losses and other unaccounted (non-revenue) water. Industrial uses (largely manufacturing) are considered in their own industrial sector. We therefore sought other data, particularly for consumptive use, as appropriate within the sectors.

Data and scenarios

Conceptually, calculation of total water use in the major sectors of agriculture, municipal use and industry requires summation across all sub-sectors and across geography (municipalities, basins or regions). Practically, there were neither time nor data resources for such an exercise. Within sub-sectors, intensity of water use (amount of water per unit of product) can vary due to age of infrastructure, nature of process and other factors. Most agricultural and many industrial users supply their own water, so their consumption does not show up in municipal or other databases. We therefore relied on other sources of provincial total water use for the major sectors:

- de Loë and Moraru (2004) estimated water use by major sub-sectors (field, fruit, vegetable and specialty crops, and livestock) in southern Ontario (where most agriculture occurs) by a coefficient method.
- Environment Canada (2005) provided municipal water use statistics based on surveys of municipal operators; these data included some industrial uses.
- Scharf et al (2002) summarized the last census of industrial water use (1996), which reported data for 14 manufacturing categories at national scale.

For each of the three sectors, we generated three scenarios. Our target year for the 'future' was 2031, not 2050 as chosen by other components of the soft path study, because reasonably reliable population, and demographically based employment projections, are available to that time. Mid-century is too far into the future to make realistic assumptions about the course of the economy. A business-as-usual (BAU) scenario merely scaled up current water uses for the projected population in 2031, naïvely assuming that current patterns and intensities of water use would remain unchanged. As Ontario's population is forecast to grow by 32.6 per cent between 2004 and 2031 (Ontario Ministry of Finance, 2005), water use was forecast to be about one-third more than at the beginning of the millennium. A demand management scenario applied estimates of the effects of available demand management strategies with assumptions of uptake or application. The soft path scenario made more rigourous assumptions about demand management and changes in patterns of water use, reflecting a questioning of services desired and whether they could be achieved with less, or no water. The target for 2031 was 'no new water' – that is, total water uses in the province are not to exceed current amounts.

In this chapter, we differentiate water 'use' as 'intake' of water from the local environment (either surface or subsurface withdrawals) or 'consumption' (cf. the definitions for the industrial sector, as in Scharf et al, 2002). The water consumed is the difference between withdrawal and that discharged (returned) to the local environment. Such distinction refers only to quantity; discharged water may or may not be of sufficient quality for other uses. Further, recycling of water means that 'gross water use' may exceed water intake. The distinctions are important in the water soft path paradigm, because the principle of matching quality to end service emphasizes reuse and thus contributes to overall measures of efficiency and conservation.

The agricultural sector

Agriculture is the second largest economic sector in Ontario, generating at the start of the millennium approximately $6.8 billion annually from soybeans, corn and wheat, as well as fruit and livestock (de Loë and Moraru, 2004). A steady decline in the number of farms in Ontario since 1970 has been matched by an increase in average farm size, so total overall area devoted to agriculture in the province has hardly changed (Ontario Ministry of Agriculture, Food and Rural Affairs, 2002). Agricultural water withdrawals are concentrated in the summer months and, although less than 10 per cent of farms reported using irrigation, calculations from available data suggest approximately one-quarter of total agricultural water use was for summer irrigation. The BAU scenario projects a growth in agricultural water use from 174Mm^3/yr to 230Mm^3/yr.

For our scenarios, we assumed no net change in total cropland and no structural changes; that is, the relative distribution of types of agriculture practised remained the same as at present. We did assume major expansion of irrigation for all cropland to meet growing demand for food and discretionary products such as nursery stock and sod (both of which are water intensive) in the face of suburbanization and climate change impacts. We assumed that the mode of irrigation for the main crop categories does not change, but that continual improvement of efficiency does occur. We assumed that half of the specialty crop water is used for sod production (the other major specialty crop, tobacco, is in decline), and that all sod production is irrigated.

The demand management scenario results in total water use nearly half again as large as the current amount, and even 12 per cent above the BAU scenario. This seemingly contradictory result arises because of our assumption of extensive increase in irrigation use from the present, even though efficient irrigation technology is used. In the soft path scenario, total water use is estimated to be some 17 per cent above the current amount, but 12 per cent below the BAU scenario. These results illustrate the sensitivity of the scenarios to the assumptions. Our assumption about expansion of irrigation, in particular, may be too large, and clearly will be a policy that will merit considerable societal debate. Two significant changes in society might occur, which would affect agricultural use: near-complete abandonment of tobacco production (already under way); and major abandonment of lawns as residential and commercial landscape features. Were such lifestyle changes to occur, the estimates of future water use by agriculture would be considerably smaller than indicated here. This sector then might not require any new water by 2031.

The municipal sector

Average daily flow (supply) for municipal use in 2001 was 533 litres/person, of which 285 litres/person was for residential use (Environment Canada, 2005). The BAU scenario thus projected total municipal withdrawals to grow from about 1000Mm^3/yr to about 1338Mm^3/yr.

For the demand management and soft path scenarios, we began with the same efficiency factors for technologies and practices used by Brandes and Maas (Chapter 9, this volume). Efficiency factors should be constant across the country, but penetration (or adoption rates) may vary by size of community, economic structure, provincial policy and support, and so on. Our target year is some 20 years earlier than that used by Brandes and Maas, so we may be overestimating penetration rates of efficient technologies and thus may overestimate water savings achieved. Because we expect an intensification of multi-unit dwellings, we adjusted the ratio of indoor to outdoor water use to 55:45. We also introduced reductions in non-revenue water use in response to the recommendations from an expert panel on the urgent and inescapable need for infrastructure renewal (Water Strategy Expert Panel, 2005).

In the demand management scenario, considerable indoor reduction results from the increased adoption of efficient water appliances. Enhanced efficiency outdoors (through reduction in landscape irrigation) is outstripped by the effect of population growth and the demand (albeit at a reduced rate) for single-family homes with green landscapes. An assumed 25 per cent reduction in municipal water loss is countered by the expansion of infrastructure to meet population growth, so the net contribution to savings is small. In total, the scenario showed 10 per cent less water use than at present.

In the soft path scenario, further uptake of indoor efficiencies and conservation measures reduces in-house use to half of the present amount. Outdoor uses, with the further adoption of xeriscaping and application of more landscape-watering restrictions, are reduced by 15 per cent. Non-revenue losses are expanded to 50 per cent, so the net contribution to water saving become significant. In total, municipal water use, under the WSP scenario, is 41 per cent less than the present amount. That is, Ontario can accommodate the assumed population and economic growth to 2031 while using considerably less water in the municipal sector than it does now. In addition to the implications for municipal water supplies, these results suggest that a considerable portion of the suggested nearly $9 billion needed for new infrastructure by 2019 (Water Strategy Expert Panel, 2005, pp7–8) might be avoided.

The industrial sector

Unlike the other core studies in the original project (Chapters 9 and 10, this volume), the industrial sector is a major player in the water budget of Ontario. In the mid-1990s, the province accounted for one-half of the national total industrial intake of water and more than one-third of national industrial consumptive use (Scharf et al, 2002). As the 1996 census of industrial water use reported data for the 14 major industrial groups only as national totals, we assumed that the amount of water used within a manufacturing category in Ontario is proportional to the concentration of activity of that category in the province, and used the provincial proportion of national employment in the group as an indicator of concentration. Paper and allied products, primary metals and chemicals and chemical products were both the largest drawers and consumers of water.

The BAU scenario sees water intake grow to 3388Mm^3/yr and consumption to 310Mm^3/yr. However, industries have been making continual improvements in efficiency, such as reusing water and thus reducing the need for fresh intake of water from the environment. In 1996, recycle rates (amount of water recirculated within plants divided by the amount of new water brought into the plants) varied from 25 per cent in the beverages category to 292 per cent in the plastic products category. In the face of our inability to undertake the analyses necessary for precise modelling either on a plant-by-plant basis, or even by manufacturing sector, we made the global assumption that, at a minimum, the water savings in 2031 compared to 2000 would be of the same magnitude as demonstrated in the period 1981–1996. In that period, water intake declined by 25 per cent but the consumption ratio (consumed:intake) increased slightly (2 per cent), meaning that industry became more water efficient in production. With this assumption, and assuming no structural change in the make-up of Ontario's industrial sector, the

Table 11.1 *Estimated water intake and consumption, Mm³/yr, by manufacturing categories in Ontario for 1996*

Sector	Employment Can	Employment ON	ratio	Intake Can	Intake ON	Consumption Can	Consumption ON
Food	149,778	49,303	0.329	269.5	88.7	29.5	9.7
Beverages	15,318	6368	0.416	73.1	30.4	16.9	7.0
Primary textile	14,733	5787	0.393	86.7	34.1	2.1	0.8
Textile prod	7136	2767	0.388	15.0	5.8	2.1	0.8
Wood prod	55,241	6888	0.125	45.1	5.6	12.1	1.5
Paper & allied prod	77,741	21,752	0.280	2421.3	677.5	214.3	60.0
Petroleum & coal prod	7353	2585	0.352	370.5	130.3	22.5	7.9
Chemicals & chem prod	57,822	30,774	0.532	1121.3	596.8	90.7	48.3
Plastic prod	42,371	23,647	0.558	13.3	7.4	1.3	0.7
Rubber prod	17,915	10,493	0.586	12.3	7.2	1.0	0.6
Non-metal mineral prod	33,779	14,691	0.435	102.3	44.5	19.2	8.4
Primary metals	73,570	44,469	0.604	1423	860.1	120.0	72.5
Fabricated metals	40,751	19,556	0.480	19.4	9.3	1.1	0.5
Transport equip	196,568	148,280	0.754	65.4	49.3	19.0	14.3
Total	**790,076**	**387,360**		**6038.2**	**2547.0**	**551.8**	**233.1**

Source: Scharf et al, 2002, Table 3, and authors' calculations

demand management scenario shows (depending on low and high economic growth scenarios) intake growing to 2740–5030Mm³/yr and consumption growing to 300–550Mm³/yr, a large increase over present values but perhaps equivalent to BAU scenarios. With an assumption of quite modest further improvement in efficiency, the soft path scenario shows water intake and use far below BAU values, but still at least 16 per cent above present levels.

Two case studies suggest the detail that could be obtained by focusing on specific industries. Pulp and paper production requires more water per tonne of product than any other industrial product and in Ontario mills water needs are mostly self-supplied. Estimates of water intensity vary widely, from 44–83m³ to as much as 400–500m³, per tonne, depending on grade of paper, process, age of mill and level of corporate responsibility (Abramovitz and Mattoon, 1999; Falkenmark and Rockstron, 2005). Mechanical pulping uses the least amount of water, but the highest amount of energy, per unit product. Chemical pulping uses 4–5 times more water than mechanical pulping, while thermo-mechanical pulping uses an intermediate amount. From reported surveys by the Forest Products Association of Canada (2004), there appears to have been a downward trend of about 34 per cent in water used (or consumed) per tonne of product over the past 20 years. Boardley and Kinkhead (2006) reported many process improvements already made or possible in the short term. As an example of an ultimate best practice, Domtar's Trenton mill in south-eastern Ontario has, since 1997, successfully used a closed-loop process water system (Rodden, 1997). Only a small amount of water from the Trent River is needed to make up water requirements (about $2m^3$/tonne). If such technologies were applied to all pulp and paper mills in Ontario, future water consumption by this industry would be significantly lower than at present. In addition, significant water quality issues that are caused by mill effluents would also be addressed.

Canada's entire automobile manufacturing sector is based in Ontario, although other subcategories of transportation equipment manufacturing are found in other provinces. As well, the volume of vehicle production in Ontario has recently been close to the largest, by jurisdiction, in North America. More than 90 per cent of water used by this sector is supplied from public sources (ie, by municipalities) and thus can represent a significant strain on municipal infrastructure and water supplies. Statistics on water intensity were very difficult to obtain; estimates based on data in annual reports of some corporations varied from 1.4 to $8.8m^3$/vehicle. This range reflects differences (and sloppiness) in what is reported (water 'use', 'intake' and 'consumption' are all terms used), and differences between single plant versus dispersed manufacture and assembly methods of production.

Taking a median value of $6m^3$/vehicle, and scaling up current levels of production and North American populations, we estimated a BAU scenario of $23.2Mm^3$/yr consumed. Very modest and conservative estimates of increased production efficiencies gave us demand management scenarios of 17–24 per cent more consumption than at present, and soft path scenarios of 4–11 per cent more. The auto industry does have a large recycling ratio (in excess of 60 per cent of gross water use is recycled water) and Toyota Canada, for one, boasts of employing exceptional water treatment and recycling efforts (Toyota, 2006). Opportunities for better performance exist: within the manufacturing process, such as waterless painting as practised by the Smart® Car Division of Mercedes Benz; and associated with the facilities, such as rainwater capture from the extensive, flat, factory roofs (a simple estimate suggested a volume of approximately 10 per cent of the estimated 1996 consumption might be harvested). Societal change away from an intensive car-based society would reduce production demands and reduce water needs in this industry; the economic implications of course are vast.

Discussion

If water use intensity continues at the present rate, by 2031 Ontario would be experiencing water use greater by 30 per cent or more than it was in 2001. While Ontario appears, to the casual observer, to be water rich, such demands would stress water utilities' ability to provide both infrastructure and supplies. As illustrated by Figure 11.1, the soft path scenarios suggest the province *can*

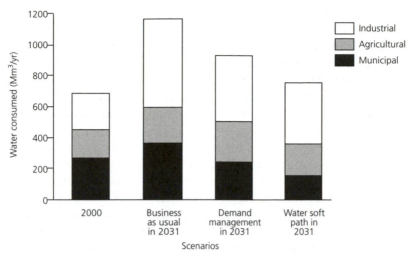

Source: Alternatives (2007) vol 33, no 4

Figure 11.1 *Comparison of Ontario's water consumption in 2031 under three different scenarios*

achieve a 'no new water' future in 2031; the magnitudes we suggest are indicative, although we recognize limitations to precision due to data issues, scale of analyses, and broadness of the assumptions. All sectors have identified technologies and demand management practices that can improve efficiencies of water use and enhance conservation of supplies. The issue for Ontario is less the *ability* to adopt soft path methodology than the *willingness* to do so. That reluctance may stem from two major, and related, sources: first, the perception that Ontario is not water stressed; and second, the lack of a foundational provincial water policy that sets the direction for future water management.

Our analyses have focused on technical feasibility; whether it is possible to imagine a sustainable water future, given efficiency and conservation tools that are currently available. We have not, in this study, addressed economic feasibility. The costs of retrofitting such a populous and urban-intensive province would be very great indeed; yet the cheapest supplies of future water will be found through conserving what we have rather than through the further exploitation of new or existing sources. A decision to implement intensive efficiency and conservation measures in all new construction and projects, for example, would be a major step in the right direction. Nor have we addressed social feasibility; that is whether the people of Ontario, and the businesses operating here, would readily accept the measures necessary to achieve a sustainable water future. The wild card of climatic change has not been factored into the scenarios, either. All these points clearly need further study and policy action.

The Ontario study illustrates the difficulty of dealing with a very large industrial sector in the attempt to identify water soft paths. Water is used for both production of first-order products, such as steel, and end-product goods, such as automobiles. Addressing efficiencies in the production of the steel may totally ignore the social questions of the need for the final products, yet the water soft principles suggest that social changes will come at the latter step before the former. Structural changes in manufacturing may make as much difference to the achievement of a sustainable water future as the variety of conservation measures implemented in agricultural and municipal sectors. The pulp and paper sector had already, over a number of years, seen the closure of many mills. The reduced demand for water in such circumstances in this sector, therefore, bears no relationship to the implementation of efficiency and conservation measures. The global financial crisis of 2008 may impose similar changes in other manufacturing sectors in Ontario. For example, the automobile sector, which is a very major component of the provincial economic and employment scene, may emerge in a greatly modified form, in terms of how much, and what is manufactured where. These changes would also affect the production of steel and other primary goods. At the time of writing, it is anybody's guess as to how North American industrial geography and thus industrial water balance will look in a decade.

For further water soft path work, moving into detailed modelling such as the urban calculator (Maas and Maas, Chapter 8) and development of planning tools, the provincial scale seems the least appropriate. Municipality or basin scales are more likely to yield significant results, because of the more nearly uniform conditions, the accessibility of focused data, the ability to implement detailed and truly integrated water and land use planning, and the ability to work with stakeholders in a participatory and integrated fashion to define a desired future and design pathways to it. The role of the province, as the constitutionally empowered jurisdiction for water management, should be to establish the conditions for the adoption and application of soft path methodologies. If Ontario were to do so, perhaps its municipalities and basin management bodies, and ultimately the province itself, would not have to run twice as fast to stay in the same place.

References

Abramovitz, J. and Mattoon, A. (1999) *Paper Cuts: Recovering the Paper Landscape*, Worldwatch Institute, Washington, DC

Alternatives (2007) vol 33, no 4, University of Waterloo

Boardley, A. and Kinkhead, M. (2006) *An Analysis of Canada and Other Water Conservation Practices and Initiatives: Issues, Opportunities and Suggested Directions*, Canadian Council of Ministers of the Environment, www.ccme.ca/assets/pdf/kinkead_fnl_rpt_2005_04_2.1_webpdf, accessed October 2008

de Loë, R. C. and Moraru, L. C. (2004) *Water Use and Sustainability Issues in the Canadian Agricultural Sector, Final Report*, Prepared for Sustainable Water Use Branch, Water Policy and Coordination Directorate, Environment Canada, Rob de Loë Consulting Services, Guelph, ON

Environment Canada (2005) *Municipal Water Use 2001 Statistics. 2004 Municipal Water Use Report*, www.ec.gc.ca/water, Cat no. En11-2/2001E-PDF

Falkenmark, M. and Rockstron, J. (2005) *Balancing Water for Humans and Nature: The New Approach in Ecohydrology*, Earthscan, London

Forest Products Association of Canada (2004) 'The ultimate Canadian growth industry', www.fpac.ca/en/who_we_are/pdfs/Publications/AnnualReview2004.pdf, accessed March 2007

Ontario (2008) 'About Ontario: The origin of the name "Ontario"', Queen's Printer for Ontario, www.gov.on.ca, accessed October 2008

Ontario Ministry of Agriculture, Food and Rural Affairs (2002) *Summary of Agriculture Statistics for Ontario*, www.omafra.gov.on.ca/english/stats/agriculture_summary.pdf#search=%22Summary%20of%20Agriculture%22, accessed June 2007

Ontario Ministry of Finance (2005) *Ontario Population Projections 2004–2031, Ontario and Its 49 Census Divisions*, www.fin.gov.on.ca/english/demographics/demog05.html, accessed January 2007

Ratliff, M. (2005) *Annual Report of the Great Lakes Regional Water Use Database Repository Representing 2002 Water Use Data in Litres*, Great Lakes Commission, Ann Arbor, MI

Rodden, G. (1997) 'Closure provides Trenton with increased flexibility, extra capacity', *Pulp and Paper Canada,* vol 98, no 5, pp8–11

Scharf, D., Burke, D. W., Villeneuve, M. and Leigh, L. (2002) *Industrial Water Use, 1996*, Environment Canada, Ottawa, ON

Statistics Canada (2007) www40.statcan.ca/, accessed October 2008

Toyota (2006) *Toyota North America Environmental Report*, www.toyota.ca/cgi-bin/WebObjects/WWW.woa/wa/vp?vp=Home.Environ.EnvironmentReport&language=english, accessed January 2007

Water Strategy Expert Panel (2005) *Watertight: The Case for Change in Ontario's Water and Wastewater Sector*, Queen's Printer for Ontario, Toronto, ON

Part III
Water Soft Paths as Planning Tool

12

Removing Institutional Barriers to Water Soft Paths: Challenges and Opportunities

Sarah Jordaan, Carla Stevens and David B. Brooks

I love the water of wells and springs
and the taste of roofs in the water of cisterns.

Wendell Berry

There are many kinds of barriers to advancing alternative water management practices and policies. In this chapter, we identify a number of the barriers relevant to water soft paths and discuss strategies that could be deployed to remove those barriers. Though the focus is water soft paths, we often make reference to demand management, as it is a more developed concept in the literature. Some barriers are general (e.g. changing human behaviour), while others are more specific (e.g. inefficient sprinklers for irrigating lawns or crops). For the purposes of this chapter, we focus on *institutional barriers* to water management, which are defined by Holtz (2007) as specific impediments that make it difficult or undesirable to implement a specific action. While we have used examples from Canada in this chapter, the issues being highlighted would be applicable in most other countries to a greater or lesser extent.

As we will see below, institutional barriers occur at many levels of society, from the general public, to managers of water utilities and up through various levels of government. There is no simple recipe for dealing with institutional barriers. Some, as in the case of public perceptions, may be amenable to public education campaigns that lay out the rationale for change. Other barriers may prove to be more intractable, as with the reluctance of consecutive Canadian federal governments to act decisively on climate change. Nevertheless, there is something to be gained by clearly identifying the barriers that confront us. Then and only then can we develop specific strategies for change.

We identify the following five categories of barriers to water soft paths:

Type 1: Attitudes and perceptions
Type 2: Organization and management
Type 3: Financial
Type 4: Data and information
Type 5: Policy and governance

The following sections discuss the characteristics of each category and identify specific barriers that meet the following barrier selection criteria:

- known to impede the advancement of alternative water management strategies;
- can be removed or addressed by taking actions that alter the situation through the implementation of an action-oriented time line;
- can be reduced through the actions of government agencies or corporate bodies over the next 5–10 years.

Type 1: Attitudes and perceptions

Society formulates attitudes and perceptions through learning, motivation, social interaction and exposure to information (Bell et al, 2001). Analysing why certain attitudes and perceptions are held, seemingly in the face of objective 'facts', can be difficult. We have only to look at the rejection of the Theory of Evolution by some segments of Western society as a case in point. Early recognition of contrary attitudes and perceptions is important in the development of water soft paths because they can be barriers to advancing change. However, completely eliminating the underlying psycho-social causes of unsuccessful efforts is difficult. Attachment to specific attitudes and perceptions can be stubborn because changing them requires a significant psychological reform by the individual or group that holds the attitude or perception and because the alternative way of thinking is unfamiliar or unacceptable for any of a variety of reasons.

The following common attitudinal and perception barriers meet the selection criteria defined above.

Myth of superabundance

In Canada, a common perception is that our freshwater sources are boundless and that no significant water problems exist (Brandes and Ferguson, 2004). This perception makes it difficult to encourage conservation behaviour.

As discussed in Chapter 1, only a small portion of Canadian water is, in fact, renewable and located close to where most Canadians live. While there is ample scientific evidence in Canada of the potential for water shortfalls, there has been little sense of urgency at any level to deal with the problem. Indeed, despite evidence that climate change is likely to increase water scarcity in western Canada (Schindler and Donahue, 2006), the perception extends to the point that many people think that Canada will be a 'winner' as the effects of climate change extend across the globe. Remedial actions may be taken when shortfalls occur during a limited period of time; for example, limits may be placed on lawn watering during a summer heat wave. However, once normal rainfall and cooler weather have 'solved the problem' by the end of the summer, the perception that something 'needs to be done' fades away.

Even those parts of the country that have experienced periodic droughts, such as the southern parts of the three prairie provinces in western Canada, are only now beginning to consider the necessity of changing the way that things are done. Farmers, ranchers and municipalities fight over the water that is available but, except to the extent that they work with regional conservation districts or other watershed management groups, local governments have not generally taken a lead role in launching a debate about the long-term sustainability of water use practices in the region. In contrast, and perhaps an indication of a new reality, each of the provincial governments has established new governance structures to deal with water use and management.

Disconnect between human systems and ecological systems

Traditionally, supply-based solutions for water management have been designed without respect to the ecological systems providing the water. The near complete collapse of Pacific salmon populations in those west coast rivers that have seen the construction of extensive hydroelectric projects is one illustration of this phenomenon, but there are many others. The neglect of these potential impacts is a result of the lack of awareness and understanding of the ecological importance of both 'renewable water supplies' (precipitation that falls and flows towards the sea or into a deep aquifer), and 'total water supplies' (renewable water plus stored freshwater in lakes and aquifers) (Brandes and Ferguson, 2004).

Flawed beliefs about the impacts of water conservation

In an interesting, but perhaps not unexpected, parallel to the attitudes expressed towards energy conservation, some Canadians believe that a reduction in water consumption resulting from conservation efforts will lead directly to economic losses in the industry sector or a reduction in standards of living in the residential sector (Wolff and Gleick, 2002; J. Kinkead Consulting, 2006; Gleick, Chapter 4 in this book). Understandably, this perception contributes to the resistance to alternative water management strategies.

Type 2: Organization and management

Organizational structures and management approaches, within any organization or decision-making authority, can create barriers to water soft paths when they conflict with existing practices and protocols. Theoretically, organizations are formal groups of people with one or more shared goals. In reality, the individuals that comprise these groups often come from different disciplines and their diverse backgrounds may inhibit the cohesion needed to design effective solutions.

Common organizational and managerial barriers that meet the defined selection criteria are discussed below.

Fragmented management

Water soft paths require the collaboration of a variety of organizations in order to be successful. Unfortunately, many management structures within and between organizations are fragmented due to traditional disciplinary or departmental segregation or 'silos'. As a result, internal structures, information systems and policies can impede some fundamental tools, such as effective communication, information sharing and innovation (Maas, 2003; Brandes and Ferguson, 2004). All levels of government in Canada are also subject to periodic changes in leadership and structure as a result of the election process, normal staff turnover or specific policy initiatives. This more-or-less constant transition in government almost inevitably results in the reorganization of both policy-making and management structures. Short-range planning cycles can ultimately result in plans, bylaws, standards and policies with inconsistent or overlapping efficiency and conservation goals. As a result, water soft path policies may be officially in place but are not fully implemented because they conflict with existing supply plans or pricing structures (Brooks and Wolfe, 2007; Furlong and Bakker, 2007).

Prominence of formulaic approaches

The focus of conventional water management approaches is meeting supply-side needs, which often leads to the further development of water-intensive infrastructure (Wolff and Gleick, 2002; Brandes and Ferguson, 2004). In this scenario, decisions are often based on known formulas rather than on integrated, interdisciplinary strategies (Brandes and Ferguson, 2004). In the past, such approaches have been effective in supplying water, while ignoring impacts to the upstream and downstream ecosystems. Depending on the organization, meeting the more holistic water management goals associated with water soft paths may require a complete change of corporate philosophy. The planning of future water management activities must involve a more diverse range of disciplines than in the past. The hiring of specialists who are conversant with both ecological issues and water suppy technologies will be a fundamental part of this corporate shift.

Performance management focused on monitoring, rather than problem solving

Organizations are often required to report and communicate their performance in relation to water management. In these kinds of situations, the focus tends to be on monitoring the current situation (eg, the amount of water used, quality of water) rather than on measuring performance based on the application of innovative approaches. 'Performance' is therefore defined in a very limited way, based on meeting the status quo rather than promoting improvements. Also, as noted below, there can be a 'Catch-22' aspect to monitoring; while a reduction in water use is a *positive* soft path result, it can simultaneously result in lower revenues for a water utility, which is the opposite of what is normally considered to be good performance.

Type 3: Financial

Financial barriers can prevent the implementation of alternative water policies and often arise from the lack of consideration of obstacles and complexities in the economic models used in decision-making (Jaffe and Stavins, 1994; Lovins and Lovins, 1998). Conventional approaches to water management, such as supply management, tend to stimulate both growth and higher levels of use. The infrastructure necessary to support supply management is generally capital-intensive and may not result in potential savings of conservation and efficiency (Brooks, 2005). Alternative approaches focused on efficiency, such as demand management, can reduce water demand and provide an alternative for economical water savings (Brandes and Brooks, 2007). Reducing costs through efficiency requires the ability to employ appropriate economic models to achieve new water conservation goals, such as the use of innovative pricing and tariff systems that help utilities and agencies as well as their customers to benefit (Savenije and van der Zaag, 2002; Howe, 2005).

The following common financial barriers meet the defined selection criteria.

Fiscal viability

Some agencies and utilities depend on the revenue from water sales to maintain their fiscal viability. Water conservation presents such organizations with a difficult financial choice. They must deliver water at rates that cover all, or some proportion, of the costs associated with the service while also promoting water conservation to their customers. Both demand management and water soft paths can result in a decline in sales, thus threatening the revenue stream necessary for utilities to remain viable, and this has caused even publicly owned water utilities in Canada to question the advisability of promoting conservation (Furlong and Bakker, 2007). Certainly utilities that have invested in significant infrastructure expansion do risk becoming overcapitalized, as they must assume responsibility for managing the large debts associated with their expansion (Tate, 1990; Brandes and Ferguson, 2004). 'Smart' pricing, such as has been proposed for electrical utilities, can help avoid this Catch-22 by ensuring that utilities share in some of the returns from conservation (Gibbons, 2004). Smart pricing can also promote conservation by adjusting the price of the service according to the time of day or season of the year – the price goes up during periods when high demand affects the capacity to deliver.

Perceived costs of initiatives and underestimation of their benefits

Though water soft paths projects and programmes may make economic sense over their life cycle, substantial changes in infrastructure may be required, something that generally implies higher initial costs. The same changes can also jeopardize stable returns. When companies are overcapitalized, the apparent higher costs associated with implementing new approaches can be significant and the benefits tend to be underestimated as a result of the perceived risks associated with anything new.

Incomplete pricing and markets

Price signals (ie, the cost of the commodity) provide consumers and producers with an indication of when it makes economic sense to increase supply or reduce demand. However, current water pricing structures rarely account for either the full cost of supply (including capital invested in infrastructure and generally paid from general tax revenues) or externalities associated with intensive water use, such as the cost of degradation to watersheds, which is paid by society at large. In other cases, activities associated with production may provide environmental benefits (commonly called ecological goods and services) for which the operators receive no returns. This is notably true for farmers and ranchers, who construct shelterbelts, protect riparian areas and avoid farming marginal land. In either case, price signals give a false representation of the real costs or benefits associated with water use.

As with energy, there is not yet a complete market for saving water (Lovins and Lovins, 1998). Energy utilities in the US do, however, provide incentives for customers to invest in energy-saving measures (US Department of Energy, 2007). Similarly, opportunities exist to develop incentives to deliver different qualities of water for different services and to charge for wastewater disposal on the basis of the type and degree of contamination. In either case, markets would require different pricing structures and likely government funding that would cover all or part of the additional cost. Tools are still being developed to determine the value of water in situ and of other ecological goods and services (Postel and Richart, 2003; Millennium Ecosystem Assessment, 2005; Katz, 2006). At present, even if a municipality wanted to price water at its real value, it would have trouble doing so. It is difficult to convince people why they should pay for the full value of water rather than just the costs of delivering it.

Gap in payback

The payback period required by a private investment in infrastructure often does not reflect a time frame that end-users are willing to accept (RMI, 1991). Supply investments made by utilities may not be paid back for 20 years or more. Homeowners, renters and industry typically want efficiency investments to be repaid within two to five years. Capital is often misallocated to increase supply rather than towards efficiency and conservation. Though payback periods for investments in supply may be equally long, or even longer, they are hidden in tax rates. Government funding of efficiency and conservation measures could also be hidden, but experience with energy suggests that they will be developed as special programmes that make the costs quite evident. Development costs and some overheads may be paid from taxes. Of course, if homeowners and other private entities are incurring the costs, they will not be hidden at all.

Misplaced incentives

Not only are markets incomplete, pricing patterns can also inhibit change. For example, those who pay costs do not receive benefits in rental situations. If the renter pays for water, he or she will receive benefits from more efficient water infrastructure. In contrast, the landlord sees no real benefits from the investment. If the landlord pays for water, the tenant has no incentive to conserve. Incentives should be designed to benefit those who have borne the costs as well as to promote conservation. One example of this approach is the ALUS programme (Alternative Land Use Services; see, among many other sites: www.deltawaterfowl.org/alus/) which pays farmers and ranchers to implement activities that reduce erosion, support fish habitat and protect drinking water sources in rural Canada.

Absence of life cycle approach to assessing environmental, social and economic costs and benefits

Life cycle assessment (LCA) is an environmental assessment tool that evaluates environmental burdens of a process or product from materials extraction (cradle) to waste disposal (grave) (Baumann and Tillman, 2004). Impacts of water use may not be fully understood without a full life cycle approach to assessing water management options. A comprehensive assessment of some activities may show that more water than anticipated has been used when upstream or downstream consumption is also included. For example, combusting gasoline in cars is not considered to be a water-intensive process. However, with the development of water-intensive tar sands technologies and biofuels from agricultural crops, unconventional fuels may have greater upstream water use than one would expect.

Life cycle approaches to accounting should also include cumulative costs and benefits to ecosystems from other activities throughout the life of the project or programme. These costs and benefits, though difficult to quantify, should be considered when developing process and product design alternatives to determine trade-offs in environmental and economic costs. The state of the watershed should be considered alongside water use. Water drawn from degraded watersheds could reflect a greater cost. Water use has been included as a component of the Economic Input–Output Life Cycle Assessment model (www.eiolca.net). Ultimately, the goal should be to include the full cost of water in pricing structures, and the life cycle framework in assessments, so that alternatives can be compared on a level playing field that recognizes both short-term and long-term effects, and both costs and benefits.

Type 4: Data and information

Access to relevant data and information remains one of the biggest challenges to managing Canada's water resources (Rosolen, 2006). Gaps in the amount of useful data available stem, in part, from the fact that some data are held under private ownership and that critical historical data are non-digitized (Rosolen, 2006). There is a need to develop a national standard for data to improve the ability to compare disparate data sets. In addition to the issue of availability and collection of compatible data, there is also concern about what constitutes acceptable use of data. The potential use of data outside the scope of its intended purpose is problematic because of the non-transferable nature of some data and its potential misinterpretation by the public. In order for both water soft path and demand management initiatives to succeed, barriers to data and information availability and use need to be considered.

The following data and informational barriers meet the defined selection criteria.

Lack of regular time series data on water withdrawals, use and consumption

Regular time series data on water withdrawals, use and consumption can allow managers to better understand how to manage water consumption and improve policies. In Canada, accurate data on current and projected water use, by sector, are limited and dated thanks, in part, to significant cuts in the budgets for monitoring water use data by the federal government. As a result, it is often unclear how much water might be available to be conserved or even how much *has* been conserved. For example, the International Joint Commission, which manages boundary and trans-boundary waters along the US–Canadian border, has reported that water conservation in the Great Lakes states and provinces appears to be much greater than expected, but it has no idea of where or how the conservation is taking place (International Joint Commission, 2004). Out-of-date data inaccurately represent the systems being investigated and can result in 'solutions' that are not appropriate for current problems. Furthermore, the common terms 'water withdrawal', 'use' and 'consumption' are not used consistently, which further confounds data collection and, especially, interpretation (Merrett, 2004; Paul Kay, Chapter 11 in this book).

Lack of access to relevant case studies and success stories

Lack of information on the cost and potential savings associated with water soft path approaches within Canada means that specialists must adapt information from other countries to develop Canadian solutions. This information may not be entirely applicable to the Canadian water context (Brandes and Ferguson, 2004). Lack of (and conflicting) information on the scale of water savings, and on associated monetary savings achievable under demand management approaches, are serious barriers to water conservation (J. Kinkead Consulting, 2006).

Success stories and studies of water conservation efforts at the local, regional and provincial level could play a useful role in the shaping of water soft path policy and initiatives. The lack of mainstream reporting of these successes helps maintain a knowledge gap between water soft path practitioners and policy-makers. Access to and sharing of relevant information about water soft paths could play an important role in reducing concerns that policy-makers might have about the implementation of alternative water management approaches (Brandes and Ferguson, 2004).

Information on the potential benefits – economic, environmental and social – of water soft paths and their implementation is not being adequately shared between users or communicated to the public.

There are numerous reasons for this lack of sharing, including the cost of acquiring data, difficulty in obtaining licence agreements for information sharing, and privacy laws, which prevent the release of certain data to the public. The current resistance to data sharing by some industry sectors is caused, at least in part, by the fear of having unflattering data made public. This has led to increased scrutiny, loss of control and, in some cases, even to the loss of funding or jobs (Rosolen, 2006; Patrick et al, 2008). For example, golf courses are significant users of water in some areas, especially during the drier summer months, and are notably secretive about their water use.

Type 5: Policy and governance

Policy refers to a plan of action that guides decision-making. The term may apply to government, private sector organizations, non-governmental organizations and individuals. For example, integrated planning, stakeholder participation, departmental capacity, utility ownership and the role of private partnerships are all governance issues that influence most aspects of demand management and soft paths (Brandes and Ferguson, 2004). Policy changes within governments are based on the associated need within society and are often fuelled by a crisis. Proactive changes to policy related to future water efficiency and conservation goals are less common and often more difficult to achieve (Holtz, Chapter 7 in this book). Strong arguments for change must be made to convince decision-makers to modify existing policies. Securing political and bureaucratic acceptance of the need for change is often the greatest barrier to both water soft paths and demand management.

The following common policy and governance barriers meet the selection criteria defined earlier in this chapter.

'Use it or lose it' policies

A significant institutional barrier to improving water conservation is the 'use it or lose it' principle. This quota-based system, used in Canada's prairie provinces for agricultural water use, effectively eliminates the incentive to reduce and reallocate water withdrawals in high rainfall years.

No room for innovation and creativity

Prescriptive policies can entrench the status quo and limit innovation (Brandes and Ferguson, 2004). Innovative and creative solutions are necessary to change policy related to water use, and they more often arise from policies that indicate the outcome to be achieved rather than telling groups how to operate. Smarter regulation sets goals and lets implementing organizations and agencies determine the best ways to meet those goals.

Lack of public participation

People need to be seen as a strategic resource rather than part of the problem. The lack of public involvement in water management decision-making may impair public support for government initiatives (Creighton, 2005; Videira et al, 2006). The inclusion of the public requires more than a single open 'consultation' session. Effective public involvement is a long-term, integrated partnership in which ideas are exchanged and public input is used to shape future initiatives, something that is by no means easy or inexpensive.

Poor enforcement

The enforcement of actions put forth in policies related to water use is critical for meeting performance criteria and overall water conservation goals. However, proper enforcement is expensive, time-consuming and difficult to monitor. Lack of funds for enforcement and lack of will to enforce present significant barriers to better governance for fresh water resources at all levels in Canada.

Disconnect between ecological and political boundaries

Political boundaries rarely coincide with ecological boundaries; a particular watershed, for example, could span multiple jurisdictions. If the water management mandates, agendas and policies for adjacent jurisdictions do not align, or if the demands of one of the jurisdictions cannot be met, political tensions can arise. This can shift the focus of political agendas away from collaborative water management and inter-jurisdictional cooperation. The creation of watershed based conservation authorities in Ontario and Manitoba, and somewhat similar bodies in several other provinces, is a positive response to overcome this barrier.

Removal of barriers

New water management approaches, such as water soft paths, can benefit many countries at a time when most are experiencing both population growth and an increasing range of environmental concerns. At the institutional level, a variety of barriers inhibit or even prevent the adoption and implementation of water soft path approaches. Three general types of action can assist decision-makers in removing barriers (and in avoiding the creation of new barriers) to the successful implementation of water soft paths. This list is not intended to be complete, but rather to show how to address some of the critical barriers outlined in this chapter.

Multi-stakeholder involvement

- Involving stakeholders with diverse backgrounds and agendas can help managers overcome many of the aforementioned barriers.
- Barriers related to attitudes and perceptions can be addressed by providing stakeholders with the context they need to dispel some of the common water supply myths, such as the myth of superabundance.
- Including a mixture of sectors in water management decision-making can facilitate communication between disciplinary silos, promote exchanges of experience and even diminish some of the distance between stakeholders on opposite sides of a water policy debate.
- Barriers related to data and information will also be addressed more effectively, as information can be shared through forums and networks.
- Some policy and governance barriers, such as the reluctance to include people and lack of partnerships, can be overcome by establishing collaborative working groups or advisory bodies composed of individuals with a variety of skills, knowledge and resources. For example, industrial firms and government agencies can engage in partnerships to invest in community-based conservation initiatives. Ideally, they will also help support the process by committing funds.

Monitoring and enforcement; rewards and punishments

- Setting clear goals and objectives, determining strategies to achieve these goals and objectives and developing relevant performance criteria should be part of any water management practice or policy.
- Monitoring should be used to determine whether the chosen strategies are meeting performance criteria and whether goals, objectives or operations need to be adjusted to ensure targets are being met on an ongoing basis.
- Make all water using sectors and organizations accountable for their impacts on a watershed, including paying the full costs for water use and disposal, on the one hand, and being rewarded for ecologically beneficial activities, on the other.
- Monitoring and enforcing targets will help managers to recognize different stresses on watersheds and to develop appropriate strategies to prevent net negative impacts. This recommendation primarily addresses policy and governance barriers. For example, audit programmes could also be used to ensure that sectors are actually contributing to the success of related water conservation initiatives and offering acknowledgement to those that meet targets.
- Financial barriers related to Catch-22 scenarios (see Fiscal viability above) can be reduced or removed by examining pricing structures to identify and correct issues that arise due to misplaced incentives or incomplete market signals.
- Water pricing incentives can be used to promote the use of lower quality water and off peak water, where appropriate.

Bring barriers to the attention of policy-makers

- Barriers can change depending on many factors such as political climate, the composition and number of stakeholder groups, industrial development and population growth. Regular evaluations should be undertaken to identify the barriers that managers are experiencing or anticipate being an issue in the future.
- Equally important, managers should seek to determine whether the policies and programmes they are managing are erecting new barriers for the groups or sectors that they are trying to influence. A regular flow of information upward can reduce or eliminate barriers that were inadvertently introduced by new laws, regulations or programmes.
- Some of these barriers can be dealt with in-house by using adaptive management strategies to develop and test alternative implementation strategies. Other barriers may require the attention of policy-makers at a more senior management level.
- Transparent working environments and multi-sector stakeholder groups can help create the conduits necessary to facilitate the transfer of this information within and between sectors. These efforts will ensure that processes are in place to not only systematically re-evaluate barriers but also to identify and implement adaptive management strategies that promote the success of water soft paths approaches.

Conclusions

Both water soft path and demand management efforts at various scales (municipal, watershed and provincial) can stimulate significant reductions in the amount of water used rather than trying to manipulate the supply (supply management). In Canada, the focus of water management needs to shift not only towards better use of existing supplies but also to changing the habits and attitudes of water users and policy-makers. This shift will require significant changes in institutions. Various types of barriers – social, organizational, technical, financial and bureaucratic – can impede change, making it difficult or undesirable to implement a specific action. Clearly identifying the barriers that confront us is critical. Though there is no simple recipe for overcoming institutional barriers, there are some general types of action that can assist in barrier removal. Multi-stakeholder involvement persuasion and barrier recognition are actions that can influence the changes society must take to move towards a sustainable future.

References

Baumann, H. and Tillman, A.-M. (2004) *The Hitch Hiker's Guide to LCA: An Orientation in Life Cycle Assessment Methodology and Application*, Studentlitteratur, Lund, Sweden

Bell, P. A., Greene, T., Fisher, J. and Baum, A. S. (2001) *Environmental Psychology*, 5th Edition, Routledge, New York, NY

Brandes, O. M. and Brooks, D. B. (2007) *The Soft Path for Water in a Nutshell*, revised Edition, Friends of the Earth Canada, Ottawa, ON, and The POLIS Project on Ecological Governance, University of Victoria, Victoria, BC

Brandes, O. M. and Ferguson, K. (2004) *The Future in Every Drop: The Benefits, Barriers, and Practice of Water Demand Management in Canada*, The POLIS Project on Ecological Governance, University of Victoria, Victoria, BC

Brooks, D. B. (2002) *Water: Local-Level Management*, IDRC Books, Ottawa, ON

Brooks, D. B. (2005) 'Beyond greater efficiency: The concept of water soft paths', *Canadian Water Resources Journal*, vol 30, no 1, pp83–92

Brooks, D. B. (2006) 'An operational definition of water demand management', *International Journal of Water Resources Development*, vol 22, no 4, pp521–528

Brooks, D. B. and Peters, R. (1988) *Water: The Potential for Demand Management in Canada*, Science Council of Canada, Ottawa, ON

Brooks, D. B. and Wolfe, S. E. (2007) *Institutional Assessment for Effective WDM Implementation & Capacity Development*, Report to the Regional Water Demand Management Initiative in the Middle East and North Africa, International Development Research Centre, Ottawa, ON

Brown, L. R., Larsen J. and Fischlowitz-Roberts, B. (2001) *The Earth Policy Reader*, Earth Policy Institute, Washington, DC

Chenoweth, J. (2008) 'A re-assessment of indicators of national water security', *Water International*, vol 33, no 1, pp5–18

Creighton, J. L. (2005) 'What water managers need to know about public participation: One US practitioner's perspective', *Water Policy*, vol 7, no 3, pp269–278

Environment Canada (2004) *Threats to Water Availability in Canada*, Environment Canada, Ottawa, ON

Environment Canada (2008) 'Indicators: Water use', *State of the Environment Infobase*, www.ec.gc.ca/soer-ree/English/headlines/ind1.cfm, accessed 9 June 2008

Furlong, K. and Bakker, K. (2007) *Water Governance in Transition: Utility Restructuring and Water Efficiency in Ontario*, UBC Program on Water Governance, University of British Columbia, Vancouver, BC

Gibbons, J. (2004) *Making Everyone a Winner: Making Energy Conservation Profitable for Ontario's Electrical Utilities*, Pollution Probe, Toronto, ON

Gleick, P. H. (2003) 'Global fresh water resources: soft path solutions for the 21st century', *Science*, vol 302, pp524–528

Hawken, P., Lovins, A. B. and Lovins, H. (1999) *Natural Capitalism: Creating the Next Industrial Revolution*, Little, Brown and Co., New York, NY

Holtz, S. (2007) Energy, Environment, Sustainable Development – Policy, Personal communication, 10 April 2007

Howe, C. W. (2005) 'The functions, impacts and effectiveness of water pricing: Evidence from the United States and Canada', *International Journal of Water Resources Development*, vol 21, no 1, pp42–53

International Joint Commission (2004) *Protection of the Waters of the Great Lakes, Review of the Recommendations in the February 2000 Task Force Report*, Ottawa, ON, www.ijc.org/php/publications/pdf/ID1560.pdf, accessed April 2007

Jaffe, A. B. and Stavins, R. N. (1994) 'The energy efficiency gap: What does it mean?', *Environmental Policy*, vol 22, no 10, pp804–810

Katz, D. (2006) 'Going with the flow: Preserving and restoring instream water allocations', in P. H. Gleick, H. Cooley, D. Katz, E. Lee, J. Morrison, M. Palaniappan, A. Samulon and G. H. Wolff (eds) *The World's Water 2006–2007: The Biennial Report on Freshwater Resources*, Island Press, Washington, DC

J. Kinkead Consulting (2006) 'An analysis of Canadian and other water conservation practices and initiatives: Issues, opportunities and suggested directions', Prepared for Water Conservation and Economics Task Group, Canadian Council of Ministers of the Environment, Mississauga, ON, www.ccme.ca/asets/pdf/kinkead_fnl_rpt_2005_04_2.1_web.pdf, accessed April 2007

Kirkland, L. H. and Thompson, D. (2002) 'Analysis of barriers', in D. Thompson (ed) *Tools for Environmental Management: A Practical Introduction and Guide*, New Society Publishers, Gabriola Island, BC

Lovins, A. B. and Lovins, L. H. (1998) *Climate: Making Sense* and *Making Money*, Rocky Mountain Institute, Snowmass, CO

Maas, T. (2003) *What the Experts Think: Understanding Urban Water Demand Management in Canada*, The POLIS Project on Ecological Governance, University of Victoria, Victoria, BC

Merrett, S. (2004) 'The demand for water: Four interpretations', *Water International*, vol 29, no 1, pp27–29

Millennium Ecosystem Assessment (2005) *Ecosystems and Human Well-Being: Wetlands and Water – Synthesis*, World Resources Institute, Washington, DC.

Mirza, S. (2007) 'Danger ahead: the coming collapse of Canada's municipal infrastructure', Report for the Federation of Canadian Municipalities, available at www.fcm.ca

Morris, T. J., Boyd, D. R., Brandes, O. M., Bruce, J. P., Hudon, M., Lucas, B., Maas, T., Nowlan, L., Pentland, R. and Phare, M.-A. (2007) *Changing the Flow: A Blueprint for Federal Action on Freshwater*, Walter and Duncan Gordon Foundation, Toronto, ON

Natural Resources Canada (2008) *Water Consumption*; available at http://atlas.nrcan.gc.ca/site/english/maps/freshwater/consumption/1

Patrick, R., Kreutzwiser, R. and de Loë, R. (2008) 'Factors facilitating and constraining source water protection in the Okanagan Valley, British Columbia', *Canadian Water Resources Journal*, vol 33, no 1, pp39–54

Pollution Probe (2007) *Towards a Vision and Strategy for Water Management in Canada*, Pollution Probe, Toronto, ON, available at www.pollutionprobe.org/Reports/WPWS%20Final%20Report%202007.pdf

Postel, S. and Richter, B. (2003) *Rivers for Life: Managing Water for People and Nature*, Island Press, Washington, DC

Rocky Mountain Institute (RMI) (1991) *Water Efficiency: A Resource for Utility Managers, Community Planners, and Other Decision-makers*, Rocky Mountain Institute, Snowmass, CO

Rosolen, S. (2006) 'Water connections: A feasibility study towards understanding and improving access to water information in Canada', available at www.waterconnect.ca/waterconnections_may2006_draft.pdf

Savenije, H. H. G. and van der Zaag, P. (2002) 'Water as an economic good and demand management: Paradigms with pitfalls', *Water International*, vol 27, no 1, pp98–104

Schindler, D. W. and Donahue, W. F. (2006) 'An impending water crisis in Canada's Western Prairie provinces', *Proceedings of the National Academy of Sciences*, vol 103, no 19, pp7210–7216

Sprague, J. (2007) 'Great white North? Canada's myth of superabundance', in K. Bakker (ed) *Eau Canada: The Future of Canada's Water*, UBC Press, Vancouver, BC

Tate, D. M. (1990) *Water Demand Management in Canada: A State-of-the-Art Review*, Inland Waters Directorate, Water Planning and Management Branch, Environment Canada, Ottawa, ON

US Department of Energy (2007) *Federal Energy Manangement Program, Utilities Management*, www1.eere.energy.gov/femp/program/utility/utilityman_em_wa.html, accessed 19 October 2008

Vickers, A. (2001) *Handbook of Water Use and Conservation*, WaterPlow Press, Amherst, MA

Videira, N., Antunes, P., Santos, R. and Lobo, G. (2006) 'Public and stakeholder participation in European water policy: A critical review of project evaluation processes', *European Environment*, vol 16, no 1, pp19–31

Wolff, G. and Gleick, P. H. (2002) 'The soft path for water', in P. H. Gleick et al (eds) *The World's Water 2002–2003: The Biennial Report on Freshwater Resources*, Island Press, Washington, DC

13
Pushing the Boundaries: Shifting Water Soft Paths Philosophy towards Hard Policy in Municipal Water Management

Sarah E. Wolfe and Kurtis Elton

Resources are not; they become.

E. W. Zimmerman

For experts dedicated to investigating and resolving resource issues, the conclusion that unsustainable resource use is one of the most pressing problems of our age is a truism. Rates of energy and water use, and resulting resource scarcities and disparities, continue to pollute the environment, bankrupt organizations, polarize populations and undermine social equity (Homer-Dixon, 1999). As emphasized throughout this book, water soft paths represent one of our best options to address our current and future water constraints. However, it is uncertain how to 'sell' soft path analysis (SPA) to a Canadian public committed to consumption and to policy-makers vested in the current system.

The research described here emerged from a colloquium on municipal soft path efforts that was attended by diverse thinkers from the academic, public and private sectors. The one-day colloquium was held in January 2008 at the Briarhurst Institute for Science, Public Policy and Global Affairs in Fergus, Ontario, Canada. Colloquium participants were asked to respond to concepts, assumptions and questions laid out in discussion documents. The focus was on SPA interventions that would be politically and operationally practical at the municipal level.

Soft path elements of energy and water management are readily understood: backcasting, living within sustainable limits, focusing on conservation and demand management first, and matching quality of water to end-use. But soft paths have not received much attention from policy-makers or technicians, such as municipal planners and engineers. To investigate the reasons for this lack of attention, we designed a survey in partnership with the Canadian Water and Wastewater Association's Water Efficiency Network (CWWA-WEN), an organization conducting research on the establishment of municipal water efficiency benchmarks. The survey questions assessed the specific water management strategies already being undertaken by municipalities and the extent to which they fit within a soft path framework. With the data provided by the survey, we hoped to be better able to translate the philosophy of soft path and design into an intervention strategy that will support existing water management efforts and move municipalities closer to the soft path ideal.

This chapter reports our early research results. We provide a brief background and rationale for the research, including some of the conclusions of the soft path colloquium. We outline the conceptual framework that guided this research project and its methodology and we present our preliminary findings. Throughout this chapter, text boxes provide examples of municipal efficiency and soft path efforts from across Canada.

Rationale and background from the Briarhurst Colloquium

Though substantive research on soft path analysis has been completed at provincial, sectoral and watershed levels, soft path advocates have recently begun to focus on municipal-level interventions. There are good reasons for this. Municipal water use, not including industrial, accounts for 10 per cent of all water withdrawals in the country; and of that 10 per cent, more than half is residential (Pleasance, 2008). A municipal focus may also constitute a more straightforward policy challenge. According to Brooks and Holtz (Chapter 9, this volume), rural uses for water are fraught with social and economic impacts because water is so much more often connected with livelihoods than it is in urban areas. Doubling water prices would hardly be noticed in cities but even measuring water in rural areas is a hot political issue.

Unfortunately, data constraints bedevil analysis. Numerous variables – existing efficiency initiatives, environmental constraints, housing stock and residential and demographic characteristics, etc. – make comparisons among municipalities difficult. And Canada currently does not have a recognized standard for water conservation and efficiency (Pleasance, 2008), let alone a policy framework that could adequately support a soft path philosophy. Along with the data constraints, dismantling an 'overbuild mentality' (Brooks, 2007), originating in the engineering culture, is also essential to moving water efficiency and soft paths into the municipal mainstream and into planning processes.

Discussions at the Briarhurst colloquium also indicated that there are substantial institutional barriers preventing the realization of a soft path philosophy and process at the municipal level. Because such barriers have been discussed in detail by Jordaan and Stevens (Chapter 12, this volume), they need not be repeated here.

In the concluding session, colloquium participants were asked to identify viable projects or partnerships that could help move the soft path agenda into the municipal mainstream. They suggested that water experts should:

- create a municipal 'Model Water Pricing Structures' exercise to illustrate options;
- develop a set of municipal Water Demand Benchmarks;
- assist the province in developing industrial performance indicators for water use;
- clarify water use terminology (subsequently discussed by Kay and Hendriks, Chapter 11, this volume);
- encourage industrial, commercial and institutional buildings to be water efficiency 'early adopters'; and
- request that government funding for infrastructure be tied to water efficiency benchmarks.

What was missing from the colloquium participants' conclusions and recommended interventions were any consideration or recognition of the underlying norms, values and knowledge that create and sustain the well-recognized barriers to soft path innovation. However, by focusing on institutional contexts, as well as on the social capital that can sustain or dismantle water management initiatives, we will be better able to achieve soft path objectives.

To address this gap, we saw the need for a new conceptual framework that would frame the research, inform our survey of municipalities, and help move the soft path agenda into the municipal mainstream. We sought to contribute additional research on the socio-political contexts of water management organizations and the knowledge, values and norms of water managers.

Conceptual framework

The value of municipal water efficiency policies has been increasingly recognized in water management research and implementation. But our understanding of what is required to improve water demand management (WDM) and to shift toward a water soft path policy has not progressed very far. For example, it may be that the obstacles preventing the implementation of WDM policies arise, at least partially, from the conventional conceptualization of WDM policy. This conventional conceptualization of WDM fails to take into account the influence of practitioners' social capital.

Refocusing our understanding of water efficiency – to include explicitly soft path principles and innovation concepts – extends the range of questions that can be asked. New questions could investigate the influence of water practitioners' social capital: their capabilities (skills and knowledge), their capacity (ability to act in a given context), their collaboration (through social networks) and their commitment (willingness to act) to water demand management and a soft path philosophy (Wolfe, 2009).

Water soft paths can be better understood as part of a social innovation. A social innovation is the development of new ways of thinking, new skills or new interventions that address complex social problems (Westley et al, 2006). The WSP qualifies as a social innovation because it:

*   challenges the norms in a society that currently value consumption over conservation (Norgaard, 1994);
*   necessitates major changes in society's attitudes, values and behaviours related to water (Nancarrow et al, 1996–7); and
*   shifts attention away from technical and economic solutions and toward explicit personal and political choices (de Oliver, 1999).

If sustainable water use is the ultimate innovation – with its complex sub-elements of soft path principles and efficiency strategies – it necessitates a revised worldview and deliberately prudent and responsible decisions at global and personal levels.

Wolfe's research (2006) shifted the focus away from the tools aimed at water consumers; it focused instead on municipal practitioners and their opportunities to move a social innovation forward. Specifically, the research assessed the influence of practitioners' social capital on their WDM decisions, their tacit knowledge, and the professional networks that structure their organizational culture. By applying insights from social capital theory, this theoretical framework draws on knowledge management, organizational theory, innovation diffusion and network theory. The new focus embeds water practitioners – with all of their quirks and inconsistencies – in the policy process and adds the question of '*how we view it*' to the conventional questions of '*how and when we do it.*'

The concept of social capital

Definitions of social capital vary widely across academic disciplines and applied research practice. The definitions usually include the substance and source of social capital and the influence of its availability (Adler and Kwon, 2002). The substance of social capital includes the norms, values, knowledge and expected or anticipated behaviours within a group. Research on the sources of social capital focuses on the relationships within a social network; these relationships are influential because they generate a group's social capital, which is an unquantifiable but appreciating resource that can be drawn upon over time. The costs and benefits associated with generating and maintaining social capital are also important. This includes the transaction costs of sharing information and nurturing the relations with other members of a group.

Indicators for assessing social capital

This conceptual framework is useful for water efficiency and soft path efforts because it encourages us to investigate a different set of questions. Rather than just asking questions about residential or institutional consumers, for example, we can focus on questions about a community and its political decision-makers. Of particular interest are the types of knowledge decision-makers have and the types of networks in which they operate. Putnam (1993), for example, argued persuasively that a network's norms and trust relations are the source of social capital.

Earlier research (Wolfe, 2008) identified four interdependent elements of a decision-maker's social capital. These four elements influence the substance, source and availability of social capital and are defined as follows, at the level of an individual decision-maker:

1   *Capability* – the explicit and tacit knowledge held by the decision-maker;
2   *Capacity* – the ability of a decision-maker to act in the context in which he or she usually works (the conventional focus of 'barriers to implementation' research);
3   *Collaboration* – the work carried out by a decision-maker within a social network (involves active collaboration with, and a drawing of intellectual or professional resources from, colleagues and peers; also involves support of research initiatives to generate new information);
4   *Commitment* – the willingness of the decision-maker to act under both negative and positive conditions and to 'go beyond the call of duty'.

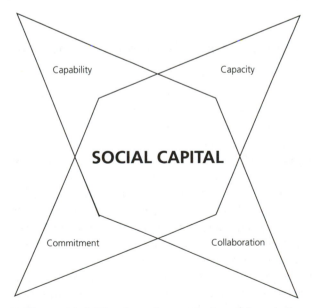

Figure 13.1 *The four elements of social capital*

Examining these four elements of social capital is not straightforward. Each is subject to an array of constantly evolving variables that must be interpreted. But they represent a valuable characterization of social capital because they provide a context for the social relations among actors. These elements also help to explain why changes do or do not occur within the network and its community.

Survey results

Over the course of the Briarhurst Colloquium, we became aware that, although soft path philosophy seemed to resonate with participants, including municipal water practitioners, there was disconnect between their apparent understanding of soft path concepts and their ability to apply them. Therefore, we designed a survey – 'Socio-political Questions for Water Practitioners' – to collect baseline data on existing municipal efforts related to water efficiency and to assess those efforts within a soft path framework. This survey was intended to provide us with a much better sense of what was happening in 'conventional' municipalities, in addition to our sense of what was happening among 'early adopters' already keen to explore soft path approaches. The information would help to formulate viable and realistic soft path interventions for municipal practitioners. The annex to this chapter provides more detail about the methodology of the survey.

The data collected from this survey was assessed according to the social capital framework outlined above. Analysis of the results from the survey used an aggregate of all respondents' answers. A wide variety of water practitioners, representing different geographical areas, employment positions and levels of experience, responded to the survey.

Capacity (ability to work within organizational context and constraints)

A total of 23 unique, official Water Efficiency Plans/Policies (WEPs) were represented in the survey. The mean year for approval of these WEPs was 2001, and the median was 2005, revealing that where they exist, WEPs are relatively new phenomena. Only 61 per cent of the 23 WEPs had specific numerical targets (eg '10 per cent of average day (2006 levels) by 2010, 15 per cent of average day by 2017, 20 per cent of average day by 2025'); the remainder had no formal or specific target, or had a nebulous goal (eg 'Integrated Water Management by 2011'). One respondent wrote that, although a WEP existed for her/his region, it had not been approved by the relevant council.

Reasons for the adoption of a WEP varied a great deal. One of the most popular reasons, cited by 58 per cent of respondents, was to 'raise awareness of water as a service'. Whereas water is conventionally thought of as a *resource*, the role of an urban water system is to provide a variety of *services* through the collection, treatment and distribution of water. Since this resource-to-service

Box 13.1 'Get Water Smart', Kelowna, BC

Susanne Porter-Bopp and Jennifer Wong

The City of Kelowna Water Utility services 64,000 water customers on the shores of Lake Okanagan. The city's biggest water challenge is one of infrastructure stress, due to residential watering in the summer. In 1996, Kelowna faced a $40-million infrastructure improvement and expansion cost over the following 10 years based on consumption patterns at the time (Get Water Smart Website, 2008).

By 2007, the Kelowna City Council endorsed the Utility's goal of reducing city-wide water use by 15 per cent by the year 2012. Its Water Sustainability Action Plan included the 'Get Water Smart' programme, which has a current annual operating budget of $198,000 (Klassen, personal communication, 2008).

The 'Get Water Smart' programme reduced water consumption through metering, rate structure, home water audits and community-based, social marketing programmes. Between 1998 and 2007, the City's total water consumption increased by 2 per cent, while the population grew by 25 per cent. Over the same period, average residential water use was reduced by 29 per cent (Klassen, personal communication, 2008).

The greatest single user of water is the municipal Parks Department, consuming 20 per cent of all outdoor water. The 'Get Water Smart' programme used its 2007 Parks Audit and Survey programme as part of a council directive, and consumption decreased by 15 per cent (Klassen, personal communication, 2008).

paradigm shift is one of the main principles required for water soft path thinking (Brooks, 2005), the fact that the majority of respondents were using this message as a reason for the adoption of their WEP is encouraging.

Other reasons cited by a majority of respondents for the adoption of a WEP were to:

- 'Defer new water supply infrastructure' (63%);
- 'Reduce environmental impacts' (75%);
- 'Become a sustainable urban water system' (63%).

The first answer is not surprising, since deferral of infrastructure costs is a common objective for urban water systems (eg 'The Dublin Statement', 1992), but the second and third responses are more difficult to interpret. Concepts of 'environmental impacts' and 'sustainability' are important yet difficult to define; their presence here at the very least demonstrates that water practitioners are concerned for the long-term welfare of their respective water systems and the users of these systems. Water practitioners seem to be stuck in a temporal 'social trap' (Platt, 1973); they must balance the immediate demands of present users with the long-term needs of future users and the welfare of the environment at large.

Regardless of the reason for its adoption, some measures taken to implement a utility's or organization's WEP were common, such as lawn watering restrictions (reported by 71 per cent of survey respondents in the category of

---

BOX 13.2 CAPITAL REGIONAL DISTRICT WATER SERVICES
DEMAND MANAGEMENT PROGRAMME

Susanne Porter-Bopp and Jennifer Wong

The Capital Regional District (CRD) Water Services organization is located on the southern tip of Vancouver Island in a northern Mediterranean climate. It is the wholesale water supplier to 320,000 consumers in the Greater Victoria Drinking Water System and acts as a retail supplier in the Western Communities. It draws surface water from the Sooke Reservoir, which was raised by 6 metres in 2002 (CRD Water Website, 2008).

Over the past decade, total water consumption has not increased, despite a growing population. Residential users currently consume 314LCD and account for 70 per cent of total water use, while industrial, commercial and institutional customers use on average 132LCD and account for 30 per cent of total use (Walker, personal communication, 2008).

The CRD's Demand Management Programme operating budget for 2008 was $1.5 million. Water conservation initiatives for residential and industrial, commercial and institutional users include education programmes, a summer watering bylaw, and toilet, washing machine and irrigation timer rebate programmes. In 2005, the CRD implemented a bylaw that requires the installation of 6-litre low-flow toilets in new buildings, a measure that the provincial government adopted in 2008. The CRD also offers free water use and efficiency audits to businesses in Greater Victoria and provides assistance with cost–benefit analysis of various water conservation measures (CRD Water Website, 2008).

Although the rights to the Leech River have been purchased for future infrastructure expansion, the CRD hopes to defer expansion of the water supply to after 2050. The interim goal is a 10 per cent reduction in water use per capita by 2023 (Walker, personal communication, 2008).

'bylaws/regulations'). A variety of measures were being taken in the category of 'public participation, awareness, and education', including:

- use of print media (79%);
- rain barrel and/or showerhead promotions (67%);
- work with local schools/boards of education (67%);
- toilet rebate programmes (67%).

In fact, at least half of the respondents were practising every measure listed in this category. That public participation strategies were much more popular than ordinances suggests that those who implement WEPs would prefer to *coax* individuals to change their water-using behaviour than to *coerce* them. The public participation programmes so widely cited by the respondents could be modified accordingly to help guide the backcasting activities necessary for the implementation of a water soft path. Involving the public at large is essential for creating a vision for the future, and education initiatives provide a basis on which to build the necessary momentum.

To reiterate, the survey reveals a conflict between serving the needs of contemporary populations and moving towards a sustainable water system to serve future populations. Exacerbating this dilemma is the municipalities' ever-present need to remain economically viable.

Capability (tacit and explicit knowledge)

Another section of the questionnaire asked questions about personal experience and knowledge. For example, when asked if their childhood home was located in a water-scarce area, 19 per cent answered that it was. Respondents were asked how and when they first learned about water efficiency strategies and options. A third of the respondents said school was their first source of information, while another 30 per cent cited the workplace. Only 13 per cent learned about it first from water conservation programmes, which suggests that historically, public education programmes have not been used to convey water-related curriculum or have not been effective.

When asked what mechanisms were found effective for sharing water efficiency strategies/options/information, respondents often cited more than one mechanism: the most cited mechanism (39 per cent) was personal conversations; conferences weighed in at 35 per cent; and publications and websites were cited by 26 per cent of respondents. While the latter three mechanisms for communication are important vehicles for the dissemination of new knowledge and information, they do not necessarily accommodate feedback. Conversely, personal conversations require speaking and listening and allow for a more balanced transfer of information. This two-way type of learning is essential for exploring the nuanced details of a water soft path.

For example, creating a shared vision, even within the water practitioner community, entails agreement on important terminology. The knowledge and language of water management, both in literature and in oral communication, is peppered with the term 'full cost', as in, 'consumers should pay the full cost of the services they consume ...' (Swain et al, 2005). Indeed, a water soft path would not be achievable without accounting for all costs incurred from the creation and operation of a water system.

This survey indicates that there is no consensus on the proper definition of the term 'full cost'. The most popular definition, with a response rate of 39 per cent, was the most comprehensive, since it included 'externalities associated with public health and ecosystem maintenance'. The next most popular definition (31 per cent) was 'operation and maintenance costs PLUS capital charges emphasizing the future costs of replacing capital stock and building new infrastructure'. The 'future' qualifier in this definition would suggest that long-term marginal cost is an important consideration for these respondents.

Unfortunately, most water in Canada is priced to cover only historical capital costs and to allow a utility to break even. Taking into account environmental externalities will be even more of a challenge, and as a result, more expensive. Further research and communication is necessary to create consensus among water practitioners.

Collaboration (within a social network)

Agreement on terminology is but one small requirement for the proper functioning of water demand management. Operational processes and structures dictate how practitioners interact in a water utility or organization and thus influence the degree of collaboration and the capacity for WDM implementation (Wolfe, 2008).

Since there are typically many departments within an organization, there are a number of different ways to implement demand management. A majority of respondents in this survey (59 per cent) had a specific department devoted to WDM. Another 37 per cent shared duties among departments, while the remaining 4 per cent outsourced to the private sector.

Brown (2008) argues that sustainable urban water management performance is related to the internal corporate commitment to these practices. Indicators of this commitment (or lack thereof) include the total staff time and the percentage of budget allocated. Our survey found that funding was poor across the board: respondents estimated that only about 1 per cent of their utility's or organization's annual budget went towards WDM. An average of only 74 person-hours was devoted to WDM practices every week, the equivalent of less than two full-time staff. Survey responses, therefore, indicated a lack of serious commitment to sustainable urban water management practices and WDM.

Respondents were asked how they would rate communication efforts across departments and between different levels of government. On a scale from one to five (1 = 'needs drastic improvement' and 5 = 'superb'), mean answers were 2.7 and 2.8, respectively. These poor ratings could indicate cases of the 'silo effect', resulting from 'horizontal fragmentation' (across departments) and/or 'vertical fragmentation' (between levels of government) (Brown, 2008), where each sub-unit of an organization or utility is focused solely on achieving its own narrow objectives (Dell, 2005). In such cases, a 'big picture' goal like demand management or the development of a soft path approach can become lost in the bureaucracy, even if a specific department is assigned to this task.

Brown (2008) names three dimensions of institutional capacity building: human resource development, institutional reform, and intra- and inter-organizational strengthening. The survey questioned respondents about the first two dimensions, asking what actions their utility or organization had taken in the effort to better implement WDM practices. In the area of human resource development, 69 per cent of respondents said that 'research building and networking (eg conferences, seminars, etc.) was being used, and 47 per cent said that 'support for participation in professional associations' was available.

In the area of institutional reform, the most popular capacity development method was 'mobilization of local political and community support' (39 per cent). The responses on the survey reveal a desire for collaboration among water practitioners. Building on the knowledge and mistakes of others intuitively makes sense. Indeed, the water soft path would not be possible without collaboration among its champions and facilitators.

Box 13.3 Early adopters in Canada: Guelph, Ontario

Matt Binstock and Susanne Porter-Bopp

Guelph is aiming to position itself as a water conservation leader in Canada and beyond (Earth Tech Canada et al, 2006). Reliant solely on groundwater, the city faces many challenges because of its designation as an 'urban growth center' under Ontario's Growth Plan for the Greater Golden Horseshoe.

With a current population of 126,000, Guelph was initially assigned a target population of 195,000, but local planners determined this level of growth would exceed the assimilative capacity of the Speed River (the city's primary receiving water) and were able to negotiate a lower growth target on these grounds (City of Guelph, 2008).

Some stakeholders have suggested that a long-term solution to Guelph's water and wastewater limitations would be a shared regional pipeline system to Lake Erie (Hemson Consulting, 2005). But Guelph has chosen to make conservation its strategic focus: the city launched a Water Conservation and Efficiency Strategy in 1999, and daily water use declined even as the population grew steadily (City of Guelph et al, 2008). Pilot programmes included a toilet replacement programme (decrease: 450m^3 per day), an ICI efficiency programme including capacity buybacks, fixture replacements and process reductions (decrease: 300m^3 per day), system leak detection and repairs (decrease: 1100m^3 per day) and an outside water use reduction programme (decrease: 800m^3 per day) (City of Guelph et al, 2008).

Water consumption in Guelph is currently at its lowest levels since 1998 (City of Guelph et al, 2008). Individuals updating the 2008 water efficiency strategy agreed that it was an aggressive water conservation plan (Blease, personal communication, 2008). Guelph has set a 20 per cent water conservation target for 2025 and is currently considering a range of options including additional toilet rebate programmes, rain barrels and xeriscaping (Earth Tech Consulting et al, 2006; City of Guelph et al, 2008). Guelph's efforts offer an example of how soft path goals can be introduced in municipalities facing growth challenges.

Commitment (willingness to act)

While it is important to have many players participating in the creation of a water soft path, almost any new endeavour will be led by a smaller group of leaders and innovators.

With this in mind, it is very interesting to note that 55 per cent of survey respondents said that they would consider their utility or organization to be a leader in WDM practices. When asked why they consider this to be true, 35 per cent answered that it had something to do with their collaboration with others! Providing a more logical answer, 18 per cent explained that they had started earlier than others, thereby providing an example of innovation for others to follow. Respondents who said they do not consider their utility or organization to be a leader were asked to explain their answer: some (29 per cent) cited 'general inadequacy'; some (29 per cent) said that WDM was given a low priority in their organization; and some (21 per cent) answered straightforwardly that they did not consider their organization a leader because it was following the leads of others.

Respondents were asked what attitudes, behaviours, experiences or beliefs are important for people who implement WDM. At 27 per cent, the most

---

BOX 13.4 LONG-TERM INTEGRATED CONSERVATION IN THE TOWN OF OKOTOKS, ALBERTA

Jennifer Wong and Susanne Porter-Bopp

The Town of Okotoks has made an explicit decision to limit growth based on an established environmental carrying capacity. Okotoks is located in the Sheep River Valley in the Alberta Foothills (pop. 19,996). It is the second-fastest growing community in Canada with a 46 per cent growth rate since 2001 (Okotoks, 2006a).

Okotoks set a water use target of 315LCD in 2008. Based on this target, the town estimates that the Sheep River has the capacity to supply water and accept treated effluent from approximately 30,000 residents. The community development plan caps Okotoks' population at this number. The current consumption rate is 373LCD for residential and non-residential uses, which represents a 30 per cent reduction from 2000 levels (Okotoks, 2008). By comparison, the average in Calgary is 510LCD.

Okotoks operates a self-funded utility system that is 100 per cent metered; the goal is a 100-per cent consumption-based rate structure. Water conservation initiatives target residential use (87 per cent of total demand) (Okotoks, 2006b). Okotoks implemented a water and wastewater programme in 1999 based on community-based social marketing principles. An outdoor watering bylaw introduced in 2001 restricted garden watering practices and created four restriction levels based on rainfall and river flow conditions. The town also introduced a water fixture bylaw in 2002 requiring low-flow water fixtures in all new home and renovation construction. Okotoks also incorporated xeriscape plantings in municipal landscaping projects and has an ongoing programme to find and fix leaking municipal water pipes (Okotoks, 2006b).

Okotoks is a leader in *whole system management* and turns its sewage into compost for residents and nearby farmers through its Integrated Waste Water Treatment Plant. This innovative initiative cost $13 million less than conventional methods and has resulted in an annual 30 per cent reduction in energy use, 28 per cent reduction in greenhouse gas emissions and 4200 tonnes of productive compost (Okotoks, 2006f; EPCOR).

---

popular answer was some form of 'belief in demand management as a driver for change'. Another 23 per cent answered that it is important to believe that water is a finite resource. The former answer is somewhat ambiguous, but important. It seems that the attitude necessary for the adoption of a water soft path is already held, in some form, by water practitioners.

Conclusions

The three most important elements for an effective water efficiency strategy, according to the professional opinions of respondents, are water loss detection and management, communication and education, and conservation-based water tariffs. Additionally, on a scale from one to five (1 = 'not at all receptive' and 5 = 'extremely receptive'), respondents rated the citizens of their utility's or organization's jurisdiction at a mean of 3.4. This positive reception reflects the value of the two public-oriented water efficiency strategies listed above.

Although respondents were not asked about the financial viability of their utility or organization as a result of WDM, one participant commented:

Utility finances are an important factor. The dilemma is that the utility's fixed costs are in the 75–80 per cent range so they have a difficult time offering an incentive for customers to reduce consumption. Rate structures need to be mandated to promote conservation. We still have many [practitioners] that still want us to build more capacity rather than [take] the 'soft' approach.

It is likely that other respondents share the concern for financial viability while still desiring to adopt the WSP. Future research should make a point of addressing this important issue.

In sum, the responses given in this survey indicate that the foundations necessary for a shift from water demand management to the water soft path exist in municipal water practitioner networks. Their experience with public participation initiatives and collaboration indicates that there is strong potential for future exchanges of information and knowledge. Survey respondents also expressed aspirations for a sustainable future, but they face many immediate hindrances: some existing WEPs lack specific targets, the 'silo effect', the lack of consensus on certain terminology, and the small amount of money and time devoted to water demand management practices stand as major obstacles. The desire for change must be coupled with the resources needed to implement it. Otherwise, nascent visions will quickly evaporate.

Annex: Survey methodology

Survey research was built on earlier work by Brooks and Peters (1988), Tate (1990), Dangerfield (1994), Waller and Scott (1998) and de Loë et al (2001). The actual survey was called 'Socio-political Questions for Water Practitioners', and sought respondents who were water management practitioners in the public and private sectors.

Data collection

While we did not have the budget to collect data across Canada or Ontario, we were able to partner with researchers at CWWA-WEN, who were administering a national survey on municipal water efficiency benchmarks. Their survey focused on identifying and assessing the feasibility of water conservation and efficiency performance benchmarks within municipalities. The performance indicators included:

- average annual and peak day demands;
- average and residential per capita demand;
- percentage water loss, including the Infrastructure Leakage Index;
- wastewater flows; and total water savings from implemented water efficiency measures.

The questions posed by CWWA-WEN were designed to identify (Pleasance, 2008):

1 What indicators are currently used in the municipal sector.
2 The benchmarks being used for each performance indicator.
3 The feasibility of developing improved water conservation and efficiency performance indicators and benchmarks in the municipal sector in Ontario and in Canada.

We complemented the highly technical questions posed by CWWA-WEN's previously administered (mail) survey. Our questions targeted the water management organizations and the knowledge, values and norms of water managers. These questions also focused on temporal and socio-political aspects of municipal water efficiency and performance indicators, and supplemental investigations of water conservation and efficiency within a water soft paths framework. These supplemental investigations included:

1 A review of the historical context of municipal water efficiency;
2 The development and administration of an additional question set to extend the survey to include socio-political data collection from municipal practitioners.

Our supplemental survey was administered at the CWWA-WEN's national conference, which took place, 3–5 November 2008, in Waterloo, Ontario. Because of CWWA-WEN's membership profile and existing campaign to bring together as many Canadian agencies and municipalities involved in water efficiency as possible, the conference provided us with a cost-effective and time-efficient method for targeting possible survey participants. The surveys were completed at the participants' leisure; some surveys were returned by the end of the conference, but most were faxed in the weeks following. Because we wanted to increase the number of responses, we also offered an online survey option but we did not differentiate between online or hardcopy responses.

Survey structure

The survey questions addressed three subjects:

- the nature of a municipality's or organization's water efficiency plan/policy (WEP);
- organizational processes and structures;
- personal experience and knowledge.

The survey consisted of multiple-choice questions. In the first section, the respondent was asked to select the main reasons for the adoption of the municipality's or organization's WEP. The range of possible answers included: conventional fiscal reasons (eg 'deferral of new water supply infrastructure', 'reduce treatment costs at wastewater treatment plants') and socio-political reasons (eg 'improve user equity', 'raise awareness of water as a service'). The available answers offered on the survey were based on the goals for water demand management as stated in Canadian water resources literature (Mackenzie and Parsons, 1994; Waller and Scott, 1998; Brooks, 2006).

Respondents were also asked what measures are included in their WEP to address municipal bylaws/regulations and public participation, awareness and education. Finally, respondents were asked to choose a definition for the term 'full cost', since this nebulous term is often mentioned as a goal in water management literature. 'Full cost' can be based on historical or future capital costs and can also include notions of opportunity costs and externalities (Rogers et al, 1997).

The second part of the survey examined organizational processes and structures. Respondents were asked how WDM responsibilities are distributed, how much budget and staff time is allocated to WDM practices, and how effective communication efforts are across departments and between levels of government. Most of the questions in this section were based on the institutional capacity-building framework as described in Brown (2008). These questions tackled the problematic 'silo effect' that often plagues the urban water sector, wherein utility departments work to fulfil their perceived function rather than to achieve a process outcome such as WDM (Dell, 2005). Survey answers were used to help understand the social networks of those actively engaged in water demand management (Wolfe, 2008).

The final part of the survey probed the influence of personal experience and knowledge on the practice of water demand management. Our future research will use this data to explore the motivators for WDM practitioners.

References

Adler, P. S. and Seok-Woo Kwon, S.-W. (2002) 'Social capital: prospects for a new concept', *Academy of Management Review*, vol 27, no 1, pp17–40

Blease, K. (2008) Resource Management Strategies Inc., personal communication, 20 November 2008

Brooks, D. B. (2005) 'Beyond greater efficiency: The concept of water soft paths', *Canadian Water Resources Journal*, vol 30, no 1, pp83–92

Brooks, D. B. (2006) 'An operational definition of water demand management', *International Journal of Water Resources Development*, vol 22, no 4, pp521–528

Brooks, D. B. (2007) *Presentation to the Water Soft Path Colloquium*, Briarhurst Institute for Science, Public Policy and Global Affairs, 16–17 January 2008, Fergus, ON

Brooks, D. B. and Peters, R. (1988) *Water: the Potential for Demand Management in Canada*, Discussion Paper #8, Science Council of Canada, Ottawa, ON

Brown, R. R. (2008) 'Local institutional development and organizational change for advancing sustainable urban water futures', *Environmental Management*, vol 41, no 2, pp221–233

City of Guelph (2008) 'Council adoption of Local Growth Strategy Recommendations', 23 June, available at www.guelph.ca/uploads/

PBS_Dept/planning/documents/Guelph%20Growth%20Management/council%
20resolution_june23_08.pdf, last accessed 4 November 2008

City of Guelph and Resource Management Strategies Inc. (2008) 'City of Guelph water conservation and efficiency strategy update', 20 November, available at http://guelph.ca/uploads/ET_Group/waterworks/WCE%20Study/WCES%20 Appendix%20D.pdf, last accessed 4 November 2008.

CRD Water Website (n.d.) Water Services Home Page, www.crd.bc.ca/water/, last accessed 13 December 2008

CRD (2002) *Drought Management Action Plan*, available at www.crd.bc.ca/reports/ water_/2001_/stage3798/STAGE3798.pdf

Dangerfield, S. (1994) 'An overview of Federal and Provincial water conservation policies', in D. Shrubsole and D. Tate (eds) *Every Drop Counts: Based on Canada's First National Conference and Trade Show on Water Conservation*, Ottawa: Canadian Water Resources Association, pp39–62

Dell, R. K. (2005) 'Breaking organizational silos: Removing barriers to exceptional performance', *American Water Works Association Journal*, vol 97, no 6, pp34–37

The Dublin Statement on Water and Sustainable Development (1992) International Conference on Water and the Environment, Dublin, January

Earth Tech Canada Inc., Lura Consulting, Lotowater Geoscience Consultants Ltd and C. N. Watson and Associates Ltd (2006) 'City of Guelph Water Supply Master Plan', available at http://guelph.ca/uploads/ET_Group/waterworks/WSMP_ Draft-Final-Report-Sep1206-rev.pdf, last accessed 4 November 2008

Environment Canada (2008) *Municipal Water and Waste Survey 2004*, available at www.ec.gc.ca/water/mwws/, last accessed on 13 August 2008

EPCOR website (n.d.) www.epcor.ca/en-ca/about-epcor/operations/operations-alberta/ water-wastewater/Okotoks/Pages/default.aspx, last accessed 27 December 2008

Get Water Smart Website (2008) www.getwatersmart.com, last accessed 13 December 2008

Hemson Consulting (2005) 'The Growth Outlook for the Greater Golden Horseshoe', available at www.hemson.com/news/GrowthOutlookForGGH%2017Jan2005a.pdf, last accessed 18 November 2008

Homer-Dixon, T. (1999) *Environment, Scarcity, and Violence*, Princeton University Press, Princeton, NJ

Klassen, N. (2008) Get Water Smart Coordinator, personal communication, 1 December

de Loë, R., Moraru, L. and Kreutzwiser, R. (2001) 'Demand side management of water in Ontario municipalities: Status, progress, and opportunities', *Journal of the American Water Resources Association*, vol 37, no 1, pp57–72

Mackenzie, P. and Parsons, F. M. (1994) 'Municipal management instruments for water conservation', in D. Shrubsole and D. Tate (eds) *Every Drop Counts: Based on Canada's First National Conference and Trade Show on Water Conservation*, Canadian Water Resources Association, Ottawa, ON

Nancarrow, B. E., Smith, L. M. and Syme, G. J. (1996–7) 'The ways people think about water', *Journal of Environmental Systems*, vol 25, no 1, pp15–27

Norgaard, R. B. (1994) *Development Betrayed: The End of Progress and a Co-Evolutionary Revision of the Future*, Routledge, London and New York

de Oliver, M. (1999) 'Attitudes and inaction – a case study of the manifest demographics of urban water conservation', *Environment and Behavior*, vol 31, no 3, pp372–394

Platt, J. (1973) 'Social traps', *American Psychologist*, vol 28, no 8, pp641–651

Pleasance, G. (2008) *Proposal to the Ontario Ministry of Environment on Municipal Water Efficiency Benchmarking*, Canadian Water and Wastewater Association, Ottawa, ON

Putnam, R. D. (1993) 'The prosperous community: Social capital and public life', *The American Prospect*, vol 4, no 13, pp35–42

Rogers, P., Bhatia, R. and Huber, A. (1997) *Water as a Social and Economic Good: How to Put the Principle into Practice*, TAC Background Papers, No 2, Global Water Partnership, Stockholm

Swain, H., Lazar, F. and Pine, J. (2005) *Watertight: The Case for Change in Ontario's Water and Wastewater Sector*, Queen's Printer for Ontario, Toronto

Tate, D. M. (1990) *Water Demand Management in Canada: A State-of-the-Art Review*, Social Science Series #23, Inland Waters Directorate, Water Planning and Management Branch, Ottawa, ON

Town of Okotoks (2006a) '2004–2006 municipal development plan review', available at www.okotoks.ca/pdf/devserv/planning/G3_MDP_Rev04-06.pdf, last accessed 27 December 2008

Town of Okotoks (2006b) www.okotoks.ca/sustainable/Water/initiatives.asp, last accessed 29 December 2008

Town of Okotoks (2006c) www.okotoks.ca/sustainable/Water/watershed.asp, last accessed 29 December 2008

Town of Okotoks (2006d) www.okotoks.ca/sustainable/Water/wastematters.asp, last accessed 29 December 2008

Town of Okotoks (2006e) www.okotoks.ca/sustainable/Water/perspective.asp, last accessed 29 December 2008

Town of Okotoks (2006f) www.okotoks.ca/sustainable/Water/wastematters.asp, last accessed 29 December 2008

Town of Okotoks (2007) 'Green guide', available at www.okotoks.ca/pdf/Sustainable/greenguide.pdf, last accessed 27 December 2008

Town of Okotoks (2008) 'Water management plan', available at www.okotoks.ca/pdf/Operations/utilities/WMPlanApr2008.pdf, last accessed 27 December 2008

Walker, D. (2008) CRD Water Demand Management Coordinator, personal communication, 1 October

Walker, D. (2008) 'Water conservation: Exploring the "wet" coast myths', presented at the Canadian National Conference and Policy Forum on Water Efficiency and Conservation, 2–5 November, Waterloo, ON

Waller, D. H. and Scott, R.S. (1998) 'Canadian municipal residential water conservation initiatives', *Canadian Water Resources Journal*, vol 23, no 4, pp369–406

Westley, F., Zimmerman, B. and Patton, M. Q. (2006) *Getting to Maybe: How the World Is Changed*, Random House Canada, Toronto, ON

Wolfe, S. (2006) 'Collaboration and commitment: Common elements in the Southern African and Canadian Water Demand Management Programs', PhD Thesis, University of Guelph at Guelph, ON

Wolfe, S. (2008) 'Capacity, capability, collaboration, and commitment: How social networks influence practitioners of municipal water demand management policy in Ontario, Canada', *Environmental Practice*, vol 10, no 2, pp42–52

Wolfe, S. (2009) 'What's your story? Practitioners' tacit knowledge and water demand management policies in Southern Africa and Canada', *Water Policy*, in press

14
Green Buildings and Urban Space: A Water Soft Path Perspective

Andrew Hellebust

Until one is committed, there is hesitancy, the chance to draw back, always ineffectiveness. Concerning all acts of initiative (and creation), there is one elementary truth the ignorance of which kills countless ideas and splendid plans: that the moment one definitely commits oneself, then providence moves too. A whole stream of events issues from the decision, raising in one's favor all manner of unforeseen incidents, meetings and material assistance, which no man could have dreamt would have come his way.

William Hutchinson Murray from
The Scottish Himalayan Expedition (1951)

A successful soft path approach starts with finding the right questions, but what questions do today's urban water and wastewater systems answer? This chapter provides some of these answers as well as a number of examples of ways in which new technology and a different attitude towards water use can further the soft path approach in urban areas.

Historically, the main goal of urban water systems was to eliminate waterborne disease in humans, a task that was managed at first by simply removing human waste from the vicinity of drinking water wells and then by disinfection of the water supply. The treatment of wastewater was then gradually introduced in situations where untreated sewage outflow resulted in unacceptable aesthetic and economic degradation to ecosystems. Once waterborne disease outbreaks were largely under control in developed countries, water authorities turned their attention to a couple of increasingly serious issues:

- the need to minimize a range of unhealthy compounds that were being introduced into the drinking water supply by industry, agriculture and even by the water treatment process itself (eg nitrates from fertilizers and the byproducts of water disinfection such as trihalomethanes (THM) from chlorine); and
- the need to define the assimilative capacity of the receiving ecosystem for wastewater contaminants and then to develop methodologies that would ensure the continued health of these ecosystems.

The understanding of what is unhealthy to ecosystems and to humans has progressed along with advances in science and improvements in detection methods. Infrastructure evolved to take advantage of economic efficiencies of scale, to maximize control and accountability and to minimize encroachment on expensive urban real estate.

In most cities, municipal water infrastructure now consists of a central water treatment plant that provides a single stream of high quality water to all users and a central wastewater treatment plant that releases effluent, generally into the same lake or river from which the water was taken. The standards for drinking water typically include zero counts of indicator bacteria and limits on toxic compounds as defined by the relevant health authorities. Ideally, the prescribed quality of wastewater effluent is limited by the capacity of the receiving water body to assimilate a relatively short list of contaminants and nutrients and the capability of current technology to remove impurities.

The urbanite fortunate enough to live in a city with modern water treatment facilities (ie those in North America, Western Europe and a few other lucky regions), generally takes for granted the availability of an unlimited supply of low-cost water of the highest quality and is commonly unaware of how the wastewater, produced by his community, is treated or of the resulting negative environmental impacts associated with its disposal. Although a fear of waterborne disease lingers, thanks to a number of well-publicized outbreaks involving deaths, statistically, the water supply in larger urban centres is essentially free of pathogens.

Though the modern urban water system is considered a success, this is the result of incremental improvements that began in the 19th century, in response to urban typhoid and cholera outbreaks, and which had the goals of supplying pathogen-free water to citizens and of using water to dilute and transport away human waste. This system may have achieved these aims, but is it efficient? Humans actually consume only a *few per cent* of all the water that is treated to drinking water standards. Our excrement is diluted in 30 times its mass of potable water and then fed to bacteria, which convert it mostly to carbon dioxide gas. If excrement, comprised of unused food nutrients, were viewed as a resource we would chose to concentrate and recover it, not dilute it. While the protection of human health will remain paramount, it is time to revisit the water treatment paradigm to address 21st-century environmental goals.

Defining a future vision for water infrastructure

If we take it as a 'given' that the current urban water system is both inefficient in its use of potable water and unsustainable in its impacts on both the upstream and downstream ecosystems, the question then becomes: what should take its place? One design approach that we believe would be more appropriate consists of a hybrid of centralized and distributed plants that are capable of supplying a variety of water qualities and of minimizing dilution of extractable resources. More generally, this design would have an expanded list of co-dependent principles, notably:

- provide an adequate supply of safe water for human consumption;
- ensure that there is a sufficient supply of water of the required quality to maintain healthy watershed ecosystems;
- match water sources and treatment level to service requirements;
- recover the resources in wastewater;
- minimize the energy used in delivering and treating water and wastewater.

Given the urban focus of this chapter, we will look at the last three principles in more detail below.

From overtreatment to appropriate treatment: Matching water sources and treatment level to service requirements

Assuming that a given service requires water at all, the source that is at, or just above, the quality required should be used to supply the service. Laundry and bathing require a certain quality, arguably non-potable, swimming water quality. This quality might be provided by rainwater in a single-residence system with minimal treatment, or by highly treated and disinfected waste-water effluent from a sophisticated neighbourhood treatment plant.

There could be serious health consequences should the quality required for a specific task deteriorate, or if there should be cross-contamination between water sources. Regulators of our future system must therefore take into consideration the potential incidence of treatment failure. Putting this new system into place will be an iterative process, keeping in mind the requirement to safeguard human health at every step. Initially, therefore, regulations designed to promote non-potable uses might allow the highest quality water source (below drinking water) available to be used for the least risk use, for example the Ontario Building Code 2006 allows grey water (wastewater excluding toilets) or rainwater for flushing toilets. Assigning a certain water quality for a task sounds attractive, but frequent testing requirements at the single unit level could make a non-potable system uneconomic. The German rainwater harvesting equipment industry resisted post-installation testing requirements in favour of working with regulators to establish what basic equipment, for example filters, cisterns and backup devices, would provide the required performance.

Recovering resources in wastewater

In many areas, agricultural land is plagued by the loss of organic material due to soil erosion. Would it be possible to return the food component of waterborne waste – that is, the non-reactive carbon and dissolved or solid nitrogen and phosphorus left after treatment (Sala and Serra, 2004) – to rebuild the soil? This would provide a valuable source of organic fertilizer using material which is currently considered as 'waste'. However, it would be challenging to recover clean organic material from municipal wastewater. Even with excellent source control on industry, trace metals find their way into raw water and food, and they can concentrate in the organic phase. Assuming a clean material *could* be recovered, it would probably only be economic to use it on nearby fields (which would nicely complement the growing emphasis on a 100km diet). Nevertheless, this material would still have to compete against commercial concentrated liquid or solid fertilizers. To be efficient, resource recycling will require relatively short transportation distances between source and food production areas and a cleaner, more concentrated organic material.

Chemical extraction from concentrated wastewater, dry toilets and urine diversion are also promising techniques to capture resources (Jönsson, 2001; Johannson, 2004; Novaquatis, 2006). Currently, many commercially available composting toilets (Del Porto and Steinfeld, 2000; Jenkins, 2005) are designed for convenience and aesthetics, and they may consume more materials and energy than a low-flush toilet connected to municipal wastewater treatment. Not only are composting toilets larger appliances, but electricity is used in some models to evaporate excess moisture to avoid overflow (urine may provide more water than is required for composting or can be absorbed by the dry material) and to run a vent fan, which pulls conditioned air from buildings. These problems can be avoided by providing capacity to store all liquid and by integrating the toilet vent with the building exhaust and heat recovery ventilator. Future dry toilets may be receptacles from which material is extracted and taken to composting plants for later distribution to farmland. The composting plants would ensure pathogen elimination through high temperature using thermophilic (heat-loving) bacteria that thrive at 55–60°C, and would properly stabilize the material for one year following composting, tasks which are difficult to guarantee with small domestic composting toilets because of the small mass of material and the constant addition of new excrement. The infrastructure to service a large-scale switch to dry toilets does not currently exist and could only be justified by backcasting from a long-term goal.

Water itself is a resource for agriculture, but irrigation with wastewater is limited by transportation costs, crop suitability and soil characteristics. For example, Israel, which has extremely limited freshwater supplies, can only reuse 65 per cent of its wastewater, due to the fact that crops don't use water in the winter, some wastewater can't be captured, and wastewater can be too toxic or salty to be used (Graber, 2005). Some analysts recommend further treatment of treated wastewater, even desalination, before use on agricultural fields (Gross et al, 2004).

Ecosystems depend on water being available in the right quantity and quality. The higher the quality, the more physical and chemical work water can do, such as carrying dissolved nutrients and minerals. However, chemicals such as pharmaceuticals, health products and endocrine disruptors (Exall et al, 2004) are now commonly found in domestic wastewater and have the potential to seriously harm the functioning of ecosystems. Though parties involved in crafting reuse quality targets are conceptually aware of the effects of toxic residuals (CMHC, 2004), they do not figure quantitatively in non-potable standards. Over the long term, therefore, the maintenance of ecosystem health will require a much more comprehensive testing regime to detect and minimize (or preferably eliminate) these compounds.

Rainwater harvesting

We have included rainwater harvesting as a subset of wastewater reuse since, in urban areas, rainwater is primarily something which has to be 'got rid of' through the (storm) sewer system. Rainwater harvesting is currently more common, particularly in new buildings, than wastewater reuse as it is a higher quality raw source and can serve more tasks. A disadvantage compared to wastewater reuse is that precipitation is less available during freezing weather and droughts, whereas wastewater production is relatively constant. Rainwater harvesting is a natural match with outdoor irrigation, which requires water during non-freezing periods, with wastewater reuse a better choice for a task such as toilet flushing that requires water both winter and summer.

With the exception of the 'first flush' – the first rain, which washes the majority of deposited air pollution and animal contamination off the roof and is generally diverted from the cistern – rainwater quality is of drinking water quality with no or minimal treatment. A rainwater harvesting system, with a cistern, pump, filters and disinfection capability, is an incremental variation on well or municipal drinking water supply. Given the decades of experience with rainwater harvesting, particularly in Australia and Germany, it is expected that this approach should achieve a rapid penetration into new markets, such as North America. In some aspects rainwater may be superior to municipal drinking water; it offers chlorine-free water to irrigate with and soft water to wash with. In some areas – for example, where groundwater is brackish – rainwater may be the highest quality drinking water source.

Though the technology to harvest rainwater is well proven, apart from rain barrels, rainwater-harvesting systems are still uncommon in many jurisdictions. Given the high quality of the raw source, rainwater harvesting deserves consideration in 100 per cent of the building stock.

Minimizing the energy used in delivering and treating water and wastewater

The more water efficient the end-user, the smaller the water technology infrastructure needs to be, saving not only operational energy, but also energy to manufacture and install water infrastructure. Wastewater reuse allows smaller sanitary sewers while rainwater harvesting allows smaller storm sewers. Leaks, at approximately 20 per cent of total water supply (FCM, 2005), are proportional to pipe length and water pressure, not flowrate. The more users there are on a given length of pipe, the smaller the ratio of leaks to total water use.

When we examine the public wastewater infrastructure assets in the Canadian province of Ontario, we find that distribution and collection system assets comprised 72 per cent and treatment assets 28 per cent of the total (WSEP, 2005). For areas of lower density, the cost of conventional sewers can be 80 per cent or more of the total cost of sewers and treatment (Crites and Tchobanoglous, 1998). With pipes and sewers being the major cost, it is cost effective to use water efficiency measures to fit more users per pipe length. Taken to the extreme, the Toronto Healthy House is an urban infill project where users were added with no added demand on municipal services. Rainwater supplies all new water, effluent is reused and excess effluent infiltrates into the ground within the property.

The amount of energy, mostly electricity, required to pump and treat water and wastewater, is in the order of $2kWh/m^3$ for a centralized municipal system (Sala and Serra, 2004; Arpke and Clerico, 2005). It would take 0.4kWh to provide the 200L/d that a Canadian might use domestically. For a household of 3.5 people, water use consumes 500kWh/yr or 6 per cent of electricity used for lighting, appliances and air conditioning of 8000kWh/yr in Ontario (ICF Consulting, 2005). Increased water efficiency will result in energy savings and associated decreased greenhouse gas production, with the caveat that alternatives to municipal water, for example some models of composting toilets (due to heaters and fans) or some treatment and reuse systems (due to pumps and blowers), can use comparable or greater amounts of electricity.

Reuse and increased water efficiency will greatly reduce the volume of water flowing to central facilities; but there is a downside to this lower volume – a proportional increase in the concentration of salts and other substances not treated or not removed in satellite (decentralized) reuse treatment plants. This may require different treatment approaches at the central plant level, perhaps with a shift from aerated suspended growth processes towards intensive attached-growth digestion processes. An environmental impact assessment will reflect the smaller volume but higher concentration of salts and recalcitrant chemicals. Source control will help: for example, the Israeli Ministry of Environment has limited the use of salt for ion exchange water softening and uses tanker trucks to discharge brine into the sea. Israel has also set limits on the salt and boron content in laundry detergents (Weber and Juanicó, 2004).

To the extent that storage and reuse flatten peak demand, capacity is freed up to serve more customers or delay system expansions. The cost of reuse water, which can be higher than the average water rate, could be justified using peak water cost. A similar argument is used with solar photovoltaics, which produce power when air conditioning raises the use of electricity. Unlike electricity where there is a real-time hourly market price with private and public power plants adjusting to meet demand, there is no publicized spot price for peak water, yet it is a real cost nevertheless.

Central treatment plants will not disappear, but they will be complemented by sophisticated, decentralized and on-site technology. Reuse treatment systems for large buildings will be compact versions of technologies already in use serving ex-urban communities. On-site treatment technology has moved well beyond the septic system. Current technology employs trickle filters or aeration under bacteria-covered media and delivers the treated effluent to the shallow, aerobic and biologically active soil layer. Drip irrigation tubing is inserted into the soil without trenching and the total area required is reduced due to superior treatment provided by the shallow soil.

Irrigating greenspace with treated wastewater solves a number of problems: it reduces drinking water demand; it accepts wastewater effluent; it displaces chemical fertilizers; and it recharges water back into the ecosystem. Residential water use can increase by 50 per cent during the growing season due to irrigation (Environment Canada, 2006). Golf courses can benefit from the water and nutrients in treated effluent. The City of Vernon, BC, irrigates selected crops with wastewater effluent (Brandes and Kriwoken, 2005), initially done as an alternative to wastewater treatment upgrades, but it has since been recognized as a valuable alternative to water supply.

Reusing wastewater: Opportunities and challenges

Compared to a centralized single water quality system, it is more complicated to manage a more distributed system with multiple water qualities. Non-potable supply introduces health risks that must be addressed with technology and management. Cross-connections with drinking water can be discouraged by using different coloured piping material and can be detected by checking for flow when one side is depressurized. Preventing a certain grade of non-potable water from being used for something it was not intended for (bathing instead of flushing) can be minimized with education and inspections. Municipal backup supply is protected with air gaps or annually tested backflow preventors.

The cost of reuse can be higher than average rates for municipal water, but the premium should be compared against the cost of peak water capacity and future expansion. For a small building supplying $10m^3/d$, the cost for on-site non-potable treatment and supply is C$2.70/$m^3$ (Hellebust, 2006) or 50 per cent more than municipal water and sewage of C$1.74/$m^3$ for the City of Toronto, 2008. The Solaire building in New York City reuses up to $95m^3/d$ sewage effluent using a GE-Zenon membrane bioreactor (Zenon, 2006). A life cycle assessment (Arpke and Clerico, 2005) showed that this technology required three times the electricity and cost 10 per cent more than New York City water supply (which charges 25 per cent less for customers that reuse at US$1.10/m^3 (C$1.24/m^3) combined water and sewer charges), but was 8 per cent less expensive than rates in Atlanta. At larger scales, the Greater Vancouver Regional District (GVRD) projected treatment costs for a 1100m^3/d scale reuse facility as low as C$0.40/m^3 (Vassos, 2006), a cost range similar to an earlier US study (Asano, 1998). Charges for recycled water in some jurisdictions in Australia were 50–80 per cent of the price for drinking water (Dimitriadis, 2005) to encourage potential users to overcome the 'yuck factor' associated with reusing sewage effluent.

Many of the challenges overcome by pioneering communities which installed district dual water distribution systems were not economic, but rather human and regulatory. Consumer acceptance is always a challenge when non-potable reuse is introduced. Dual supply systems in Florida (Asano, 1998) were implemented only after decade-long debates over the issues of water sharing and the discharge of effluent into sensitive natural water bodies. Reaching agreement on these systems required significant consensus-building efforts among powerful interest groups and regulators. In Australia, where waste-water reclamation has a relatively long history, new projects are still introduced in a step-wise fashion with education as a key component. In Port Macquarie, New South Wales, the first stage of a reclaimed water system will service only public buildings which the public will tour along with the treatment plant to gain a better understanding of this 'water product' (Thompson, 2005).

Developing policy and standards for non-potable supply – Canadian and international efforts

Incorporating the term 'non-potable reuse' into regulations would legitimize this option for local regulators and practitioners and prevent it from being quickly dismissed as carrying too high a liability. Regulations in British Columbia have included water reuse for a number of years (Brandes and Kriwoken, 2005) although initial frequent testing and bonding requirements (as in BC, 1999) discouraged building scale systems. More recently, British Columbia announced that by 2010 it would require larger new buildings to incorporate purple non-potable plumbing. Canada has a draft water reuse standard meant for incorporation into the National Building Code (Health Canada, 2007). The Canada Standards Association produced standard B128 in 2006 that details construction and testing for dual plumbing systems.

Non-potable reuse will affect other areas of regulation, as it should allow smaller sewers for municipalities and smaller leaching beds for on-site systems. Higher concentration of salts and solids in smaller volumes of water will have design implications for drains, treatment systems and environmental discharge points. Buildings can be future-proofed to be ready for non-potable supply by installing non-potable designated piping. To go even further, the municipality could run dual water supply lines (potable and non-potable) for new developments or where drinking water pipes are being replaced, with supply stubs at each property for future hook-up. Regulations are used around the world to promote or even require non-potable plumbing systems.

- Australia has 500 sewage treatment plants that recycle at least part of their effluent, totalling 150–200GL/yr, yet there is still call for greater awareness in the industry, for streamlined planning instruments, and for ensuring greater public participation and confidence (ATSE, 2004).
- In New South Wales, Australia, one must demonstrate a 40 per cent reduction over conventional water use through water efficient technology and design, rainwater harvesting and/or reuse in order to obtain a residential or commercial building permit (BASIX, 2006).
- Korea and Japan require reuse in buildings over a certain size, e.g. 5000m^2 floor area for Fukuoka, Japan (Noh et al, 2004).
- In China, Beijing has a policy to use reclaimed water in large hotels and public buildings (Jia et al, 2004).
- Irvine California requires new developments to be built with dual water systems for drinking water and reclaimed water (Asano, 1998).
- In Germany, where water can cost up to €5/m^3, 300–400 grey water recycling systems are in operation and 40,000–50,000 rainwater harvesting systems are installed each year (Nolde, 2004).

Non-potable reuse of treated wastewater effluent – some Canadian examples

Meeting conceptual green or water saving objectives appears to be the prime motivator to implement non-potable reuse of effluent, but there are also site-specific reasons why reuse can enhance a development or allow it to be built at all. Reducing water charges was a minor motivator in the non-industrial sector (Hellebust, 2006). Many Canadian communities, companies and organizations have already implemented use and reuse of non-potable water. For general papers on non-potable reuse of wastewater in Canada, see Schaefer et al (2004), Marsalek et al (2002), Vassos and Soroczan (2004) and Hellebust (2006).

The GE-Zenon Oakville Ontario office and the Earth Rangers building in Kleinburg Ontario treat sewage with a GE-Zenon system to reuse for toilet flushing in order to gain experience with reuse and to demonstrate green technologies. Dockside Green, a large urban development in Victoria BC, will use treated sewage in landscaping, flowing through natural watercourses to the ocean. Jonathan Westeinde of Windmill Developments wanted to demonstrate a distributed treatment model that could reduce heavy investment in a central plant. Rainwater harvesting is used at Dockside as well as at their projects in Calgary and Ottawa.

A grey water reuse system at the 19-unit condominium Quayside Village in North Vancouver, BC, uses technology derived from the Toronto Healthy House water reuse system. Although the intent was to supply toilet flushing, laundry, bathing and irrigation, the city and health authorities restricted reuse to toilet flushing (Vassos and Soroczan, 2004).

Sewage effluent was reused for toilet flushing at The Toronto Waldorf School (Thornhill, Ontario) to extend the life of a failing leaching bed by reducing the volume and increasing the quality of the effluent discharged. Area limitations, nitrogen loading to groundwater, and lack of high-quality groundwater were reasons for reusing treated sewage for toilet flushing for an expansion of the Husky Oil truck stop near London, Ontario (Harsch et al, 2005). The expansion would not have been approved without the reduction in effluent and nitrate loading achieved through reuse. Recirculated nitrate is converted to nitrogen gas in the septic tank. A reuse target of 80–85 per cent at the York Region Works and Transportation Centre in East Gwillimbury, Ontario, allowed discharge to soil infiltration rather than surface discharge, drastically decreasing approval time and cost (West et al, 2006).

About 20 per cent of GE-Zenon's over 200 on-site wastewater systems in the US north-east involve wastewater reuse (Millar, 2006) because regulators allow development on smaller lots if buildings do not increase demand on municipal infrastructure.

A pilot project in Nova Scotia aimed to establish that a simple sand filter can reliably produce effluent of acceptable quality for reuse and that reuse for toilet flushing can reduce household water use by 40–80 per cent (Sheppard, 2006). A leaching bed for septic tank effluent requires up to six times the area required for tertiary filtered effluent and ten times the area for tertiary filtered effluent with 40 per cent reuse (Hellebust, 2006). Reuse could allow a reduction in the traditional 2-acre (0.8ha) lot to 0.2 acres (0.08ha), approaching the density of municipally serviced suburban lots. Soil infiltration areas for clustered rural developments would also provide habitat and public greenspace.

Water supply is the most expensive home utility in the Canadian north, higher even than heating. Water servicing would drop from $80,000 to $47,000 per lot if homes were connected in clusters to on-site wastewater recycling systems instead of using conventional trenched pipes (Gleeson, 2001). The average cost of water in Iqaluit in 2000 was $25/m^3, and the cost in outlying communities was $50/m^3 (Spitzer, 2000) or ten times what is charged in the south.[1] The Northwest Territories Housing Corporation and Canada Mortgage and Housing Corporation supported a demonstration of five First Nations residences in Ndilo and Dettah, near Yellowknife with trucked-in water and sewage.[2] Reusing treated wastewater to flush toilets saved an estimated $8,000 per year per home (Vassos and Soroczan, 2004).

Goals for urban water infrastructure

In the future, water infrastructure will become more integrated with environmental and agricultural requirements. It will have a less hierarchical structure, moving from complete reliance on single large treatment plants to a hybrid, interdependent system of central and distributed technologies, which requires a corresponding shift in human management and regulation to design and monitor a more diverse, but a more resilient infrastructure.

Centralized treatment will improve in terms of energy efficiency, contaminant removal, biosolids processing and dilute resource extraction. Upstream and end-user tools will include demand management through pricing, substitution of dry techniques for water-based techniques, displacement of drinking water with various non-potable sources and recovery of relatively undiluted and unmixed resources at their point of generation.

Long-term goals related to water infrastructure from which we are to backcast and foster current and innovative solutions are:

- provide appropriate raw water source and treatment for different services;
- guarantee health protection and supply through a robust, resilient and diverse system;
- minimize the material cost of pipes and sewers;
- minimize energy use and associated environmental impact of water supply and treatment;
- minimize area taken up for water infrastructure and allow compact rural servicing;
- minimize the distance of water supply by increasing local and building-scale capacity;
- maximize the life of existing infrastructure;
- recover resources in a concentrated, high quality state;
- use water and waterborne resources to irrigate and fertilize greenspace and agricultural land;
- maintain watershed water quality and quantity requirements.

Some of these goals can be met with incremental improvements on our current approach to water servicing, whereas other goals, such as recovering nutrients from wastewater, will require leadership to bring a shift to management and technology.

Notes

1 Iqaluit is the capital of Nunavut Territory, which occupies the eastern part of the Canadian Arctic; it is characterized by nine months of winter and an average January temperature of −31°C.
2 Yellowknife is the capital of the Northwest Territory, which occupies the central part of the Canadian Arctic; average January temperature is −25°C.

References

Arpke, A. and Clerico, E. (2005) 'Life cycle cost and life cycle assessment of decentralized water reuse systems as a sustainable cost effective alternative', Water Environment Federation's Technology 2005 2nd Joint Specialty Conference for Sustainable Management of Water Quality Systems for the 21st Century, San Francisco, CA

Asano, T. (ed) (1998) *Wastewater Reclamation and Reuse*, CRC Press LLC, Boca Raton, FL, Water Quality Management Library, vol 10 (originally published by Technomic Publishing, Lancaster, PA)

ATSE (2004) *Water Recycling in Australia*, Australian Academy of Technological Sciences and Engineering, Special Report

BASIX (2006) New South Wales, Australia: www.basix.nsw.gov.au

Brandes, O. M. and Kriwoken, L. (2005) *Changing Perspectives – Changing Paradigms*. Canadian Water Resources Annual Conference, Kelowna, BC

British Columbia (1999) *Environmental Management Act. Municipal Sewage Regulation. B.C. Reg. 129/99.* www.qp.gov.bc.ca/statreg/reg/E/EnvMgmt/129_99.htm, Victoria, British Columbia, Canada; see also companion guide: *Code of Practice for the Use of Reclaimed Water*, May 2001, British Columbia, Ministry of Environment, Lands and Parks: www.env.gov.bc.ca/epd/epdpa/mpp/pdfs/cop_reclaimedwater.pdf

Canada Mortgage and Housing Corporation (CMHC) (2004) *Water Reuse Standards and Verification Protocol*, Technical Highlight, Technical Series 04-131, December 2004 (contact Cate Soroczan, CMHC, for full report by NovaTec Consultants which accompanies this highlight)

Crites, R. and Tchobanoglous, T. (1998) *Small and Decentralized Wastewater Management Systems*, WCB/McGraw-Hill, Toronto, ON

Del Porto, D. and Steinfeld, C. (2000) *The Composting Toilet System Book*, The Center for Ecological Pollution Prevention, Concord, MA

Dimitriadis, S. (2005) *Issues Encountered in Advancing Australia's Water Recycling Schemes*, Parliament of Australia, Department of Parliamentary Services, Research Brief, Canberra

Environment Canada (2006) *The Management of Water*, Water efficiency/conservation section, www.ec.gc.ca/water/en/manage/effic/e_retro.htm. See also www.crd.bc.ca/reports/water_/crdwathgowu/CRDWat_HGOWU.pdf. Compare with 'outdoor water consumption can account for up to 50% of water use in summer months' Green Venture, Wise Water Use, in partnership with the City of Hamilton, ON, www.greenventure.ca/wwu.asp?ID=5

Exall, K., Marsalek, J. and Schaefer, K. (2004) 'A review of water reuse and recycling, with reference to Canadian practice and potential: 1. Incentives and implementation', *Water Quality Research Journal of Canada*, vol 39, no 1, pp1–12

Federation of Canadian Municipalities (2005) *2005 Policy Statement on Municipal Infrastructure*: www.fcm.ca/english/policy/muninfra.html

Gleeson, R. (2001) Yellowknife, 18 July 2001, newspaper article 'Healthy housing: meet the team behind the North's environmentally-friendly home', Comment by Aleta Fowler, CMHC Yellowknife office, regarding the Northern Healthy House, Yellowknife, Northwest Territories, Canada: www.nnsl.com/frames/newspapers/frames/newspapers/2001-07/jul18_01hou.html

Graber, E. (2005) *Water Re-Use and Sustainability in Israel*, lecture, Environmental Seminar Series, University of Toronto Centre for Environment, 2 November

Gross, A., Azulai, N., Oroni, N., Roneni, Z., Armolds, M. and Nejid, A. (2004) 'Environmental impact and health risks associated with greywater irrigation – a case study', 'Proceedings of the IWA Biannual Meeting', Marrakech, Morocco

Harsch, D., Ip, I., Jowett, C., Millar, H. and Straw, K. (2005) 'Husky oil truck stop in Belmont, Ontario', *Onsite Wastewater News*, vol 6, no 3, pp2–3

Health Canada (2007) *Canadian Guidelines for Household Reclaimed Water for Use in Toilet and Urinal Flushing*, Draft for consultation, Federal-Provincial-Territorial Committee on Health and the Environment: www.hc-sc.gc.ca

Hellebust, A. (2006) *Wastewater Reuse in Residential, Institutional and Commercial Buildings in Canada: Current Motivations, Future Scenarios and Initiatives*, Report for the Water Soft Path Project, Friends of the Earth Canada, Ottawa, ON; available in CD Format, *Lexicon of Water Soft Path Knowledge*, vol 1 (2007)

ICF Consulting (2005) *Factor Analysis of Ontario Electricity*, Report for Ontario Power Authority, Toronto, ON, Canada

Jenkins, J. (2005) *The Humanure Handbook*, 3rd Edition, Jenkins Publishing, Grove City, PA

Jia, H., Guo, R., Xin, K. and Wang, J. (2004) 'Research on wastewater reuse planning in Beijing Central Region', *Water Science and Technology*, vol 51, no 10, pp195–202

Johannson, M. (undated, ca. 2004) *Urine Separation: Closing The Nutrient Cycle, for Stockholm Vatten, Sweden*: www.stockholmvatten.se/pdf_arkiv/english/ Urinsep_eng.pdf

Jönsson, H. (2001) 'Urine separation: Swedish experiences', *EcoEng Newsletter* 1, October 2001, www.iees.ch/EcoEng011/EcoEng011_F1.html. See also Gebers Housing project case study at www.iees.ch/cs/cs_4.html

Marsalek, J., Schaefer, K., Exall, K., Brannen, L. and Aidun, B. (2002) *Water Reuse and Recycling*, Canadian Council of Ministers of the Environment, Winnipeg, Manitoba. CCME Linking Water Science to Policy Workshops Series. Report No. 3

Millar, D. (2006) Personal communication, Duncan Millar, Zenon Corporation

Noh, S., Kwon, I., Yang, H.-M., Choi, H.-L. and Kim, H. (2004) 'Current status of water reuse systems in Korea', *Water Science and Technology*, vol 50, no 2, pp309–314

Nolde, E. (2004) 'Greywater recycling systems in Germany: Results, experiences and guidelines', *Water Science and Technology*, vol 51, no 10, pp203–210

Novaquatis Project (2006) www.novaquatis.eawag.ch/english/NoMix_e.html; (see also 'Ecosan' or ecological sanitation initiatives in Europe)

Sala, L. and Serra, M. (2004) 'Towards sustainability in water recycling', *Water Science and Technology*, vol 50, no 2, pp1–8

Schaefer, K., Exall, K. and Marsalek, J. (2004) 'Water reuse and recycling in Canada: A status and needs assessment', *Canadian Water Resources Journal*, vol 29, no 3, pp195–208

Sheppard, W. J. (2006) 'Evaluation of the suitability of using recycled wastewater for toilet flushing', Unpublished Report: bill.sheppard@ns.sympatico.ca

Spitzer, A. (2000) 'For Jens Steenberg, no water is waste water: Jens Steenberg's recycling device turns sewage into clean – and technically, drinkable – water', *Nunatsiaq News*, 20 October: www.nunatsiaq.com/archives/nunavut001031/ nvt21020_13.html

Thompson, M. (2005) 'Port Macquarie's urban reclaimed water supply scheme', Proceedings IPWEA NSW Division Annual Conference 2005, New South Wales

Vassos, T. (2006) NovaTec Consultants, Vancouver, personal communication

Vassos, T. and Soroczan, C. (2004) 'Canadian on-site and small-scale decentralized water reuse case studies', Proceedings of 1st International Conference on Onsite Wastewater Treatment and Recycling, Fremantle

Water Strategy Expert Panel (WSEP) (2005) *Watertight: The Case for Change in Ontario's Water and Wastewater Sector*, Ontario Ministry of Public Infrastructure Renewal, Publications Ontario, Toronto, ON: www.pir.gov.on.ca

Weber, B. and Juanicó, M. (2004) 'Salt reduction in municipal sewage allocated for reuse: The outcome of a new policy in Israel', *Water Science and Technology*, vol 50, no 2, pp17–22

West, B., Masini, M. and Kobilnyk, T. (2006) 'Case study: Compact, onsite MBR system enables rapid permitting and water recycling', Ontario Onsite Wastewater Association annual conference 2006, Kitchener, ON

Wilsenach, J. and van Loosdrecht, M. (2003) 'Impact of separate urine collection on wastewater treatment systems', *Water Science and Technology*, vol 48, no 1, pp103–110

Zenon (2006) www.zenon.com/resources/case_studies/water_reuse/Solaire_Apartments_Battery_Park.shtml

15
Water Soft Path Thinking in the United States

Peter H. Gleick

Civilizations are built on a combination of water, land, and people. When the combination ceases to be infused with a moral relationship between man and man, and man and nature, civilizations decline.

President's Water Resources Policy Commission (1950)

Introduction

The world is in the midst of a major transition to a new way of thinking about global freshwater resources. This new age requires a change in direction if we are to find a way to manage and use our vital and limited freshwater resources sustainably. New sources of supply, such as recycled water, will have to supplement traditional ones. New thinking about how we use water must replace thoughtless water policy. The efficiency of water use will have to improve so we can feed more people with less water. Our aquatic ecosystems will have to be restored and protected. New technological, economical and institutional approaches will have to be tried. And in the end, the transition to a sustainable planet will require a transition to sustainable water use. This approach is called the Water Soft Path.[1]

This chapter will provide some on-the-ground experience in the US that supports the idea that the fundamental concepts of the water soft path are not only practical, but are being implemented – whether water managers and planners call it the soft path or not. This is great news, but we still have a long way to go.

One dimension of the soft path in practice: Efficiency of use in the US

There are many dimensions to the soft path for water. Often, writings on the soft path focus on one or another of these dimensions, but in my writings, I support the need for a comprehensive set of technologies, policies and institutions to tackle water problems. This broader view can be seen in various references (below) and in other chapters of this book. For example, Lens et al (2001) and Wright (1997) are excellent introductions to the wastewater dimension of the soft water development path. Gleick et al (1995) present a detailed quantitative assessment of future soft path water development in California, and the first volume of *The World's Water (1998–1999)* included a qualitative global vision of a sustainable water path: 'Moving toward a sustainable vision for the Earth's fresh water' (Cooley and Gleick, 2008). Wolff and Gleick (2002) offer a comprehensive summary of soft path issues, while Gleick (2002) is more concise. A sizeable literature has also emerged in Canada, including both theoretical treatments (e.g. Wolfe and Brooks, 2003) and semi-popular summaries of water soft path concepts (Brandes and Brooks, 2007). In all of these discussions, a key element is improving the efficiency of water use.

Definitions and concepts

Improving efficiency is not a new concept, but until now it has not played a central role in water planning. In 1950, the Water Resources Policy Commission of the US published *A Water Policy for the American People*, which noted that:

> We can no longer be wasteful and careless in our attitude towards our water resources. Not only in the West, where the crucial value of water has long been recognized, but in every part of the country, we must manage and conserve water if we are to make the best use of it for future development. (WRPC, 1950)

In the early 1960s, Gilbert White, an early leader in applying economic analysis to water policy, called for broadening the range of alternatives examined by water managers who had previously only focused on structural solutions to water problems (White, 1961). White called on managers to consider both structural and non-structural alternatives, including zoning, land use planning and changing water use patterns. Unfortunately, traditional water management has, in general, continued to concentrate heavily on the construction of physical infrastructure.

One of the first challenges along the soft path is to define conservation and water use efficiency. Baumann et al (1980) defined water 'conservation' using a benefit–cost approach: 'the socially beneficial reduction of water use or water loss'. In common vernacular, however, the term *water conservation* is often used to refer to reducing water use by any amount or any means (see further in Brooks, 2005). *Technical efficiency* is a measure of how much water is actually used for a specific purpose compared to the minimum amount necessary to satisfy that purpose.[2] *Water use efficiency* is sometimes synonymous with technical efficiency. Under these definitions, the theoretical maximum water use efficiency occurs when society actually uses the minimum amount of water necessary to do something. In reality, however, this theoretical maximum efficiency is rarely, if ever, achieved because the technology isn't available or commercialized, because the economic cost is too high, or because societal or cultural preferences rule out particular approaches.

Though technical efficiency and water use efficiency can be useful concepts, they offer little guidance as to how much reduction in water use is 'enough' (Dziegielewski, 1999). In theory, a society could conserve too much water – expending resources on saving water that would be better spent on other goods or services. Consequently, the best use for numerical measures of technical efficiency is to provide a comparison over time or between locations.

The concepts of *water productivity* and *water intensity* are more useful to soft path planners, and come close to what economists called economic efficiency in contrast to the engineering concept of technical efficiency. Unlike technical efficiency, which is a percentage, water productivity is the amount of measurable output per unit of water that is used. The units of output can be physical (e.g. kilograms of wheat) or economic (e.g. the dollar value of the good or service produced). Figure 15.1 shows water productivity for the US economy from 1950 through 2000 measured in (1996) dollars of gross

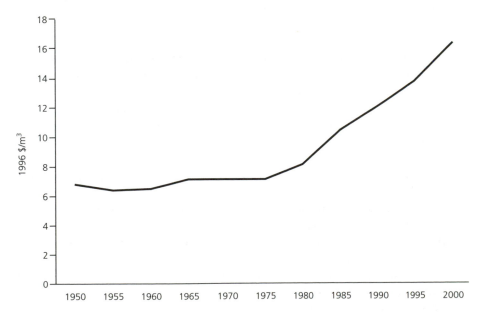

Figure 15.1 *US economic productivity of water 1950–2000 in dollars (1996) of GNP per cubic metre of water used*

national product (GNP) per unit of water used. This figure shows that productivity was relatively constant until the 1970s, when a combination of factors (such as rising environmental awareness, advances in technology, and the shift toward a service economy) caused water productivity to rise steadily. It is now more than double the value in the 1970s.

Recent efficiency improvements in agriculture

As noted previously, agriculture is the largest user of water worldwide: often 80 per cent of water use in a country or region. Agriculture's place as the largest water use sector implies that each 1 per cent decline in agricultural water use reduces demand for water much more than each 1 per cent decline in municipal, commercial, institutional or industrial water use. For example, a 25 per cent reduction in agricultural water use in an area where agricultural use is 80 per cent of the total use makes possible a doubling (100 per cent increase) of water use in all other sectors combined.

The potential for water efficiency improvements in agriculture is large, but there has been a serious reluctance on the part of water agencies, irrigation districts and even individual farmers either to evaluate that potential, or to explore policy and economic options for capturing it. Efficiency improving techniques include furrow diking, land levelling, no till, direct seeding, drip irrigation, better soil moisture monitoring and management, regulated deficit irrigation, low-energy precision application sprinklers, low-pressure sprinklers, water accounting and many others. Postel (1999) provides examples from around the world of the gains from some of these techniques. A new study released in September 2008 makes the first comprehensive attempt to evaluate a range of 'soft path' approaches to improving the efficiency of water use in California's agricultural sector (Cooley et al, 2008). This analysis computes potential efficiency savings from a range of efficiency scenarios for farmers in the Central Valley of California based on actions, programmes and technologies already in use by growers.

Four scenarios were evaluated, starting from the fundamental assumption that the objective was to maintain agricultural production at current levels, but to do so using less water:

1   modest shifts in crop type, along the lines of the trend in cropping patterns in California between 1960 and 2000;
2   changes in irrigation technologies, again using historical trends from flood to sprinkler to drip irrigation on appropriate crops;
3   regulated deficit irrigation used on those crops where this water-savings technique has proven effective; and finally,
4   improved irrigation management techniques including better timing of deliveries, improved soil moisture monitoring and application, tailwater reuse and so on.

The assumptions used in this study were conservative; based on current experience that shows improved food production with less water.

The results of this analysis were dramatic: each scenario identified substantial potential to improve the efficiency of agricultural water use. Annual water savings from the four scenarios ranged from 0.6 to 3.4 million acre-feet (a million acre-feet is equivalent to 1.2 billion cubic metres). These scenarios, by themselves and in combination with one another, can help satisfy the growing constraints on California water supply, reduce groundwater overdraft in the region, and help restore the health of the ecosystems, while still maintaining a strong agricultural economy – precisely the objectives of a soft path approach. Moreover, these savings are larger in magnitude, and lower in cost, than any of the hard path alternatives currently being proposed in California and much of the western US. For example, these savings are equivalent to the water that could be provided by between 3 and 20 new dams of the size currently under consideration at two sites in California – and there simply aren't many more sites that would be economically, environmentally or politically acceptable. Finally, the report clearly acknowledges that there are barriers to capturing these efficiency improvements that have to do with cost, communications problems between farmers and irrigation districts, the lack of markets for some kinds of crops, inadequate information and data and so on. Recommendations for overcoming these barriers are also presented for policy-makers, academics, growers and water managers.

Recent efficiency improvements at the municipal scale

Substantial amounts of water are also used in our urban settings for residential, commercial, industrial and institutional end-uses. As with agriculture, a wide range of technologies, policies and strategies are available to reduce urban water use while continuing to satisfy needs and demands for goods and services.

A number of municipal water suppliers have implemented aggressive water conservation programmes. Municipal conservation programmes that are fully integrated have shown impressive successes. Box 15.1 lists elements of comprehensive programmes. Postel (1997) and Cooley and Gleick (2008) provide details of successful municipal programmes or more narrow but successful efficiency efforts in specific sectors, in Jerusalem, Seattle, Las Vegas, Atlanta, Mexico City, Los Angeles, Beijing and many other cities. Reductions in water demand varied from 10 to 30 per cent.

A comprehensive assessment of urban water use potential was also prepared for California by the Pacific Institute (Gleick et al, 2003). This analysis was based on end-use reviews of all major urban water uses and applied existing, cost-effective technologies and policies, including leak reduction, to estimate potential savings. Despite the fact that many urban agencies in California have been implementing a wide range of conservation programmes for many decades, the report concluded that there was still significant untapped potential for savings, of the order of 30 per cent. For example, despite the fact that national standards in the US have required new construction to use ultra-low-flow-toilets using 1.6 gallons per flush or less since 1994, the report estimated that as many as 7 million old toilets using as much as 6 gallons per flush still remain in California homes. Similarly, high-efficiency washing machines can save substantial amounts of water, energy and detergent, but most residents still have not purchased them. Examples of indoor and outdoor savings were identified in every sector, for every end-use, from hospitals, schools and office buildings to the semiconductor, chemicals and food processing industries.

Overall, the report estimated that urban water use in California could be reduced by 2.3 million acre-feet per year, or around 30 per cent of total urban water use at costs less than that of building new water supply capacity to meet additional demand. A substantial fraction of these savings, around 900,000 acre-feet, come from indoor residential actions. Between 350,000 and 600,000 acre-feet could be saved by changing outdoor landscape water use practices, and as much as a million acre-feet combined would result from improvements in the efficiency of commercial, industrial and institutional water use (Gleick et al, 2003). The results of this study were so compelling that the numbers were adopted by the official State California Water Plan, which is used for projecting future needs and policies.

Many water planners still believe that using less water somehow means a loss of prosperity. The traditional assumption, repeated over and over in water plans and discussions about the risk of future water shortages, is that continued improvements in well-being required continued increases in water use. The reality is that the link between water use and economic well-being (often measured as some form of GDP) is not immutable. It can be modified and even broken, as it already has been in the US. This is shown clearly in Figure 15.2, which presents the data behind Figure 15.1 (water productivity in the US) in another way. Figure 15.2 shows total water withdrawals (white line) and GDP in 1996 dollars (black line) for the US from 1900 to 2000. From 1900 to 1980,

---

BOX 15.1 SOME KEY ELEMENTS OF INTEGRATED WATER MANAGEMENT PLANS

Elements of fully integrated water-management plans can include:

- comprehensive monitoring and evaluation of water use;
- establishment and enforcement of indoor and outdoor efficiency standards;
- development of water budgets for non-residential customers;
- implementation of conservation rate structures;
- availability of a technical assistance programme;
- availability of educational programmes, such as landscape seminars, demonstration gardens and garden contests;
- availability of rebates for decentralized investments that displace or delay centralized investments.

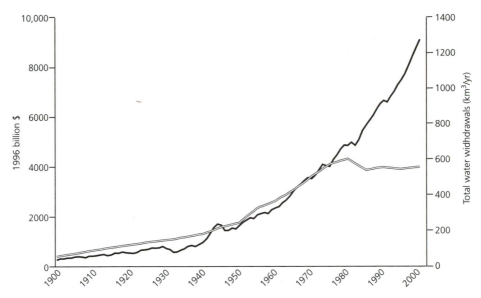

Figure 15.2 *US GDP and water withdrawals, 1900–2000*

these curves rose in lockstep – increases in national income were matched by similar increases in water withdrawals. Then, in 1980, this relationship was broken, with continued rapid increases in national income, but a levelling off – even a decrease – in total (as well as per capita) water withdrawals.

Similar patterns are emerging around the world. For example, Japan used nearly 13 million gallons of water to produce a million dollars of commercial output in 1965; by 1989 this had dropped to 3.5 million gallons per million real (inflation-adjusted) dollars of commercial output – almost a quadrupling of water productivity. Data from Hong Kong exhibit this pattern as well (Wolff and Gleick, 2002).

Implementing comprehensive soft path programmes

Successful water management inevitably requires combinations of regulations, economic incentives, technological changes and public education. Considerable experience in every sector of the economy suggests that the most effective programmes include combinations of all of these approaches (Gleick et al, 1995; Owens-Viani, 1999a, 1999b; Owens-Viani et al, 1999; Vickers, 2001).

Regulatory tools include policies taken by governments to encourage water conservation and efficiency improvements, better water quality management, groundwater oversight, as well as a variety of initiatives, including raising appliance efficiency standards, adopting landscape ordinances that promote less water use and changing building codes to mandate higher energy and water efficiency. Economic incentives for smart water use include marginal cost, volumetric water prices, rebates for water saving end-use devices or practices, low-cost loans or assistance in obtaining credit for capital investments by customers, environmental fees or surcharges that allow compensation for those damaged by additional water withdrawals (e.g. fishermen) and trading of water rights or water use permits.

Technological tools include all of the devices that permit us to use water more efficiently or manage it more effectively than in the past, and advanced media and informational techniques to communicate with and persuade water users to behave in ways that are socially desirable (ie, achieve the social objectives chosen in each locale). Education of the public means ensuring that information on options, costs, technology and regulations are fully available to water users. Smart choices will only be made when those choices are known and understood. Finally, unless demand management is fully integrated with water-supply planning, it will remain an underused and misunderstood part of our water future.

Conclusions

We must make a choice about which water path to take. We know where the hard path leads – to a diminished natural world, concentrated decision-making and higher economic costs. The soft path leads to more productive use of water, transparent and open decision-making, acceptance of the ecological values of water and new institutions.

Soft path water approaches are inherently more democratic than large centralized capital projects and require a much wider range of professional skills to implement. The soft path requires institutional change, not just better technology. But most institutional changes, historically, take place only with concerted social action or after crises force the changes to occur.

Despite the difficulties of changing paths, examples of soft path successes are becoming more common and pressure to pursue them is growing. Some of them have been touched on in this chapter and in other chapters in this book, but there are many more to be studied, generalized and disseminated. Humanity in the 21st century will either choose the soft water path or pay dearly – in both money and a diminished natural world – for clinging to the more familiar hard path.

Notes

1 As noted in Chapter 3, Amory Lovins (1977) originally coined the term 'soft path' for energy use. I warmly acknowledge his paternity in the terminology and many of the concepts discussed here.
2 The numerical measure of technical efficiency is calculated by dividing minimum use by actual use. Since actual use is larger than or equal to minimum use, reducing actual use will increase the ratio up to a maximum of 1.0 (100 per cent efficiency). This measure has one mathematical oddity, however. When the minimum use is zero, the ratio will always be 0 (0 per cent efficiency), no matter what actual water use is! Should actual water use fall to zero, the ratio will become undefined since 0 divided by 0 is undefined.

References

Baumann, D. D., Boland, J. J. and Sims, J. H. (1980) 'The evaluation of water conservation for municipal and industrial water supply- procedures manual', Contract Report 80-1, USACE Institute for Water Resources, Fort Belvoir, VA

Brandes, O. M. and Brooks, D. B. (2007) *The Soft Path for Water in a Nutshell*, Friends of the Earth Canada, Ottawa, ON and The POLIS Project for Ecological Governance, Victoria, BC

Brooks, D. B. (2005) 'Comment on "Using economic instruments for water demand management: Introduction" by B. Cantin, D. Shrubsole and M. Aït-Ouyahia', *Canadian Water Resources Journal*, vol 30, no 2, pp1–10

Cooley, H. and Gleick, P. H. (2008) 'Urban water-use efficiencies: Lessons from United States cities', *The World's Water 2008–2009*, Island Press, Washington, DC, pp100–122

Cooley, H., Christian-Smith, J. and Gleick, P. H. (2008) 'More with less: The potential for agricultural water conservation and efficiency in California', The Pacific Institute, Oakland, CA

Dziegielewski, B. (1999) 'Management of water demand: Unresolved issues', *Water Resources Update*, vol 114, pp1–7

Gleick, P. H. (2000) 'The changing water paradigm: A look at twenty-first century water resources development', *Water International*, vol 25, no 1, pp127–138

Gleick, P. H. (2002) 'Soft water paths', *Nature*, vol 418, pp373

Gleick, P. H., Loh, P., Gomez, S. V. and Morrison, J. (1995) 'California water 2020: A sustainable vision', A report of the Pacific Institute for Studies in Development, Environment, and Security, Oakland, CA

Gleick, P. H., Haasz, D., Henges-Jeck, C., Srinivasan, V., Wolff, G., Kao Cushing, K. and Mann, A. (2003) 'Waste not, want not: The potential for urban water conservation in California', The Pacific Institute, Oakland, CA

Gleick, P. H., Cooley, H. and Groves, D. (2005) *California Water 2030: An Efficient Future*, The Pacific Institute for Studies in Development, Environment, and Security, Oakland, CA

Hirsch, A. (1959) 'Water legislation in the Middle East', *The American Journal of Comparative Law*, vol 8, no 2, pp168–186

Lens, P., Zeeman, G. and Lettinga, G. (eds) (2001) *Decentralised Sanitation and Reuse: Concepts, Systems and Implementation*, IWA Publishing, London

Lovins, A. (1977) *Soft Energy Paths: Toward a Durable Peace*, Harper Colophon Books, New York, NY

Owens-Viani, L. (1999a) 'Reducing water use and solving wastewater problems with membrane filtration: Oberti Olives', in L. Owens-Viani, A. K. Wong and P. H. Gleick (eds) *Sustainable Use of Water: California Success Stories*, report of the Pacific Institute for Studies in Development, Environment, and Security, Oakland, CA, pp113–119

Owens-Viani, L. (1999b) 'Marin Municipal Water District's innovative integrated resource management program', in L. Owens-Viani, A. K. Wong and P. H. Gleick (eds) *Sustainable Use of Water: California Success Stories*, report of the Pacific Institute for Studies in Development, Environment, and Security, Oakland, CA, pp11–26

Owens-Viani, L., Wong, A. K. and Gleick, P. H. (eds) (1999) *Sustainable Use of Water: California Success Stories*, report of the Pacific Institute for Studies in Development, Environment, and Security, Oakland, CA

Postel, S. (1997) *Last Oasis: Facing Water Scarcity*, W. W. Norton, New York, NY

Postel, S. (1999) *Pillar of Sand: Can the Irrigation Miracle Last?* W. W. Norton, New York, NY

Ricciardi, A. and Rasmussen, J. B. (1999) 'Extinction rates of North American freshwater fauna', *Conservation Biology*, pp1220–1222

Vickers, A. L. (1999) 'The future of water conservation: Challenges ahead', *Water Resources Update*, vol 114, pp49–51

Vickers, A. L. (2001) *Handbook of Water Use and Conservation*, WaterPlow Press, Amherst, MA

Water Resources Policy Commissions (WRPC) (1950) *A Water Policy for the American People, The Report of the President's Water Resources Policy Commission, Vol 1*, US Government Printing Office, Washington, DC

White, G. F. (1961) 'The choices of use in resource management', *Natural Resources Journal*, vol 1, pp23–40

Wolfe, S. and Brooks, D. B. (2003) 'Water scarcity: An alternative view and its implications for policy and capacity building', *Natural Resources Forum*, vol 27, no 2, pp99–107

Wolff, G. and Gleick, P. H. (2002) 'Soft water paths', in P. H. Gleick (ed) *The World's Water 2002–2003*, Island Press, Washington, DC, pp1–32

World Commission on Dams (2000) *Dams and Development: A New Framework for Decision-Making: The Report of the World Commission on Dams*, www.dams.org/report/wcd_overview.htm

World Health Organization and United Nations Children's Fund (2008) 'Progress on drinking water and sanitation: Special focus on sanitation', Joint Monitoring Programme for Water Supply and Sanitation (JMP), UNICEF, New York, NY and WHO, Geneva

Wright, A. (1997) *Toward a Strategic Sanitation Approach*, United Nations Development Program, World Bank Water and Sanitation Program, Washington, DC

16
Water Soft Path Thinking in Other Developed Economies

As I travel around the world, people think the only place where there is potential conflict [over] water is the Middle East, but they are completely wrong. We have the problem all over the world.

Kofi Annan

Editor's Note: *This chapter points to several indications of water soft path thinking in other developed economies, each of which is undertaking significant reforms in approaches to national water management: Australia with its innovative adaptation of market mechanisms; England with its ongoing experiment with privatization of water delivery systems; and Europe with its Water Framework Directive that seeks, among other things, to use economic instruments to achieve environmental objectives. In none of these nations or regions did the concept of water soft paths play an explicit role, but in each there are elements of soft path thinking, and, what is probably more important, suggestions that water soft paths could play a greater role as the respective reform processes take hold, and as available fresh water per capita continues to decline. It almost goes without saying that all three jurisdictions are trying to keep withdrawals of water from the ecosystem and returns of water to the ecosystem within sustainable limits, even as a large share of the water is used for household, industrial and agricultural purposes. Another common objective is to ensure that water treatment, delivery and disposal is not just undertaken in a cost-effective manner, but that tariffs for water delivery and wastewater removal are sufficient to ensure the viability of the operating utilities or companies. If these reforms prove to be as effective as early reports suggest, one of the lessons will have to be that ownership of the delivery and treatment facilities is less important than appropriately designed (and of course implemented) regulatory and management structures with clear lines of responsibility to senior levels of government. However, it has already been shown that, if the public and their governments take environmental, social and economic objectives seriously, and if they are imaginative and innovative in their efforts to achieve them, ecology, equity and economic development can be compatible. That alone provides a platform on which water soft paths could readily be built. D.B.B.*

Part A: England

Gareth Walker

In 1989, England[1] added the provision of water and sanitation to its growing list of public services deemed to be better provided by the private than the public sector. Alongside energy, transport and telecom, the water industry was to be guided by the 'invisible hand' of free market economics and driven by the introduction of incentives for performance and efficiency thought to be previously lacking in the public sector. All capital assets previously owned by government were sold and a new regulatory framework established, in which the environmental, economic and water quality standards of companies were to be monitored and controlled by the Environment Agency (EA), the Water Services Regulatory Authority (Ofwat) and Drinking Water Inspectorate (DWI) respectively.

Until recently, privatization has been relatively successful in delivering its promises. The private sector has indeed provided England with some of the most secure and safe water supplies in the world. By 1998, figures showed privatization in England to have introduced an annual investment of around £3 billion in capital expenditure, almost double pre-1989 levels (Ofwat, 1999). In addition, Ofwat has observed a reduction in operational costs in water service provision (Ofwat, 1999), which presumably reflects increased efficiency. As private sector involvement in water services grows globally, the English experience has been cited as a case example of how privatizing water services, right down to the pipes in the ground, is effective in providing an initial surge in capital investment, followed by an increased efficiency in management and service provision. However, the remit of the water industry is gradually changing, and with it the standards by which it will be judged.

Gradual reductions in available water

The gap between demand and available supply is rapidly narrowing in England. As public water supply for mainly domestic use represents the largest proportion of demand for water (Figure 16.1), continued growth of both per person-day demand for water and net population means room for further extraction from the environment is dwindling. Use rates per person-day have been rising by about 1 per cent per year since the 1930s, something that is attributed to decreasing household occupancy rates, more water-using appliances in the home, and changing patterns of use. Since about 2005, the per capita rate of water use has been stable but it will be some time before one can assert that the change is significant.

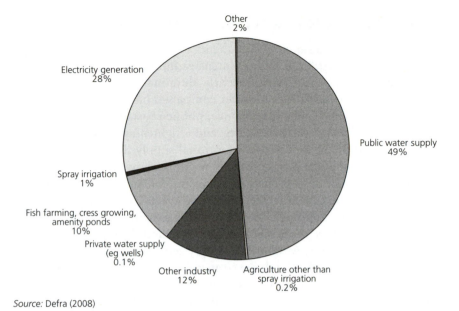

Source: Defra (2008)

Figure 16.1 *Licensed withdrawals: England and Wales (%)*

Water extraction is managed and regulated by the EA and distributed between surface and groundwater according to the geology of the region. The densely populated southern regions of England sit on porous chalk and clay aquifers and are therefore heavily dependent on groundwater withdrawals, whereas the reverse applies to the north of the country, which tends to rely on surface water. In the south, the EA has acknowledged that groundwater extraction is now approaching full capacity, with many aquifers exploited to unsustainable levels. Some hydrologists argue that the need for capping, and in some cases even reduction in withdrawal rates, is evident in the majority of English aquifers. Surface water is also under pressure; modelling carried out by the EA suggests that during dry summer periods the majority of English surface water is either already over-withdrawn or that no additional resources can be withdrawn without damaging the environment (EA, 2001).

Most of the water-stressed areas of England occur in the east and south-east of parts of the country, with intermediate levels of stress in the west-central parts and in Cornwall. Only the northern part of England and some places in the south are relatively free from water stress.

Water quality issues are also affecting available resources. England has enjoyed success in addressing point source pollution in rivers and coastal areas, but increased use of fertilizers has meant that oxidized nitrogen and phosphate levels have been steadily rising in many areas, which increases the cost of treatment. Ironically, England's self-image as a 'rainy nation' has masked many of these issues to the point where the public finds it hard to believe that per head availability of freshwater in the UK as a whole is now comparable to that of Spain or Mexico (WRI, 2008).

Growing resistance to new supply infrastructure

In the past, issues of water quality and quantity have been addressed through the development of centralized, capital-intensive infrastructure, such as reservoirs, treatment plants and more recently desalination plants. However, previously marginal externalities to water companies have all grown in influence. The environmental limits listed above, public resistance to development in greenfield sites, land scarcity and costs, and a tightening of regulation have all made it more difficult to justify conventional supply-driven options from either economic or political perspectives. In response, government and regulatory bodies have sought to steer companies toward demand-side solutions.

The government's current strategy, 'Future Water', has outlined what it calls the 'twin track' approach to water management, in which demand management and further resource development should play equal roles in ensuring security of supply. As domestic supply represents the largest proportion of water extracted in England, the strategy has emphasized a reduction in domestic per person consumption. The target is a reduction from the current 150 litres per person-day to 130 litres by 2020 (Defra, 2008). Within industry, Ofwat has set a voluntary target of a 1 per cent reduction in domestic demand through water company actions, and plans the future introduction of similar mandatory targets (Ofwat, 2008). Environmental regulation has followed a similar trend, promoting the introduction of time limited withdrawal licences by 2021, which will either cap, or in some cases reduce, net withdrawals. In these same regions, government has granted water companies operating in water-stressed areas the right to apply for licences to make metering compulsory for its customers. At present, only about 30 per cent of households are metered. The companies will also be allowed to introduce economic incentives for domestic efficiency and assist in achieving the government target of universal metering in water-stressed areas by 2030. At a higher level, obligations under the European Water Framework Directive call for member states to achieve 'good ecological status' in all catchments by 2015, which will apply to both quality and quantity.

The result of this political and regulatory push has been a sharp increase in water company pilot projects involving demand management. As of 2008, six private water companies have begun to report on the results of 18 demand management projects, with an average of 1000 homes per project.[2] Activities include adding rainwater harvesting systems in existing social housing complexes, dual-flush toilets and water-efficient showerheads and the provision of home self-audits and efficiency advice. In delivering these projects, water companies have a duty not only to meet regulatory requirements, but to carry them out as efficiently as possible. Therefore, a secondary focus has been on the cost effectiveness of investment in demand-side measures and a comparison with conventional capital-intensive solutions.

Waterwise, a not-for-profit group set up by industry to promote water efficiency, is currently compiling the results of the projects to develop the UK's first attempt to justify water efficiency in economic terms. The results so far look promising; based on the data received, the average incremental costs ($£$ per m^3) and net present values of efficiency retrofits over a 25-year period compare favourably with scenarios of augmented supply (for example, desalination or reservoirs).

This increased investment in demand management signals a positive change in the way private companies operate, but there remains a substantial amount of change to the entire regulatory, economic and institutional frameworks that surround companies in order to move significantly closer to the water soft path approach.

Waterwise's database argues for demand management under the rationale that it postpones the need for further capital investment. Unfortunately, this argument hinges on capital and operational costs being compared on equal grounds, which currently they are not. The gap is a result of the problem of regulatory asset value. At present, the construction of new infrastructure, such as pumping stations and treatment plants, provides water companies with an increase in value against which loans can be sought; demand management projects offer no such regulatory value. Indeed, in the short run bankers might see reduced sales as a threat. Until this problem is resolved, the development of further supply systems may continue to appear more economically attractive.

The problem of regulatory asset value reflects a wider challenge in introducing water soft paths to a privatized water industry: how do we shift the focus of cost–benefit analysis away from the isolated perspective of the water company and towards society and the environment as a whole? This question arises not only in maintaining the supply–demand balance, but also in areas such as flood risk and water quality. In 2007 England experienced widespread flooding which in some areas compromised supply. Somewhat ironically customers had to queue for freshwater supplies in a manner only previously seen in droughts. As the government-commissioned review later observed, the effects of these floods were heightened by a highly fractured attempt to address surface drainage, composed of at least five different responsible bodies ranging from transport, to local government, to the water companies themselves (Pitt, 2008). As each body operates under its own terms of risk management and cost, inevitably these costs and risk were transferred to society as a whole, with consequent adverse effects on security of water supply. The EA has been criticized for failing to engage with other groups, such as local authorities, drainage boards and riparian owners, that together share responsibility for managing UK waterways (Pitt, 2008).

In terms of water quality, one English water company did establish a whole-watershed management programme under the European-led Water Resources Management in Cooperation with Agriculture project (WAGRICO). This programme used similar economic arguments to those made by proponents of demand management in terms of the potential to avoid capital investment in treatment plants thanks to reduced nitrate runoff through altered farming techniques. Ultimately this project came to a close due to similar problems concerning the attractiveness of capital investment as described above.

In the short term, there are a number of means to encourage water companies to move towards the soft water approach. National accounting rules could be changed to allow decentralized investments in demand management and watershed management to be counted as capital assets; however, this seems unlikely, given its wider impacts on private industry in England. Markets for savings in water could be introduced, perhaps employing a shadow market of carbon. This has worked in regions of California and Australia, where private firms have funded mass water efficiency retrofits to homes and claimed the resulting carbon credit due to reduced hot water consumption as a means of making profit. This approach has not yet been perused under the UK Carbon Emissions Reduction Trading scheme. Finally there is the further tightening of regulation in order to force companies to consider soft options alongside capital investment; however, this may become another case of the regulatory creep which has already become so extensive that some have suggested that there is very little private enterprise left in the industry (Bakker, 2002).

In the long term, an essential change will be to redefine private water companies as service providers rather than water and sewerage suppliers. In England, this will most likely have to be integrated with Ofwat's plans to separate upstream and downstream services. Under this plan, the water industry will operate under a model similar to other utilities; the management and wholesale of water resources will be separated from the retail end of water service provision. The desired impact of such a separation from Ofwat's perspective is the introduction of competition in an industry that has previously operated under a natural monopoly, with the expectation that separation will introduce clearer market drivers for efficiency. From the perspective of wholesale retailers, a well-regulated trade in licensed withdrawals will help to signal the real costs of water extraction while capping net impacts on the environment. Such price signalling may lead to innovation in provision of resources, such as improved efficiency in pumping and perhaps even the sale of varying qualities of water for different end-uses. Water service providers who have bought water in bulk will receive incentives to distribute that water among as many customers as possible. They are therefore likely to provide demand management solutions to their customers, the resulting economic savings being shared between the customer and the provider.

Though the introduction of competition may well encourage greater efficiency in both supply and consumption, experience has shown there are limits to how much markets can address the environmental and social aspects of water. As Bakker (2005) observes, privatization in England has so far failed to commodify water resources accurately, a gap that results in the environmental damage seen to date. Water's hybrid status as an economic good, environmental resource and a social asset, and its geography as a continually circulating resource, make it different from many other resources. Price signalling through licence trading may fail to capture the full environmental value of water, which will require the development of further evaluation techniques. Where this valuation is possible, it may still be the case that the protection of the environment will not make economic sense. When defining a service provider's remit, the customer's willingness to pay for environmental services will determine the level of protection afforded to the environment. Given the public's past reactions to rising water prices, and the resulting impact on water poverty, it is likely they are not willing to pay for a service that would independently guarantee environmental protection. There is therefore a risk that attempting to encourage market environmentalism may fall short of providing the substantial changes needed to achieve a water soft path.

Recent water company initiatives to encourage water efficiency give some hope for privatization's ability to incorporate demand management into their economic models; however the wider protection of the environment and the coordination of a comprehensive strategy for managing environmental integrity, flood risk and water resources will still require a strong government and regulatory role. The verdict on England's ability to incorporate the soft water approach into a privatized industry will therefore be passed on to the government and regulator's ability to set the right rules, rather than on the company's ability to operate within them.

Notes

1 To some degree, the information in this chapter is applicable to Wales. However, Welsh Water is a single, publicly owned limited company, whereas English companies are the fully privatized models which the bulk of the paper refers to. Scotland and Northern Ireland, also part of the UK, are not covered in this discussion.
2 The results of the corporate studies are available on the Waterwise web site: www.waterwise.org.uk/reducing_water_wastage_in_the_uk/research/publications.ht ml

Part B: The European Union

Economic elements of the European Water Framework Directive: Soft path instruments to enhance sustainable water use?

Simone Klawitter

Following a long debate, the European Water Framework Directive (WFD) was adopted in 2000 with the objective of promoting the use of economic principles, tools, methods and instruments to enhance sustainable water management and enforce respective policy development in the European Union (EU) member countries.

As part of the WFD, EU Member States are being asked to (EC, 2000):

- undertake an economic analysis of water uses;
- select measures for achieving economically efficient management of water through use of cost effectiveness analysis;
- promote an adequate recovery of the costs of water services from water users and a water-pricing model that enhances the sustainability of water resources.

Political history of the Water Framework Directive

Water legislation was one of the first sectors covered by the EU environmental policy, and it comprises a number of water-related directives and decisions. Based on the first environmental action programme, a dual approach was used taking into account Environmental Quality Standards (EQS) and Emission Limited Values (ELV). No economic issues were considered. The dual approach faced immense implementation problems, however, mainly because of the patchwork of legislation that had existed in the EU since the 1970s. A major revision of the EU water policy was undertaken and finally resulted in the development of the WFD. The WFD not only repealed a number of earlier directives but also provided the basis for subsequent legislative initiatives once all Member States implemented the directive.

From the beginning of the legislative process, the WFD had to strike a compromise between a number of special interests and very demanding technical requirements. The result is a very complex and ambiguous legal text, reflecting the comprehensive process that led to it (eg Lenz and Scheuer, 2001).

General elements of the WFD – draft outline

The general elements of the Water Framework Directive are:

- integrated river basin management;
- ecological objectives for surface waters;
- chemicals policy;
- groundwater protection;
- use of economic instruments.

The WFD covers most important issues related to integrated water management. The main objectives are as follows:

- protection and improvement of the aquatic environment;
- sustainable, balanced and equitable water use;
- meeting the objectives of relevant international agreements.

New instruments are introduced in the EU water policy to protect and improve European waters, including:

BOX 16.1 THE EUROPEAN WATER FRAMEWORK DIRECTIVE

The Water Framework Directive establishes a legal framework to protect and restore clean water across Europe and ensure its long-term and sustainable use. (Directive 2000/60/EC of the European Parliament and of the Council of 23 October 2000).

The directive introduces an innovative approach to water management based on river basins, natural geographical and hydrological units and sets specific deadlines for Member States to protect aquatic ecosystems. The directive addresses inland surface waters, transitional waters, coastal waters and groundwater, and establishes innovative principles for water management, including public participation in planning and economic approaches.

Article 9 of the directive calls for the recovery of the costs of providing water services.

Article 5 requires an economic analysis of water use and Annex III lists the elements that Member States should include in this analysis.

Source: EC (2008)

- ecological and holistic water status assessment approach;
- river basin planning;
- strategy for elimination of pollution by dangerous substances;
- public information and consultation;
- financial instruments.

In addition, the WFD allows for wide-ranging exemptions and derogations, for example for developing environmental objectives for 'heavily modified' waters and for shifting important decisions to subsequent political processes, as with the criteria for assessing groundwater quality.

WFD and the use of economic instruments

The use of economic instruments is of growing importance for environmental policy in many industrialized nations. In line with these initiatives, the Water Framework Directive enforces a strict water pricing policy to achieve a more demand-driven water management and more efficient use of water.

The WFD emphasizes two main economic elements:

1. the use of prices and charges (Article 9) for enhancing the sustainability of water resources, and
2. the economic analysis of water uses (Article 5 and Annex III) to identify the most cost-effective manner for achieving the environmental objectives of the WFD.

Furthermore it integrates economics into planning and decision-making and suggests optional economic principles, economic approaches and economic instruments for future water policies.

History

Although the two key economic elements of the new policy; use of prices and charges (Article 9), and economic analysis of water uses (Article 5 and Annex III), are closely linked, they were discussed separately during the negotiations leading to the WFD. Most of the debate took place around the role that water pricing could and should play in the context of European water policy. A wide range of views from stakeholder groups and Member States, each of which benefit in different ways from different water pricing policies, was gathered. Discussion was complicated by differences in understanding related to the definitions of key concepts as well incomplete understanding of those concepts and of the principles of pricing (eg Strosser, 2000).

The WFD came into force when it was published in the *Official Journal of the European Communities* on 22 December 2000 as Directive 2000/60/EC (OJL 327/1). However, deadlines for implementation of the economic elements of the WFD are very ambiguous (see Figure 16.2).

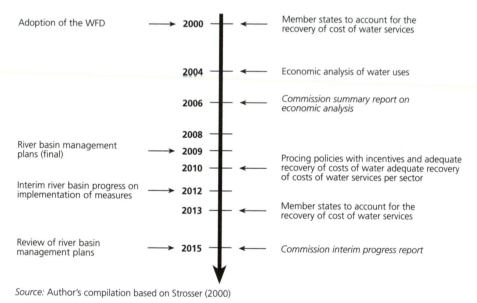

Source: Author's compilation based on Strosser (2000)

Figure 16.2 *Deadlines related to the implementation of the economic elements of WFD*

Pricing policy and the principle of cost recovery

A major shift in water policy marked by the WFD was the introduction of water prices high enough to cover all costs including environmental and resource costs (Article 9; see Figure 16.3). Already integrated in the Amsterdam Treaty as foundation of all European environmental policies, the Polluter Pays Principle determines the assignment of costs of water services (See also Roth, 2001; Lallana et al, 2001).

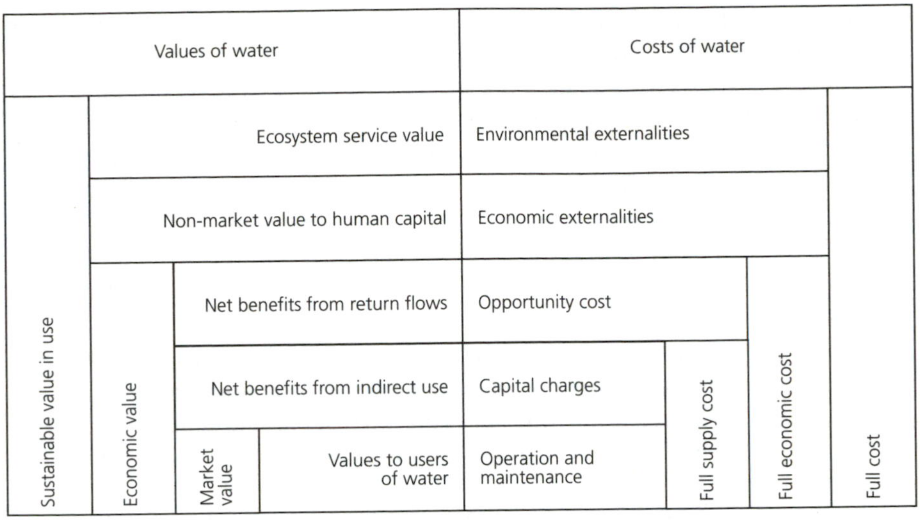

Values of water				Costs of water			
Sustainable value in use			Ecosystem service value	Environmental externalities			Full cost
	Economic value		Non-market value to human capital	Economic externalities		Full economic cost	
			Net benefits from return flows	Opportunity cost			
		Market value	Net benefits from indirect use	Capital charges	Full supply cost		
			Values to users of water	Operation and maintenance			

Source: Authors compilation based on Rogers et al (1998), Lant (2004), modified

Figure 16.3 *General principles of full cost of water*

Article 9 further specifies that Member States have to ensure by 2010:

- that a water pricing policy is formulated in such a way as to serve as an incentive for efficient water use and thereby contributes to the stated environmental objectives;
- that an adequate contribution to recover the cost of water services is paid by all water users.

The first obligation makes it clear that water pricing has to be seen as an instrument to strengthen environmental issues within the WFD. The second specifies that water users have to be classified at least in sector classes – for example, industry, households, agriculture – to make the pricing system efficient and transparent. The cost recovery objective is limited to water services, which are defined in Article 2(3) as 'all services (withdrawal, impoundment, storage, treatment and distribution of surface water or groundwater, wastewater collection and treatment facilities) which provide for households, public institutions or any economic activity'.

Weakened implementation

Exemptions to the obligations might include:

- the funding of particular remedial and preventive measures in order to achieve the objective of the directive;
- situations, where proposed established pricing policies for given water use do not compromise the environmental objectives of the directive.

Furthermore the article specifies strict reporting obligations for the Member States with respect to river basin management planning.

The initial objective of implementing a full cost recovery regime was weakened and Member States are now only required to ensure that the price charged to consumers for water supply and wastewater treatment 'takes into account' the full environmental costs. Opponents argued that the requested shift in pricing policy would interfere in social as well as environmental objectives. Therefore, provision was made for exemptions from full cost recovery. In addition, the WFD only says that Member States must ensure that pricing policies provide an 'adequate incentive' to use water efficiently. However, the European Commission is pursuing more ambitious plans to introduce full-cost pricing. The Commission does not state that pricing is the only instrument that can solve water resource problems, but rather that it plays an important role in moving from a technological problem solution and supply orientation to a demand orientation.

Due to strong opposition from Member States with a low level of cost recovery or water services, exemptions from the application of the full-cost recovery principle are possible under the following scenarios:

1   While establishing a pricing policy for water, Member States can take into account social, environmental and economic impacts as well as special geographic and climatic conditions. These factors provide some leeway for Member States to avoid meeting the pricing guidelines, but they may be necessary in some cases due to large differences in the economic and social capacities of some Member States to implement the directive's requirements.

2   A Member State can also simply decide not to establish any water pricing policy or a specific water use activity if this decision does not compromise its ability to meet the objectives of the WFD. In this case, the Member State has to justify its decisions in a report to the river basin management plan, which opens the discussion to public scrutiny and possibly to challenge through the conventional political process.

Economic analysis of water use

By 2004 for each river basin, an economic analysis had to be implemented as a precondition for application of the principle of full-cost recovery and the polluter pays principle (Article 5 and Annex III).

The economic analysis has two main objectives:

1   to support the development of water pricing policies that comply with the requirements specified under Article 9;
2   to identify the set of measures that will reach the objectives of the directive in a cost-effective manner.

According to Annex III of the WFD, the economic analysis has to contain sufficient information to fulfil the economic requirements of the directive, which includes an estimation of environmental and resource costs and a long-term forecast of water supply and demand. The economic analysis and full-cost recovery process must be incorporated in the river basin management plan.

Economic elements of the WFD – a soft path approach?

The soft path approach represents a new water management paradigm requiring society to balance water use, social needs and ecological sustainability over the long term. It also goes beyond traditional water demand management approaches in recognition of social goals and the need for participatory decisions. The soft path approach incorporates three overarching concepts: human vision, analytical method and planning tool (Gleick, 2000; Brooks, 2005a, 2005b).

Human vision
With the WFD, the European Commission has assigned an increasing role to the use of economic instruments that aim to enhance sustainable use of water resources by creating a legal framework for community actions. The objective of efficient water pricing is to act as an incentive to reduce pollution and improve the efficiency of water use. Thus, it reduces the pressure on water resources and the environment and it ensures that available resources are efficiently allocated between water uses and users. The provision of water services and protection of the environment are dealt with together in the development of more cost-effective practices. Based on the legal framework provided by the WFD, more financial resources can be mobilized to ensure the financial sustainability of water infrastructure and service suppliers, and to pay for environmental protection. Ecological sustainability is a fundamental criterion within the WFD.

Analytical method
The WFD provides not only for implementation of its economic elements but also the methodology for assessing progress. The Water Framework Directive introduces two key economic principles. First, it calls on water users to pay for the full costs of the water services they receive. Second, the directive calls on Member States to use economic analysis in the management of their water resources and to assess both the cost effectiveness and overall costs of alternatives when making key decisions.

Under the Directive, the obligation for an economic analysis also underpins the Member States' work to prepare basin management plans for their rivers. Member States will need to estimate the costs of implementing different possible measures to be integrated into the planning process. They will use these estimates to identify the most cost-effective set of measures that can improve the quality and quantity of their water bodies to at least reach 'good status'.

Planning tool

To reach the 'good status' of their water bodies, Member States can choose among many measures, for example new investment projects, regulations, establishment of economic instruments and the negotiation of agreements with polluters. Carrying out an economic analysis to assess the cost effectiveness of alternative measures will be vital in ensuring that available funds are used efficiently. In addition, Member States are obliged to make forecasts of long-term water supply and demand, based on the future population and economic scenarios of each river basin. These scenarios will provide an important way to identify expected pressure changes – due to population growth or changes in agricultural production – and the estimated impacts of climate change on future water conditions. In their 2005 reports only a few Member States presented detailed scenarios for the future.

Ongoing activities in EU member states stress that significant efforts have taken place so far for ensuring adequate implementation of the economic elements of the WFD. Most countries are adopting water-pricing systems that encourage economic efficiency and more sustainable use of water resources. However, the integration of economic and environmental objectives into the water-pricing policies of individual Member States is still uneven and, even though transparent full-cost recovery is being increasingly accepted, it has only been partly achieved. Further improvements and shifts in the focus of the analysis are required to ensure that it fulfils the basic principles of integration, proportionality, policy relevance, gradualism, public participation and transparency.

Part C: Australia

Henning Bjornlund and Geoff Kuehne

Introduction

Australia, the driest inhabited continent in the world, has since the mid 19th century been determined in its pursuit of irrigation as the means to increase agricultural production. Early experience implied that irrigation was neither economically viable nor in many cases suitable for the landscape, as indicated by early problems with salinity, waterlogging, low productivity and even economic failure. It was therefore pointed out that irrigation might not be the best solution under Australia's climatic, physical and population conditions (e.g. Davidson, 1969). However, the political determination was very strong. The general perception at the time, as later expressed by Davidson (1988), was that: 'if irrigation could not be justified on economic grounds then economics, and not irrigation, was at fault.'

Hence, to achieve political objectives, such as settlement of remote areas and accommodating soldiers returning from the two world wars, governments bailed out failing irrigation enterprises, invested in water storage and supply infrastructure and promoted irrigation particularly within the Murray-Darling Basin (MDB). This supply management approach continued at least until the early 1980s when the last of the major dams in the MDB was constructed. Within the federal structure of the nation, states continued to issue water entitlements with the immediate result of overcommitted water resources and escalating environmental problems that not only damaged ecological systems but also threatened the economic viability of the farming communities dependent on irrigation.

In response to the increasingly evident problems, water policy reforms have accelerated since the early 1990s with emphasis on a shift from supply to demand management. This reform process has taken on renewed urgency from the beginning of this millennium as Australia has experienced the worst drought in recorded history. Agriculture accounts for close to 80 per cent of water use so it is not surprising that much of this policy attention was initially focused on this sector. With irrigation so entrenched and thousands of families depending on it, there are no easy fixes.

In Australia the term 'Soft Path' has rarely been used in the context of water management. However, elements of what Brooks and Brandes (2007) call Demand Management and Soft Path are strong in current water policy reforms. Water planning processes in Australia have not asked the questions '*how*' or '*why*', but rather '*how much*' and '*of what*'. The starting point for water planning is now to define how much water is needed of what quality to achieve acceptable water dependent ecosystems. Once this has been agreed upon, backcasting has been employed, which allows the consumptive pool of water to be defined and shared among competing users. If the consumptive pool is lower than the volume of water entitlements previously issued to irrigators, the gap is resolved by defining water entitlements as a share of the consumptive pool, rather than in volumetric terms. It is then left to the individual water users to figure out *how* to reduce their current water needs to what is available to them.

From a policy perspective it could be argued that the job is done; however, it is not that simple. From a societal perspective it is important that the consumptive pool of water is used as efficiently and productively as possible so that economic activity can be maximized with the least environmental and socio-economic impacts. This requires government policies that change the way people use and interact with water – managing people rather than the water – something that implies the need for better understanding of the values that underlie decision-making by irrigators.

A brief history of Australian water policy reforms

First generation of solutions

This policy reform process has been driven by two institutions: (1) the Council of Australian Governments (CoAG); and (2) the Murray-Darling Basin Ministerial Council (MDBMC). In 1994 CoAG agreed on a water reform agenda that consolidated the shift from supply to demand management (CoAG, 1994):

- consumers should be charged according to consumption at prices set on a full-cost recovery basis including environmental costs and providing a real return on the written-down replacement costs of the assets;
- water entitlements should be separated from land and associated with clear specifications of ownership, transferability, reliability and, where appropriate, quality;
- trading in water entitlements should be encouraged to ensure that water is used to maximize its contribution to national income and welfare within social, physical and ecological constraints;
- integrated catchment management should underpin natural resource management, and irrigators should be given greater influence over management of irrigation areas;
- communities should be involved in water management, and education programmes should be implemented to improve their ability to participate in decision-making processes; and
- entitlements should be given to the environment, acknowledging it as a legitimate water user.

The MDB came under increased stress from overuse during the period from the 1970s to the 1990s. Media images of large blue-green algal blooms in the early 1990s brought the health of the Basin to national prominence. An audit of water use concluded that the level of extraction for consumptive use far exceeded what was ecologically sustainable (MDBMC, 1995). The volume of water that could be extracted for consumptive use was therefore capped at the 1993/94 level (MDBMC, 1996).

Second generation of solutions

It soon became evident that the 1993/94 cap was too high. In 2002, the MDBMC started the 'Living Murray' process (MDBMC, 2002) to determine how much more water should be allocated to the environment, how such reductions should be paid for and implemented, and what the socio-economic implications would be. Under the cap all catchments within the Basin had to develop water-sharing plans that defined how much water was needed for the environment and how much water remained for consumptive use. Many of these plans resulted in reductions in irrigators' entitlements.

In 2003 CoAG reviewed the 1994 reform agenda and found that existing water market mechanisms still prevented water markets from maximizing their beneficial impact and that there were still serious concerns about the pace of introducing processes to ensure adequate environmental flows and adaptive management systems. In 2004, CoAG approved two Intergovernmental Agreements, one on a National Water Initiative (NWI) that identifies the needs for (CoAG, 2004):

- nationally compatible water access entitlements defined as a perpetual share of the consumptive pool;
- a statutory water planning process defining the consumptive pool;
- statutory provisions for environmental and public benefits;
- assignment of risk arising from future changes in the consumptive pool;
- nationally functioning water markets including the progressive removal of barriers to trade; and
- a return of all currently overallocated or overused systems to environmentally sustainable levels of extraction.

A second agreement, 'Addressing Water Over-allocation and Achieving Environmental Objectives' provided $500 million to recover 500Mm^3 to protect six key ecological assets, the first step in the Living Murray process.

Third generation of solutions

The need to secure water for the environment was given added impetus in 2008 by the *Water for the Future* plan to spend $12.9 billion to secure Australia's long-term water supply. This Plan provides $3.1 billion for the buyback of 1500Mm^3 of entitlements from willing sellers and $5.8 billion to invest in upgrading outdated, leaky irrigation systems. However, it is becoming apparent that this quantity is inadequate (CSIRO, 2008).

In compliance with CoAG and MDBMC reforms, State water policies and legislation have undergone considerable change. Traditionally, seasonal allocations were announced as a percentage of total entitlement, at the beginning of the season, based on water availability in the reservoirs and historical inflows during the season. This policy provided certainty for irrigators when planning their production for the season. Today, the allocation at the beginning of the season is based only on what is available in the reservoirs and minimum expected inflows. This allocation is then revised during the season as additional water enters the reservoirs. While this is sounder environmental policy, irrigators have to make planting decisions without full knowledge of how much water is available. For the last six seasons the opening allocation within parts of the Goulburn-Murray Irrigation District (GMID) has been zero while closing allocations for three of these seasons still reached 100 per cent. This policy has increased the need for efficient markets to help irrigators manage the increased uncertainty.

To allow water markets and price mechanisms to operate more effectively, and to allow irrigators better management tools, the traditional water entitlements are now being unbundled into four components: (1) an access entitlement which is the long-term right to receive annual allocations; (2) a water allocation which is the right to extract a certain volume of water during the season; (3) a water use right, which is the right to use water for a certain purpose in a certain location, something that in principle requires proof of best management practices; and (4) a capacity entitlement, the right to a certain share of the supply capacity to get water delivered to the point of use.

Elements of the soft path approach in Australia

There is little emphasis in Australia on resolving the water crises by increasing supply from fresh water sources. Most solutions define minimum requirements for the environment in the form of instream flows and environmental events, such as floods, prior to defining the amount available for the consumptive pool. The political process has devolved these planning processes to the local community so as to involve all major stakeholders, but with the final decision left to the relevant Minister. In many instances this process has left irrigators feeling frustrated, confused and uncertain (Kuehne and Bjornlund, 2006).

Once the consumptive pool is defined, the issue becomes how to stay within its limits. In most instances the consumptive pool is less than the current level of use, which imposes the need to reduce use with least possible socio-economic impact. To achieve this goal, water markets and water pricing have been used.

The role of water markets and pricing

During periods of scarcity, markets have been instrumental in allowing irriga-tors to manage low allocations while maximizing economic output. Within the GMID, during seasons with very low allocations, well over a third of all water used for irrigation is purchased in the allocation market. The entitlement market has, over the first 16 years of its operation, reallocated nearly one-fifth of all water entitlements (Bjornlund and Rossini, 2008).

Whereas the entitlement market has had a small but growing impact on who owns water entitlements, the allocation market has rapidly developed a significant role in determining who uses the water. Combined, the two markets have allowed irrigators to manage the risk associated with declining access to water (Bjornlund, 2006) and thereby helped communities to remain sustain-able (Bjornlund, 2004). Irrigators with investment in high-value crops or dairy herds and producers with contracts to deliver vegetables to processors have been able to buy water and thereby achieve long-term viability. Those with lower-value crops can sell their allocation with far higher net gain than they could have earned from using the water, so they too increase their ability to remain viable. Thus, water trading reallocates water from less to more efficient and productive farmers and thus increases net return per unit of water (Bjornlund, 2007, 2008).

Full-cost recovery prices send signals to low-value and inefficient producers that they are not profitable irrigators. Water markets have helped these irrigators to manage their exit from irrigation; they have had the option either to sell their land and water separately, thereby achieving a higher price, or to stay on the farm and within their community by a combination of selling their allocation, off-farm work and dry land farming (Bjornlund, 2004). In this way, unbundling of water entitlements into its components has allowed both the market and the pricing mechanisms to become more efficient. The subse-quent arrival of market intermediaries has helped the process. For example, several electronic water exchanges and brokers are now in operation for both entitlements and allocations, and they serve to make market prices transparent and to facilitate easy identification of buyers and sellers.

Government investment

Though the government had committed a large amount of money to buy water from farmers to meet environmental needs, the initial call for tenders had trouble reaching its objectives. Many irrigators were reluctant to sell their entitlements, either because they perceived them to be an inherent part of their farms, or because they believed that prices would continue to increase (Tisdell and Ward, 2003; Bjornlund, 2003). Furthermore, the increasing demand for 'environmentally acceptable' water risks disrupting 'normal' market operations as the planned rate of purchase far exceeds the current level of willingness to sell. To achieve the current objective of buying 1500Mm^3, the government will have to buy all available water for the next 14 years at the current level of trading. This will put upward pressure on price and restrict supply for traditional buyers (Water Find, 2008), which will, in turn, will impair the market's ability to reduce the socio-economic impact of increasing scarcity within already suffering rural communities.

The government is also planning to invest $5.8 billion in improving irrigation systems to reduce water losses. From an environmental perspective this approach is questionable, unless the saved water results in reductions in the entitlements held by these systems. It is likely that improved system efficiency will result in a net *increase* in water use, and a *decrease* in river flows, as most of these savings are in the form of reduced return-flow or seepage, which both end up as river flow.

Can investment in hard infrastructure be part of the soft path?

Existing infrastructure has been used to help ensure that available water is used in the most efficient and profitable industries. For example, in South Australia irrigators who cannot otherwise be supplied from the River Murray can now use the off-peak capacity of the urban water authority's infrastructure to transport raw water to on-farm storages in vine growing regions. This has facilitated a growth in the wine industry, one of the most profitable agricultural water users. Infrastructure has also been built to convey treated effluent for use in high-value horticulture and viticulture.

The role of urban centres

As urban centres are also required to stay within the consumptive pool, they are now active in the market. Adelaide is particularly dependent on the MDB, with 40–90 per cent of its annual water use supplied from the River Murray. The city of Adelaide has purchased approx 24 Mm^3 of MDB entitlements from the farming sector (Hamstead, 2006). To obtain a permit for a new subdivision in the City of Mildura in Victoria, developers must provide the water authority with sufficient entitlements to supply the new development. Most other towns currently have excess water and are therefore major sellers in the allocation market; in effect, they transfer the seasonally available excess water to the agricultural sector.

As a consequence of the recent drought, severe water restrictions have been in place in most major urban centres, and alternative supply options are being actively pursued. The city of Adelaide recycles 29 per cent of its wastewater (more than double the national average) and uses it for irrigating public areas or for sale to farmers (Marsden Jacob Associates, 2008). Some new subdivisions have introduced onsite reticulation of waste- and storm water and homes designed with dual supply systems that use treated water for garden use and flushing toilets. Most Australian cities have also seen demand management and educational programmes introduced to reduce usage through more efficient fixtures, rainwater tanks, less garden watering, etc. The suggestion has emerged that urban users should be subject to the same market discipline as irrigators (Young et al, 2008).

Conclusions

The last 15 years have seen such significant water reform in Australia that it represents a paradigm shift from supply management to demand management. It is increasingly acknowledged by both government and stakeholders that the emphasis ought to be on managing the people using the water rather than managing the water. The new water planning process has taken a soft path approach by defining the amount of water needed for environmental services before determining how much is left for consumptive use. There is also an acknowledgement that the process is adaptive and that plans are therefore subject to regular reviews that reflect improved knowledge about climate change and environmental needs. The development of water markets is the key strategy allowing water users to stay within the consumptive pool while maximizing economic output from the limited resource. Water prices, emerging water market platforms, water registers and the unbundling of water entitlements are the major elements that enable this strategy to achieve its objectives.

References – England

Bakker, K. (2002) 'From public to private to ... mutual? Restructuring water supply governance in England and Wales', *Geoforum*, vol 34, pp359–374

Bakker, K. (2005) 'Neoliberalizing nature? Market environmentalism in water supply in England and Wales', *Annals of the Association of American Geographers*, vol 95, no 3, pp542–565

Defra (Department for Food, Environment and Rural Affairs) (2008) 'Future Water: The Government's water strategy for England', www.defra.gov.uk/Environment/water/strategy/

Environmental Agency (2001) 'Water resources for the future: A strategy for England and Wales', Environmental Agency, London

Environment Agency (2003) 'Water resources for the future: Annual review 2003', www.environment-agency.gov.uk/default.aspx

Ofwat (Water Services Regulatory Authority) (1999) 'Financial performance and capital investment of the water companies in England and Wales 1997–1998', www.ofwat.gov.uk/aptrix/ofwat/publish.nsf/ Content/1997-98financialperformance-capitalinvestment, accessed 16 October 2008

Ofwat (2008) 'PN 16/08 Ofwat plans water efficiency targets for water companies', www.ofwat.gov.uk/ aptrix/ ofwat/ publish.nsf/ Content/ prs_pn1608_watefftgts, accessed 16 October 2008

Pitt (2008) 'Lessons learned from the 2007 floods', Cabinet Office, UK, http://archive.cabinetoffice.gov.uk/pittreview/thepittreview.html

World Resources Institute (WRI) (2008) 'EarthTrends: Actual renewable water resources: Per capita, http://earthtrends.wri.org/ searchable_db/ index.php? theme=2&variable_ID =694&action= select_countries, accessed 16 October 2008

References – European Community

Brooks, D. (2005a) 'Beyond greater efficiency: The concept of water soft paths', *Canadian Water Resources Journal*, vol 30, pp83–92

Brooks, D. (2005b) 'Comment on "Using economic instruments for water demand management: Introduction"', *Canadian Water Resources Journal*, vol 30, pp263–264

EC (2000) 'Water Framework Directive (2000/60/EC)', *Official Journal*, OJL 327, pp1–73

EC (2008) 'Economics in water policy: The value of Europe's waters', Water Note 5, http://ec.europa.eu/environment/water/water-framework/pdf/water_note5_economics.pdf

Gleick, P. H. (2000) 'The changing water paradigm: A look at twenty-first century water resources development', *Water International*, 25, pp127–138

Lallana, C., Kriller, W. and Estrella, T. (2001) 'Economic approaches', in EEA (ed) *Sustainable Water Use in Europe*, EEA, Copenhagen

Lant, C. (2004) 'Water resources sustainability: An ecological economics perspective', *Water Resources Uupdate*, pp20–30

Lenz, K. and Scheuer, S. (2001) *EEB Handbook on EU Water Policy under the Water Framework Directive*, European Environmental Bureau (EEB), Brussels

Rogers, P., Bhatia, R. and Huber, A. (1998) *Water as Social and Economic Good: How to Put Principles into Practice*, Global Water Partnership (GWP), Stockholm

Roth, E. (2001) *Water Pricing in the EU – A Review,* European Environmental Bureau (EEB), Brussels

Strosser, P. (2000) *The Economic Elements of the Water Framework Directive: EEB Open Seminar on EU Water Policy under the Water Framework Directive*, European Commission, DG Environment, Brussels

References – Australia

Bjornlund, H. (2003) 'Farmer participation in markets for temporary and permanent water in southeastern Australia', *Agricultural Water Management*, vol 63, no 1, pp57–76

Bjornlund, H. (2004) 'Formal and informal water markets – Drivers of sustainable rural communities?', *Water Resources Research*, vol 40, W09S07

Bjornlund, H. (2006) 'Can water markets assist irrigators managing increased supply risk? Some Australian experiences', *Water International*, vol 31, no 2, pp221–232

Bjornlund, H. (2007) 'Do markets promote more efficient and higher value water use? Tracing evidence over time in an Australian water market', in C. A. Brebbia and A. G. Kungolos (eds) *Water Resources Management*, WIT Press, Southampton, UK, pp477–488

Bjornlund, H. (2008) 'Markets for water allocations: Outcomes and impacts', *Proceedings from the International Conference*, Water Down Under, Adelaide, Australia

Bjornlund, H. and Rossini, P. (2008) 'Are the fundamentals emerging for more sophisticated water market instruments?', *Proceedings from the 14th Annual Conference of the Pacific Rim Real Estate Society*, Kuala Lumpur, Malaysia, www.prres.net

Brandes, O. M. and Brooks, D. B. (2007) *The Soft Path for Water in a Nutshell*, Friends of the Earth, Canada, Ottawa, ON, and POLIS Project on Ecological Governance, University of Victoria, Victoria, BC

CoAG, Council of Australian Governments (1994) 'Communiqué', meeting of CoAG in Hobart, 25 February

CoAG, Council of Australian Governments (2004) 'Communiqué', meeting of CoAG in Canberra, 25 June

CSIRO (2008) *Water Availability in the Murray*, www.csiro.au/files/files/pllx.pdf, accessed 17 September 2008

Davidson, B. R. (1969) *Australia Wet or Dry*, Melbourne University Press, Melbourne, Australia

Davidson, B. R. (1988) 'Historical aspects of irrigation, agriculture and river regulation in the Murray-Darling Basin, Australia', *Regulated Rivers*, vol 2, pp131–140

Hamstead, M. (2006) 'Using agricultural water for urban growth in Australia: Opportunities, issues', Proceedings from the 9th International River Symposium, Brisbane, Australia, www.riversymposium.com/

Kuehne, G. and Bjornlund, H. (2006) 'Frustration, confusion and uncertainty: Qualitative responses from Namoi Valley irrigators', *Water*, vol 33, no 3, pp78–82

Kuehne, G. and Bjornlund, H. (2007) 'One size does not fit all: Recognizing heterogeneity in Australian farmers', Proceeding from the Conference of the US Commission on Irrigation and Drainage, Sacramento, CA

Kuehne, G., Bjornlund, H. and Cheers, B. (2008) 'Identifying common traits among Australia irrigators using cluster analysis', *Water Science and Technology*, vol 58, no 3

Marsden Jacob Associates (2008) *National Snapshot of Current and Planned Water Recycling and Reuse Rates*, Marsden Jacob Associates, Melbourne

MDBMC, Murray-Darling Basin Ministerial Council (1995) *An Audit of Water Use in the Murray-Darling Basin. Water Use and Healthy Rivers – Working Toward a Balance*, MDBMC, Canberra

MDBMC, Murray-Darling Basin Ministerial Council (1996) *Setting the Cap. Report of the Independent Audit Group*, MDBMC, Canberra

MDBMC, Murray-Darling Basin Ministerial Council (2002) 'The Living Murray. A discussion paper on restoring the health of the River Murray', MDBMC, Canberra

Tisdell, J. G. and Ward, J. R. (2003) 'Attitudes toward water markets: An Australian case study', *Society and Natural Resources*, vol 16, pp61–75

Young, M., McColl, J. and Fisher, T. (2008) 'Urban water pricing: How might an urban water trading scheme work?', *Droplet*, vol 5, University of Adelaide, Adelaide

Water Find (2008) 'Water Find analysis of the Federal Government buy back', http://waterfind.com.au

17
Water Soft Path Thinking in Developing Countries

Let the rain kiss you.
Let the rain beat upon your head with silver liquid drops.
Let the rain sing you a lullaby.

Langston Hughes

Editor's Note: Most developing countries are trying to cope with a set of inter-related, and, one might say, synergistic challenges: rising populations, expectations of economic growth and new technologies, as well as ongoing problems of inadequate water supplies and poor quality water that is inequitably distributed to people living in cities and working on farms and in factories. Though seemingly behind in the application of water soft path approaches to today's problems, in many instances, traditional practices, with an emphasis on participation in decision-making, equity in distribution and ecological protection, foreshadow what would today be sound soft path practice. Three developing countries or regions are surveyed in this chapter: South Africa with its difficult mix of a highly developed sector that resembles the economies surveyed in Chapter 16 and a grossly underdeveloped sector; India with one of the world's fastest growing economies yet also with one of the largest populations of largely rural poor people; and the Middle East and North Africa which is, by almost any measure, the most water-short region of the world.

In principle, water soft paths are equally applicable to developing as to industrialized countries. However, the situation is very different in practice, and largely because of great differences in governance. The gap between policy development and practical application is much wider in developing countries, and the number and effectiveness of safety nets to alleviate problems among those adversely affected by change are less effective, if they are in place at all. Moreover, with large numbers of people depending on water for their liveli-hoods, simplistic application of what may appear to be cost-effective shifts of water can be the wrong strategy. The value of water in industrial uses may be greater than that in subsistence farming, but losses may still be greater than gains if farm families are thereby forced into already overcrowded and under-serviced cities. Such observations do not mean that soft paths have no role to play in developing countries, only that their application must be evaluated in a much more nuanced manner than is the case in industrialized countries. D.B.B.

Part A: South Africa

Inga Jacobs and Anthony Turton

Southern Africa is characterized by three facts. First, it contains at least 15 international river basins, which results in hydrologic linkages across political borders (Turton, 2008a). Second, the four most economically developed southern African states – South Africa, Botswana, Namibia and Zimbabwe – are all water scarce and are fast approaching the limits of their readily available water resources (Turton, 2008a). Third, a spatial development pattern exists where several large cities or centres of economic development (such as Johannesburg, Pretoria, Harare, Bulawayo, Francistown, Gaborone and Windhoek) are located not on rivers, lakes or seafronts but on watershed divides (Turton, 2008b; Turton et al, 2008; Oberholster and Ashton, 2008). This translates into a dependency on water that has to be pumped uphill and, subsequently, into sewage return flows as these rivers are additionally burdened with transporting waste material, most of which enters downstream water storage reservoirs (Oberholster and Ashton, 2008).

These and other regional characteristics pose several challenges and opportunities for South Africa, which shares six of its river basins (Incomati, Limpopo, Orange-Senqu, Thukela, Maputu and Umbeluzi) with six neighbouring countries (Botswana, Lesotho, Mozambique, Namibia, Swaziland and Zimbabwe). Four of these river basins (Incomati, Maputo, Orange-Senqu and Limpopo) sustain the economic heartland of South Africa where a large proportion of South Africa's population and its industrial, mining, power generation and agricultural activities are located. These basins are approaching 'closure' (Ashton and Turton, 2008) as all utilizable water has been allocated to current users. Even now the water storage and supply infrastructure that has been developed in the South African segments of the shared river basins is insufficient to meet all of the existing demands for water. Not surprisingly, the current solution is to extend the supply management approach through dam construction and inter-basin transfers. Though this approach may offer short- and medium-term solutions for those in the formal water economy, it will place further stress on the country's already stressed water resources (Ashton et al, 2008). Coming up with water soft path approaches therefore becomes increasingly important as the implementation of effective management strategies by institutions already in place proves to be more and more challenging.

Current infrastructure not meeting current needs

South Africa has outgrown the capacity of its existing infrastructure due to:

- *Influx of people and population growth*: Current estimates suggest that there are between 3 and 5 million 'illegal' immigrants living in South Africa (STATS-SA, 2007). Because these individuals have mostly subsistence lifestyles, they seldom exert additional demand on the water used in formal sectors. However, access to effective sanitation and waste disposal is minimal, so many of their activities have adverse impacts on the quality of localized water (Ashton et al, 2008). Moreover, the South African segments of the four river basins contain approximately 24.5 million people or 55 per cent of the national population (year 2000 data). Low growth estimates project a 32 per cent increase and high growth estimates, a 73 per cent increase in population size by 2025 (DWAF, 2003a–2003k; STATS-SA, 2007). Nearly three-fifths of the population living in these basins is urbanized and just over two-fifths live in scattered rural communities, in areas that formed part of the former Apartheid homelands (Turton et al, 2006). If economic development and environmental justice continue to grow at today's rates, both urban and rural populations will place increasing pressure on already limited supplies of water.
- *Non-maintenance of sewage and treatment works leads to reduced capacity to dilute effluent naturally*: A survey conducted by the Council for Scientific and Industrial Research revealed that, though wastewater treatment plants in some regions, such as Gauteng, operate successfully, many other wastewater treatment plants do not meet effluent standards and some do not even measure effluent quality (Wall, 2005). This results in high levels of eutrophication with microsystin-producing cyanobacteria emerging in most of the major dams (Oberholster and Ashton, 2008). Moreover, reticulation systems are not being maintained, which results in unnecessary wastage. For example, night flow (the off-peak in-flow of unused water into sewage treatment works) is a serious concern for water managers because the higher the proportion of night flow, the greater the number of leaking toilets, missing taps, etc. in the reticulation system. Some areas in South Africa have recorded night flow rates at up to 70–80 per cent of peak in-flow (McKenzie et al, 2004).
- *Skills flight, loss of corporate memory, and inadequate retraining*: The loss of intellectual assets is a major threat to effective water demand management, particularly in water-scarce countries such as South Africa where the onus is on the scientific community to find technological solutions (Turton, 2008b; Walwyn and Scholes, 2006). There has been a large skills flight from South Africa in recent years as a result of increased crime, lack of confidence in the government and little or no career path opportunities. The repercussions for the water sector include high staff turnover, the loss of skills and institutional memory as experienced staff depart, appointment

of non-technical personnel to management positions requiring technical experience, as well as the absence of well structured educational and training programmes suitably targeted to all stakeholders in the water management chain (Mwendera et al, 2003; Gumbo and Van der Zaag, 2002). These factors affect institutional effectiveness, as they require major efforts to relearn and rebuild trusting relationships.

Implementation is the problem, not *institutions*

Despite the above-mentioned infrastructural dilemmas, South Africa's political transformation, formalized by the country's first democratic elections in 1994 brought with it a host of progressive reforms in the water sector.

The Water Services Act was ratified in 1997 and the landmark National Water Act in 1998 (Republic of South Africa, 1998). The National Water Act prioritizes common property aspects of water; separates ownership of land from ownership of water; confirms the need to ensure that aquatic ecosystems receive sufficient water to function properly; stipulates the need to ensure that neighbouring states utilize shared water resources equitably; and prioritizes the right of all South Africans to have adequate access to wholesome supplies of water (DWAF, 1997). It is regarded, along with the EU Water Framework Directive (EU, 2000), as a pioneer of an international wave of reform and one of the most innovative and far-reaching water laws in the world, which has set the benchmark for new ways of managing water resources (Woodhouse, 2008; Ashton et al, 2008; Postel and Richter, 2003).

However, the necessary goal of redressing past racial and gender inequality means that South Africa's water reform is expected to deliver on changes in process (holistic, decentralized, participatory and economically cost effective) and social outcomes (Woodhouse, 2008), as well as ensuring higher environmental standards as stipulated in the 1998 National Water Act. According to Philip Woodhouse, 'The prospect of redistribution from existing "haves" to "'have nots" raises considerably the political risks and expectations attached to the implementation of reform' (Woodhouse, 2008, p3). The challenge in reconciling process and social outcomes plays itself out in recent xenophobic and other violent attacks. Most of the causes cited for these outbreaks include poor service delivery (particularly of clean water and sanitation), poor governance and a lack of capacity at the local level (Johnston and Bernstein, 2007), which, compounded with an influx of foreigners from neighbouring African countries, has resulted in localized hotspots for conflict.

Institutional reform

In line with the reforms of the 1990s, and an attempt to promote social efficiency between alternative and competing demands, 19 water management areas (WMAs) were established, each with its own Catchment Management Agency (CMA) (Republic of South Africa, 1998), though ultimate responsibility for shared river basins remains with central government. Water user associations (WUAs) were also established at a subsidiary level to CMAs to promote further devolution of water management. The core responsibilities of the CMAs are (1) to investigate and advise on the protection, use, development, conservation, management and control of water resources in its WMA; (2) to develop a catchment management strategy; and (3) to coordinate the related activities of water management institutions within a particular WMA, that is to provide scope for greater public participation (Republic of South Africa, 1998; Woodhouse, 2008; Turton et al, 2003). Each CMA was to be financed through management charges payable by all water users in the catchments. Unfortunately, the majority of CMAs are not yet fully functional, and as a result, the intended benefits not yet realized.

Emerging dynamics of reform

The Inkomati WMA situated in the north-eastern part of South Africa in the Mpumalanga and Limpopo Provinces and bordering Mozambique (in the east) and Swaziland (in the south-east) provides an excellent example of the burgeoning problems associated with these early transitions to CMA management. Largely attributable to its major topographical feature – the Great Escarpment – this WMA is marked with a highly varied climate, from temperate Highveld in the west to subtropical in the eastern Lowveld. The mean annual rainfall ranges from 400mm to 1000mm over most of the WMA, reaching close to 1500mm in the mountainous areas along the escarpment. Very significantly, the irrigation sector is the biggest water user in the region, using 57–62 per cent (with some estimates at 70 per cent) of the available water (DWAF, 2004b; Woodhouse, 2008).

Efforts to manage the existing water supply have to overcome two significant constraints:

1   A lack of precise and compatible information exists as to the actual amount of water used by commercial agriculture and, as such, there is little clarification of water availability to farmers (Turton et al, 2003; Woodhouse, 2008). The information that does exist is guarded by certain irrigation boards and individual farm operators, which creates an asymmetry of information, favouring existing water users over emerging users such as residents in ex-homeland areas who seek water for agricultural or domestic use (Woodhouse, 2008).
2   Emerging farmers remain concerned about dependency and the continued dominance of white commercial farmers, who still constitute the majority of members on the Irrigation Board. This problem of limited stakeholder involvement is compounded by existing finance structures that rely on member levies, which smaller farmers can ill afford (Turton et al, 2003).

In an attempt to combat these and other effects resulting from the lack of information and insufficient voice for emerging farmers, the DWAF are in the process of undertaking compulsory licensing of all water use. The purpose of this initiative is to make water available to previously disadvantaged people who need it either for domestic or small-scale agricultural use, by reducing the amount of water which commercial agricultural operators are licensed to use (Woodhouse, 2008). This reallocation is, however, likely to be negatively affected by the fact that land and water governance in ex-homeland areas is still formally under tribal authority. Since authorization for individuals to use water will not involve individual licences but rather 'general authorization' applicable to a defined area, access to water, and therefore power, will still be in the hands of local chiefs and not decentralized to the individual level (Woodhouse, 2008).

Steps toward Integrated Water Resources Management (IWRM) and its challenges

The National Water Act recognizes the hydrological cycle in its entirety and the need to manage water as a single resource, thereby promoting the philosophy of IWRM and encouraging all stakeholder participation in decision-making processes (Ashton, 2007; Ashton et al, 2008). Ideally, this process should mobilize communities by enabling them to participate in processes that affect their lives and livelihoods. However, because the rural sector is the least influential in governmental processes, merely having the opportunity does not necessarily translate into tangible influence in water allocation (Ashton et al, 2008).

Free basic water and its challenges

Although there was a strong commitment to develop community-based, demand-driven institutional frameworks after the publication of the 1994 White Paper on Community Water Supply and Sanitation – which provided the first 'political mandate' to supply domestic water supply to households – it has not been without challenges (Turton et al, 2003).

From 1994, the Department of Water Affairs and Forestry took over the custodianship of water and sanitation services in the former black homeland areas, a former responsibility of the rural service council (RSC). The provision of free basic water to rural communities particularly became a strong political slogan in late 2000 (Turton et al, 2003) after water as a basic human right was enshrined in the South African Constitution (Republic of South Africa, 1996). The DWAF therefore committed itself to providing every household with 6000 litres of free water per month (DWAF, 2001). Achieving this has been an incremental process and local governments have been tasked with the responsibility of deciding if free basic water would be made available only to the poor, and how the poor would be defined and identified, or if it would be granted to all water users. The financing of this policy has been coordinated through subsidies from the national government from the 'equitable share' automatic transfers, through cross-subsidies from other users, or local taxes. As of March 2009, the DWAF's water sector information system reported that 41,968,683 people (approximately 85 per cent of the total population) were served with free basic water of 6kL per capita per month.

Other challenges include monitoring water consumption, and ensuring that those who consume more than the basic volume pay for any additional usage (Turton et al, 2003). This requires effective metering systems, billing and credit control systems. This is no easy feat, particularly in areas where water is provided by public standpipes (outside yard taps), making metering expensive compared to the relatively small income that can be accrued from this kind of service (Turton et al, 2003). The installation of water prepayment metering systems in disadvantaged communities has received considerable public opposition, as the constitutionality of these and other water privatization mechanisms (which are seen as contrary to free basic water commitments) have been put into question. In December 2007, the Johannesburg High Court heard one such application by residents of Phiri, Soweto, and supported by a local NGO, Coalition Against Water Privatisation (CAWP), challenging the lawfulness of prepayment meters and the sufficiency of the free basic water allocation to poor residents (Gowlland-Gualtieri, 2007). According to the residents of Phiri, everyone in the community had previously received an unlimited amount of water for which a flat-rate was charged, but with the imposition of the prepayment meters, their water supplies can be automatically disconnected when they cannot afford water credit (Gowlland-Gualtieri, 2007). Furthermore, since the per household free basic water allocation cannot sustain the large households prevalent in poorer communities (of 8 or more people on average resulting in less than the allocated 25L per person per day), these communities are often without water once their free basic allocation has been used.

Recognizing ecological demands

Despite these and other challenges to South Africa's water reform, positive results are also evident. One such outcome is the institutional awareness of the necessity to maintain the ecological reserve in order to preserve the ecological health of the environment. According to the DWAF National Water Resource Strategy, the current provisional ecological reserves are on average roughly 20 per cent of total river flow, but range between 12 and 30 per cent, depending on the ecological needs of each catchment and riverine environment (DWAF, 2004a). The translation of institutional awareness into compliance and recognition is more challenging. The ecological reserve has been subject to severe debate in South Africa with much of the discussion focused around the law's requirement for allocating water to aquatic ecosystems in a country where demands on water are high and where, in many instances, rights of use of available water have already been allocated, confounding attempts to reallocate water for development among marginalized groups (Van Wyk et al, 2006).

Backcasting our way back to the present

Institutional reform in South Africa's water sector has been progressive and provides a sound legislative model for the southern African region. However, implementation of policies remains one of the country's greatest challenges to ensure that both past inequalities are addressed and practical outcomes for economic development are achieved. Education and training are critical for improving the capacity of people to effectively participate in decision-making processes. Meeting the capacity building challenges of integrated water resources management in South Africa requires sustainable skills transfer policies in all institutional tiers. Institutional awareness of the need to maintain the ecological reserve needs to be translated into sound practices and policies that enforce this. Perhaps most importantly, water soft path approaches require not only an institutional mindset change, but also a change in public perceptions around water. Everyone needs to know the destination before we can plan for our holiday.

Part B: India

Re-forming water, transforming women: Towards a water soft path in India

Sara Ahmed

Introduction

Water is a state subject in India; that is, while the Union or Central government in India's federal structure provides guidelines on how water resources should be developed and managed, individual state governments determine their own priorities for water allocation among competing sectors (Iyer, 2007). In 1999, as part of the global Vision 21 process,[1] civil society, research institutes and water bureaucracies in the western state of Gujarat in India came together to articulate their vision for water – the Gujarat Jal-Disha[2] – where access to safe water, sanitation facilities and improved hygiene practices would be available to all citizens, irrespective of caste, creed or gender. At its core, Gujarat's Vision 2010 reiterated the belief that decentralized water management needs to be based on principles of equity, environmental integrity, sustainable and appropriate technological options and good governance. For the first time, civil society in India sought to counter the overarching paradigm of water sector reforms in India, initiated by the state in line with the global discourse, that water is a scarce resource and needs to be 'valued'. That is, cost recovery from users in a demand responsive framework, facilitated by the state in partnership with NGOs and/or the private sector, would be the new mantra underlying decentralized water management, a significant policy shift from centralized water supply. Vision 2010 acknowledged the need for efficiency in water management, but called for equity in water allocations and empowerment of citizens, particularly women and marginalized groups, through informed participation in the new community institutions that were being created under decentralization.

In many ways, this vision statement reiterated some of the principles underlying a *water soft path*, particularly the need for multi-disciplinary approaches which respect water as a service rather than an end, and which were based on stakeholder consultation where ecological sustainability was fundamental to all economic, political and socio-cultural choices (Brandes and Brooks, 2007, p12). However, the complexities of planning in an institutional vacuum, coupled with poverty, the increasingly visible impacts of climate variability and growing competition over water (all of which are typically embedded in larger societal conflicts), mean that implementation of a water soft path in the context of Gujarat, India, or indeed much of South Asia, would be a challenging, less trodden, path.

As India globalizes and opens its markets, the urban landscape is rapidly changing. Glitzy, air-conditioned malls are appearing as well as supermarkets selling imported vegetables and fruit, that are replacing local grocers, as well as raising questions about how we account for our water footprints (virtual water). Multi-storey residential blocks are being built with little attention being paid to water reuse, recharging or conservation, despite recent urban policies calling for water harvesting as part of any new residential or institutional construction. Meanwhile, for most urban and rural poor, access to potable water and sanitation remains, ironically, a distant dream. And, numerous efforts by NGOs and grassroots groups across the country, to address growing inequalities through thinking innovatively about alternative water supply and conservation systems, remain pilots or isolated islands of 'best practices'.

What, then, are the challenges in India of thinking differently about water and moving towards a water soft path? Drawing on insights from a research project on the decentralization of water management and gender rights in Gujarat, this chapter looks at the challenge of facilitating participation, particularly by poor women and marginalized groups in the new water commons.[3] Do women representatives on village water committees articulate an alternative, more gender-just, socially inclusive and sustainable water order, or is their participation merely token? Has participation in water governance been a transformatory process for water users or has the state merely co-opted civil society in its project of liberalizing and commodifying water?

Why is gender a water issue?

> *Gender mainstreaming in water management is the process of assessing the implications for women and men of any planned action, including legislation, policies or programmes, in all water sectors and at all levels (global, national, organizational, commu-*

nity, household). It is a strategy for making women's as well as men's concerns, experiences and priorities around water an integral dimension of the design, implementation, monitoring and evaluation of policies and programmes in all political, economic and societal spheres so that women and men from diverse social and economic groups benefit equally, and inequality is not perpetuated. The ultimate goal is to achieve gender equality by transforming the mainstream, that is, policies, procedures and institutional practice. (GWA, 2003, adapted)

The universal symbolism of water as the primal fluid – purifying, regenerating, creating and destroying – is closely intertwined in different cultures with women's roles as bearers and nurturers of life, as collectors and managers of household water, and as responsible for sanitation and hygiene (Ahmed, 2005). The Dublin Principles (Solanes and Gonzalez-Villareal, 1999), enunciated as part of a review of the UN International Decade on Water and Sanitation (1980–1990), maintained that 'women play a central part in the provision, management and safeguarding of water' but that this pivotal role of theirs has 'seldom been reflected in institutional arrangements for the development and management of water resources'. It further called for 'positive policies to address women's specific needs and to equip and empower women to participate at all levels in water resources programmes, including decision-making and implementation, in ways defined by them' (WEDO, 2003, p14).

While policy-makers and the water supply sector have increasingly sought to involve women in domestic water management, the institutionalization of participation through quotas for women on water committees (ranging from 30 to 50 per cent of seats) has largely overlooked the intersection of gender with other social stratifiers that constrain women from articulating voice. The roles of women – and men – and their rights to water, are shaped by numerous factors including, caste, class, faith, age and physical ability. Deeply embedded gender inequalities in terms of access to education, economic opportunities or control over resources such as land, place poor, marginalized women in India at multiple levels of disadvantage, discrimination and exploitation vis-à-vis men even within the same socio-economic category. Water supply interventions have the potential to improve the lives of poor women and men, but these are often based on assumptions of what women need – safe, accessible water – rather than *also* what women want – sharing of domestic responsibilities around water and the care economy – thus, reinforcing gender inequities in access to water and decision-making on water governance.

Gujarat: The institutional terrain

Over 77 per cent of the total drinking water requirement for Gujarat is met from groundwater sources, but these have been extensively exploited since independence by enterprising farmers encouraged by the Green Revolution strategy of intensive agriculture (Dubash, 2002; Shah, 1993). In addition, saline intrusion in several low-lying, coastal regions of the state has affected the quality of drinking water, forcing rural poor women to walk longer distances to fetch water, particularly during the summer. However, in many upper caste households it is men who collect water because of the practice of *purdah* or female seclusion that restricts their mobility in the public domain. But, unlike women who head-load water up to 25kg at a time, men have access to bicycles, motorcycles, tractors or bullock carts to transport water.

While the provision of drinking water has traditionally been the responsibility of the Gujarat Water Supply and Sewerage Board (GWSSB), the Ghogha Rural Water Supply project launched in the late 1990s marked the beginning of the shift towards sector reforms. Implemented by the GWSSB under the Indo-Dutch bilateral aid programme, the Ghogha project sought to build local institutional capacities to manage community piped water supply systems based on local sources in 81 villages and Ghogha, an old port town, in Bhavnagar district. Three NGOs were enlisted as Implementing Support Agencies to facilitate village water committees or *pani samitis*. Their role would be to support capacity building on technical and financial aspects of water management with women making up one-third of the committee members. Water users were expected to contribute 10 per cent of capital costs as well as full operations and maintenance (O&M) costs by means of water tariffs levied by *pani samitis*.

However, *re-engineering* water engineers to think about and work with communities proved to be a significant challenge and progress was slow until the quasi-autonomous Water and Sanitation Management Organisation (WASMO) was formed in 2002. WASMO was designed as a *learning* organization to facilitate the critical software, that is, partnerships between the state (district level community mobilization units of engineers and sector specialists), NGOs and village *pani samitis*. WASMO is now engaged with some 30 NGOs in the Earthquake Reconstruction and Rehabilitation (ERR) project in 1260 villages affected by the devastating Kutch earthquake of 2001. In addition, it is spearheading other sector reform projects as well as collaborative partnerships with networks such as Pravah (which means 'flow' in Hindi). Formed in the mid-1990s to promote informed advocacy on the right to water and sanitation through campaigns, and knowledge dissemination, Pravah has recently tried to demonstrate, through pilot rural water and sanitation projects implemented by members, what gender-just, equitable and sustainable water alternatives would entail in practice. However, these projects have also been framed under the same principles of cost efficiency, namely, community contributions to capital and O&M costs.

Interrogating decentralization: Gender and participation

In India it is estimated that the national costs of women fetching water is 150 million woman work days per year, equivalent to a

> *national loss of income of 10 billion rupees, approximately US$208 million.* (WASMO, 2007, p1)

According to WASMO, women's participation in village *pani samitis* is more than meeting the statutory objective of one-third membership: 'Women have the right to ask for (safe) water at their doorstep: WASMO hopes that by 2010 75 per cent of the villages in Gujarat and women in these villages will have access to safe water at their doorstep' (WASMO Project Director, interview, Gandhinagar, June 2008). So who are the women who participate, and what do they do? As part of our research project we conducted in-depth interviews with 68 women *pani samiti* members from 13 villages spread over six diverse agro-ecological districts in Gujarat. The villages were selected in consultation with NGO partners to meet a number of different criteria including population diversity and strong women's participation. Eight of the villages fell under the WASMO Ghogha and ERR projects, while five villages had NGO-facilitated decentralized alternatives, three of which were part of the Pravah demonstration pilots. Our research team included NGO field staff who helped us facilitate focus group discussions with both women and men on *pani samitis* and undertake village transects to look at water distributional issues (equity, sustainability) and talk to non-members on their perceptions of village water governance.

The majority of women *pani samiti* members in our sample are married (82 per cent), fall in the age group of 30–45 years (75 per cent) and have not had any formal schooling (66 per cent). Married and older women have a higher degree of mobility in the social domain and more time as they are past their child-bearing and nurturing years; they are also not necessarily water carriers. Prior institutional experience is the most significant factor in determining *which* women are selected; having time and leadership skills, being articulate, willing and able to work effectively are also important determinants. In terms of their diversity, at least 40 per cent of the women members come from marginalized caste and tribal categories, while some 37 per cent are from households below the (income) poverty line; that is, earning less than $1–2/day.

For most women, attending *pani samiti* meetings is seen as their primary responsibility, but many are not able to do so because of the timing and location of meetings, or their workload. Others deliberately choose *not* to attend, as they find meetings a waste of time with little opportunity or support for them to speak, given prevailing socio-cultural norms of 'appropriate female behaviour'. Upper caste women are often prevented from attending meetings by their husbands because of the strong norms regarding female seclusion that govern their mobility in the public domain. In villages where there has been a past history of women's mobilization, women use other strategies for articulating their concerns – sometimes key issues are discussed in women-only spaces (eg, self-help groups for savings and micro-credit loans) and a 'representative', typically an older, experienced woman, is appointed to speak on their behalf.

Apart from meetings, women are responsible for monitoring the construction of village water works, ensuring that the area around water infrastructure is kept clean, resolving conflicts over siting of community water distribution points and collecting financial contributions. Interestingly, these roles are seen to extend women's unpaid work beyond the household arena as well as defining them as *natural* environmental caretakers who are *accustomed* to doing voluntary work and generally more honest than men (Rocheleau et al, 1996).

For some women, like Shivuben ('ben' is the colloquial for 'sister' in Gujarati), participation in *pani samitis* has meant new responsibilities:

> *People have started respecting me more now. My extended family members ask me for suggestions for all decisions. Now I can speak up, when required. I can go out for meetings/ trainings. First time I went out alone to Botad* [nearby market town] *for buying raw materials for our water supply project. Now I have an independent identity as 'Shivuben', rather than just a relative of a male family member* (Shivuben, *pani samiti* member, Janada village, Bhavnagar district, Gujarat).

For other women it has brought status and public recognition, as actors and not just victims of water degradation and poverty. Many women are elated at the fact that they can now sit on a chair while in a meeting 'just like educated women from cities like you' (Hansaben, *pani samiti* member, Navagam village, Surendranagar district, Gujarat).

While participation in *pani samitis* has been an empowering process for some women, changes in women's lives, and their access to decision-making both at the household and community level cannot be attributed to these new institutions alone. Much has to do with the role of strong, gender-sensitive NGOs that have been able to link women's participation to larger questions of gender and water rights, for example access to safe water and sanitation not only has implications for health and education (particularly for girls), but is equally important in addressing women's security in conflict and disaster-prone environments. For example, in 2002, after the worst communal riots between Hindus and Muslims that Gujarat has ever witnessed, many Muslim women asked NGOs for independent sources of water and household sanitation as they were being denied access to community wells in predominantly Hindu villages and they were fearful of attacks (rape) against them and their daughters. In contrast, in some villages which I visited as part of a review for CARE of their Gujarat Harmony Project on reconciliation and rehabilitation, Muslim women maintained that they had no community water sources – village ponds or tanks – which could have provided them with valuable space for dialogue with their Hindu sisters (Ahmed, 2004).

Support from men, such as the sharing of household chores, has not changed much, and most of the 'costs' of women's participation (e.g. time spent in attending meetings) continue to be borne by the next generation – their daughters and daughters-in-law who are in effect the *actual* water collectors. In the Darbar (upper caste) dominated Jasapara village, men stated that women's participation in *pani samiti* meetings should not be at the cost of their primary responsibility – looking after their homes: 'We men have to wait for our meals if women go to meetings!' retorted Mohanbhai (*pani samiti* member, focus group discussion, January 2007). And, across all villages, most women continue to collect water and assume responsibility for sanitation, health and hygiene, particularly of children, the elderly and the sick, with little questioning of the growing burden of this unpaid economy in a context where access to primary healthcare, especially for women, is limited.

Engendering water governance: Implications for policy and practice

Decentralization, like democracy, is a *process* and not a destination. Building 'technical' capacity to develop, manage and maintain village water supply is not the same as building the capacity of *pani samitis* to constructively engage in the process of decentralization as citizens and subjects rather than 'objects' of participatory water planning. Political articulation – the degree to which communities of water users, women and men from diverse socio-economic groups, represented through *pani samitis* can influence water policy – is determined by the institutional architecture which facilitates articulation between civil society, the state (polity and bureaucracy) and citizens in a wider democratic context. The impact of water sector reforms and the space for rural women to participate in decentralized institutions, as well as their empowerment, has to be looked at within this larger framework; namely, is decentralization contributing to more efficient, effective, equitable and sustainable water management and governance? However, in asking this question, one needs to be cautious as the good governance agenda, and water is no exception, is often framed in terms of normative principles (accountability, transparency) rather than a more nuanced understanding of how water is embedded in relations of power structured by gender and other social inequalities (Cleaver and Franks, 2005). Decentralization is a process, which needs to be *negotiated*, and the hard reality is that, for poor and marginalized women, negotiation is being contested in an economic environment where policies of privatization, pricing and centralized, technocentric delivery systems dominate the political discourse on water management.

Efficiency, effectiveness and equity in access to water
In terms of efficiency, as defined by short-term cost effectiveness, developing demand-responsive community water works has required tremendous financial and human resources as well as time in rebuilding collective solidarities around water. It is clear that, without the involvement of NGOs in Gujarat, decentralization would not have been able to meet its intended goals. Local *panchayats*

(elected village councils) and *pani samitis* lack managerial and technical capacity or information on appropriate technological innovations – for example, solar panels, which can generate power to pump water, were introduced by Sahjeevan, an NGO in Kutch district. Other alternatives include small-scale, reverse osmosis plants that can be used to provide safe drinking water in coastal villages where saline intrusion has affected water quality.

Problems in the delivery of water (timing), in access (costs), availability and quality persist in many villages, raising questions about the effectiveness of sector reforms. While most rural water users in the villages we surveyed, even diverse women representatives on *pani samitis*, had internalized the dominant discourse on 'valuing' water, that is that all users should pay, there were concerns about the ability of the very poor to pay. In some villages, *pani samitis* had decided – and villagers had agreed – that there should be flexibility in payments of water tariffs and very poor households, typically the landless or those dependent on daily casual labour, should be excluded.

Caste conflicts in some villages persist – for example, in Surendranagar district in Gujarat, *dalit* communities argued that the location of their Cluster Water Storage tanks was determined by the powerful upper castes and the facilitating NGO could do little despite its attempts at bridging differences through multi-stakeholder dialogues.

Accountability and transparency

Accountability and transparency, while important in framing the normative principles underlying good water governance, are difficult to measure. Accountability channels operate at many levels – between the state water bureaucracy and villages, between *pani samitis* and water users, and between NGOs and the state on the one hand, and community institutions, including *pani samitis*, as well as the larger polity, on the other.

In villages where water supply works had been completed, for example the Ghogha project, *pani samiti* meetings are not held regularly and there is little information sharing between members and non-members, beyond mandatory decision-making in *gram sabhas* (village assemblies of all enfranchised adults, often seen as the lowest tier in decentralized governance). And even these are not always well attended, particularly by women and marginalized groups. While there are rules on water use, for example no direct pumping of water from distribution pipelines or water storage tanks, no washing of clothes, utensils or livestock at community drinking water sources such as village ponds or wells – these are often difficult to enforce and fines are limited.

More importantly, however, although village water works are designed to meet the government rural water supply norms of 40 litres per person per day,[4] given the irregularity of water delivery, none of the villages had any rules on how much water a person or household was entitled to. While informal norms about sharing or taking only as much water as you need could work when water is available, water scarcity can again lead to the kind of conflicts that women had to contend with in the past. Although it is difficult to find concrete examples that link women's participation in *pani samitis* to declining corruption or malpractices, perceptions of women's honesty abound: 'If one-third of the members on the water committee are women, it automatically brings the corruption down by one-third so it is essential to provide reservations (quotas) to ensure that women are able to come up in public spheres' (Hansaben, *pani samiti* member, Navagam village, Surendranagar district, Gujarat).

Argued another woman member: 'Men try to figure out where they can make money through cuts in the project allocations while women make sure that the work is done properly' (Prabhaben, Janada village, Bhavnagar district, Gujarat).

Re-forming water, transforming women?

Empowering rural women through water management initiatives requires more than providing access to decision-making or technical training – it needs strategic reflection on the micro discourses of power (Rowland, 1997). This means questioning notions of a 'hegemonic masculinity', understanding how gendered identities are continuously reconstituted by institutional change, and how women themselves perceive their transformatory potential. Empowerment cannot be achieved by separating and isolating women from the complex social relations underlying their myriad and diverse relationships with water, the environment and the larger socio-economic, political and cultural context within which a gendered analysis of decentralized water governance is embedded. And good governance, based on active stakeholder participation, integrated, equitable and gender-just planning, is at the heart of a water soft path that goes beyond the *rhetoric* of demand management to facilitate an enabling environment for water sustainability.

Notes

1 Initiated by the Water Supply and Sanitation Collaborative Council (www.wsscc.org) just before the Second World Water Forum at The Hague (2000), the global Vision 21 process was an intensive effort to bring together diverse voices and priorities to identify collective global, national and regional water agendas.
2 '*Jal*' is one of the many words for water in Hindi commonly used to refer to sacred or pure water while '*disha*' means direction.
3 '*Water Rights as Women's Rights? Assessing the scope of women's empowerment through decentralised water governance in Maharashtra and Gujarat, India,*' a two-year research project (2006–08) undertaken by SOPPECOM (Society for Promoting Participative Eco-system Management, Pune), Utthan (Gujarat) and TISS (Tata Institute of Social Studies, Mumbai) and supported by the IDRC (the International Development Research Centre, Ottawa).
4 These norms are being revised to 50LCD in line with global standards for daily water provision to meet personal needs.

Part C: Middle East and North Africa (MENA)

David B. Brooks

The World Bank's 'flagship' development report on water shows that nations in the Middle East and North Africa (MENA) already withdraw nearly 80 per cent of their renewable freshwater resources (World Bank, 2007). Next closest is South Asia, which withdraws less than 30 per cent. Half of MENA nations withdraw more than 100 per cent, which means they are 'mining' nonrenewable water (UNDP, 2006; Elhadj, 2008). Per capita renewable fresh water fell from 4000m^3 per year in 1950 to 1100 today, and it is still falling. Moreover, poverty is endemic to the region. The Human Development Index for the Arab States shows that most rank between 100th and 150th place in the list of 177 countries (UNDP, 2006). Clearly, this situation is neither physically nor socially sustainable.

Institutions as part of the problem

Water scarcity is chronic in MENA, but physical scarcity can be mitigated by institutions that are capable of implementing effective management strategies (Wolfe and Brooks, 2003). To quote from the Human Development Report (UNDP, 2006, p3):

> *There is more than enough water in the world for domestic purposes, for agriculture and for industry ... scarcity is manufactured through political processes and institutions that disadvantage the poor.*

Though appropriate political processes and institutions are not common in MENA, there are signs that they are beginning to change in ways that seem likely to improve the situation (Brooks et al, 2007). Notably, they have begun turning their attention from technical and engineering methods of coping with chronic water shortages to political and managerial strategies. Demand management is receiving more attention than it ever has before, and there are steps toward decentralization and wider stakeholder involvement. Water soft paths are still far in the future, but those are the kinds of reforms that would be essential first steps if soft paths are ever to take hold.

Institutional design

National water agencies in MENA are, for the most part, oriented to large-scale, capital-intensive supply systems for urban water supply and for commercial irrigation – a top-down 'masculine' approach (Zwarteveen, 2008) that goes back to ancient Sumer and that has, until recently, worked passably well. However, as watersheds come to be fully allocated, as costs of additional supply continue to mount, and as demands for water become more diversified, its deficiencies become evident.

Agriculture requires special attention partly because it dominates water use across the region, and partly because institutional reform is slower in rural areas. In cities, institutional change affects a critical but small portion of people's lives and incomes. (Exceptions include people engaged in urban agriculture and local water-dependent industry, such as brewing.) Land use decisions can be separated from water use decisions, and there is a demonstrated willingness in urban areas to pay for better water services. As a result, one can more easily adopt conventional economic advice about pricing and allocation.

None of these characteristics applies nearly so well outside the city. In rural areas, water availability and livelihoods are almost the same thing, so land use decisions must be coupled with water use decisions. Institutional change for water must therefore be introduced cautiously in rural areas, with parallel attention to agricultural policy and explicit attention to rural poverty (Brooks and Wolfe, 2007; de Châtel, 2007).

Urban water use and institutions

Despite their low ranking on the overall Human Development Index, MENA nations do reasonably well in providing drinking water services. Even in the poorest nations, two-thirds of the population had 'sustainable access to improved water sources' in 2004 (UNDP, 2006, Table 7), and many nations had between 90 and 100 per cent coverage. The availability of 'sustainable access to improved sanitation' is more limited. Only Algeria, Israel, Jordan, Lebanon, Libya and Syria, plus the oil-rich states, have rates above 90 per cent, and many MENA nations have rates below 50 per cent.

Urban water utilities are typically either quasi-independent agencies or part of an urban affairs ministry. In either case, they seek to provide a basic level of service for all residents regardless of ability to pay, while treating water as an economic good for richer people and for commercial and industrial clients. The main problem is less an inability or unwillingness to pay than irregular delivery and poor quality of water, which creates a vicious circle of non-payment of bills and thus even worse service. Equally problematic, few urban water delivery agencies consider water conservation by consumers as any part of their responsibility; concern stops once the water leaves their mains. In few MENA nations is there a specific agency with a mandate to deliver water demand management, and in none does such an agency rate highly in budget or bureaucratic standing (Brooks et al, 2007; Brooks and Wolfe, 2007).

Rural water use and institutions

The starting point for rural water institutions is not so much the economic value of water as the national plans for agriculture and rural development. If, as in Israel, it is accepted that export agriculture will no longer lead rural development, options for water use are much wider than if agriculture is seen as a critical source of foreign exchange. In either case, the agencies in charge of irrigation water are typically broadly oriented and powerful enough to dominate the agricultural sector, and they commonly provide extension services with an emphasis on water use and efficiency.

Despite the dominance of irrigation as a use for water, three-quarters of all farmland in Arab nations depends exclusively on rain (UNDP, 2006, p177). Productivity on rain-fed farms is far below that for irrigated farms, but they offer great potential for improvement, which in turn has potential for alleviating poverty. A roughly proportionate reduction in rural poverty can be demonstrated to occur with every increase in agricultural-water productivity (Thirtle et al, 2002). With a higher proportion of women working in rain-fed rather than in irrigated agriculture (Institute for Agriculture and Trade Policy, 2007), women's poverty can be alleviated with the same increase.

Other institutional reforms

Some forms of decentralized management are beginning to appear in MENA. Algeria and Morocco have built river basin agencies. Lebanon, Tunisia and Yemen have decentralized water management to sub-national administrative units (World Bank, 2007). In addition, in most of these countries, traditional forms of clan or family control still exist over specific wells or springs, and they typically follow unwritten rules for distributing water with reasonable equity and efficiency (Trottier, 1999; de Châtel, 2007).

Steps toward improved water resources management

One happy result of the centralized management of water in MENA is a new focus on those strategic issues for which clear directions and management are most necessary. This shift typically involves the creation of a water planning document that looks 20 or 30 years into the future and that is cast within the framework of integrated water resources management and, within that framework, explicit programming for water demand management. The process is most evident in Egypt, Israel, Jordan, Lebanon, Morocco and Tunisia. The experience of Morocco is encouraging. According to Doukali (2005, p87):

> *The reform experience of Morocco suggests that although undertaking initial reform can be difficult, subsequent reforms are relatively easier as the country consolidates and adjusts with the earlier reforms.*

Of course, barriers to implementation of institutional reform remain strong. Though water agencies may now be mandated to work with other ministries and to incorporate environmental considerations, they are largely staffed by the same people who have spent their careers focusing on supply management.

It is hardly likely that they will promote demand-side approaches, local management and environmental protection with enthusiasm (Brooks et al, 2007; de Châtel, 2007).

Water users' associations

Water management in MENA has always had both centralized and decentralized components. However, the latter were neglected after the Second World War when governments and donor agencies concluded that modern irrigation was just too complex for peasant farmers. Subsequently, with the failures of top-down management to achieve its objectives, the same agencies rediscovered the benefits of local water management. The most common adjustment was the creation of Water Users' Associations (WUAs) to enable farmers to participate in the operations and maintenance of local irrigation systems (Attia, 2003; Salman et al, 2008).

Water use productivity typically increases by 30–50 per cent in areas where WUAs have been organized, and energy used for pumping is cut by half or even more (Attia, 2003; Doukali, 2005). The increase in water efficiency does not necessarily yield a reduction in water use; more commonly, it means that tail-enders on the water system get water regularly – greater equity and efficiency, but not less water use. Women say they get a better break inside WUAs, and there are improvements in family health (van Hoffwegen, 2003). On the other hand, WUAs reinforce traditional power structures; richer farmers benefit most.

Pricing of drinking water

Many MENA nations revised their urban water pricing within the last decade to obtain not just higher prices but smarter pricing. Even so, prices remain below costs in most countries – comparable to the prices paid in Canada or the US, and far below what Europeans pay (Saghir, 2002). However, poverty imposes a constraint on raising prices high enough to cover full costs. As a partial step, many MENA nations are adopting increasing block rates for the domestic sector with the lowest block set very low (a 'social tariff') to ensure even poor households have some water. Jordan and Tunisia avoid subsidizing richer households by requiring consumers who use more water than that covered by the initial block to pay at the higher rate for the full, not the marginal, volume. There is much less activity toward reform of pricing for irrigation water and none on water markets.

Recognizing ecological demands

Few MENA nations recognize that a large share of the water in natural ecosystems must be left in place to provide services ranging from sanitation to flood control and habitat protection, or that the value of those services to society is typically much greater than the private values achieved after land is converted to purportedly 'more productive' uses (Millennium Ecosystem Assessment, 2005). However, there are signs of change. Israel amended its 1959 water law to recognize the ecosystem as a beneficial use of water and it now requires annual reports on allocations of water to the ecosystem. Jordan, Morocco, Tunisia and Turkey have all adjusted water management projects to protect nature reserves or increase flows into lakes and wetlands. Generally, however, MENA nations rank low in terms of the ecological protection afforded their water bodies (UNESCO, 2003).

Refocusing agricultural research

For many years there has been a bias against investing in agricultural research for less favoured areas, such as the rain-fed farms in MENA (Pender and Hazell, 2000; Comprehensive Assessment, 2007). It is time to shift priorities. As one example, three-quarters of all wheat in MENA is grown under rain-fed conditions with typical productivity of one tonne per hectare, a rate that can at least be doubled and possibly quadrupled by coupling additional research with supplementary irrigation (Comprehensive Assessment, 2007). Moreover, in many areas, agricultural productivity is limited more by the lack of nutrients than by lack of water, and improved water use efficiency depends on changes in agronomic practices (Warner et al, 2006; Elhadj, 2008). Investment in rain-fed techniques is particularly important for small farmers, who make up the bulk of the rural poor (Smith, 2004). They can also be helped by modest improvements in such traditional approaches as rainwater harvesting (Oweis et al, 2001) and in such modern ones as drip irrigation (Postel et al, 2001).

From boardroom to homes and fields

Institutional change to improve water management is occurring in the Middle East and North Africa, but not to the extent nor with the speed required by the situation. The problem is less a lack of good policy design than ineffective policy implementation. Almost everywhere, the needed institutional changes find support among senior planners and in the minister's cabinet, but those changes are not carried through to lower levels of the organization. Nor, in most cases, do the changes incorporate an explicit pro-poor bias. What one can see is promising for the future of fresh water management in MENA, but it is long overdue and far short of a soft path approach.

References – South Africa

Ashton, P. J. (2007) 'The role of good governance in sustainable development', in A. R. Turton, J. Hattingh, G. A. Maree, D. J. Roux, M. Claassen and W. F. Strydom (eds) *Governance as a Trialogue: Government–Society–Science in Transition*, Springer-Verlag, Berlin
Ashton, P. J. and Turton, A. R. (2008) 'Water and security in Sub-Saharan Africa: Emerging concepts and their implications for effective water resource management in

the southern African region', in H. G. Brauch, J. Grin, C. Mesjasz, H. Krummenacher, N. C. Behera, B. Chourou, U. O. Spring, P. H. Liotta and P. Kemeri-Mbote (eds) *Facing Global Environmental Change: Environmental, Human, Energy, Food, Health and Water Security Concepts – Volume IV*, Springer-Verlag, Berlin

Ashton, P. J., Hardwick, D. and Breen, C. (2008) 'Changes in water availability and demand within South Africa's shared river basins as determinants of regional, social and ecological resilience', in M. J. Burns and A. B. Weaver (eds) *Exploring Sustainability Science: A Southern African Perspective*, Stellenbosch University Press, Stellenbosch

Asmal, K. (1998) 'Water as a metaphor for governance: Issues in water resources management in Africa', *Nature and Resources*, vol 34, no 1, pp19–25

Busari, O. and Jackson, B. (2006) 'Reinforcing water and sanitation sector reform in South Africa', *Water Policy*, vol 8, no 4, pp303–312

Department of Water Affairs and Forestry (DWAF) (1997) White Paper on a National Water Policy for South Africa, Government of the Republic of South Africa, Pretoria

Department of Water Affairs and Forestry (DWAF) (2001) 'Free Basic Water Implementation Strategy', May 2001, DWAF, Pretoria

Department of Water Affairs and Forestry (DWAF) (2003a) 'Limpopo Water Management Area: Overview of water resources availability and utilisation', Report no P WMA 01/000/00/0203, September 2003, DWAF, Pretoria

Department of Water Affairs and Forestry (DWAF) (2003b) 'Luvuvhu and Letaba Water Management Area: Overview of water resources availability and utilisation', Report No P WMA 02/000/00/0203, September 2003, DWAF, Pretoria

Department of Water Affairs and Forestry (DWAF) (2003c) 'Crocodile (West) and Marico Water Management Area: Overview of water resources availability and utilisation', Report no P WMA 03/000/00/0203, September 2003, DWAF, Pretoria

Department of Water Affairs and Forestry (DWAF) (2003d) 'Olifants Water Management Area: Overview of water resources availability and utilisation', Report no P WMA 04/000/00/0203, September 2003, DWAF, Pretoria

Department of Water Affairs and Forestry (DWAF) (2003e) 'Inkomati Water Management Area: Overview of water resources availability and utilisation', Report no P WMA 05/000/00/0203, September 2003, DWAF, Pretoria

Department of Water Affairs and Forestry (DWAF) (2003f) 'Usutu–Mhlatuze Water Management Area: Overview of water resources availability and utilisation', Report no P WMA 06/000/00/0203, September 2003, DWAF, Pretoria

Department of Water Affairs and Forestry (DWAF) (2003g) 'Upper Vaal Water Management Area: Overview of water resources availability and utilisation', Report no P WMA 08/000/00/0203, September 2003, DWAF, Pretoria

Department of Water Affairs and Forestry (DWAF) (2003h) 'Middle Vaal Water Management Area: Overview of water resources availability and utilisation', Report no P WMA 09/000/00/0203, September 2003, DWAF, Pretoria

Department of Water Affairs and Forestry (DWAF) (2003i) 'Lower Vaal Water Management Area: Overview of water resources availability and utilisation', Report no P WMA 10/000/00/0203, September 2003, DWAF, Pretoria

Department of Water Affairs and Forestry (DWAF) (2003j) 'Upper Orange Water Management Area: Overview of water resources availability and utilisation', Report no P WMA 13/000/00//0203, September 2003, DWAF, Pretoria

Department of Water Affairs and Forestry (DWAF) (2003k) 'Lower Orange Water Management Area: Overview of water resources availability and utilisation', Report no P WMA 14/000/00/0203, September 2003, DWAF, Pretoria

Department of Water Affairs and Forestry (DWAF) (2004a) *National Water Resource Strategy*, 1st Edition, DWAF, Pretoria

Department of Water Affairs and Forestry (DWAF) (2004b), *Inkomati Water Management Area: Internal Strategic Perspective*, DWAF, Pretoria

European Union (EU) (2000) Water Framework Directive, http://europa.eu.int/comm/environment/water/water-framework/index_en.html, accessed 20 September 2008

Gowlland-Gualtieri, A. (2007) *South Africa's Water Law and Policy Framework: Implications for the Right to Water*, IELRC Working Paper, International Environmental Law Research Centre, Geneva, www.ielrc.org/content/w0703.pdf, accessed 25 September 2008

Gumbo, B. and Van der Zaag, P. (2002) 'Water losses and the political constraints to demand management: The case of the City of Mutare, Zimbabwe', *Physics and Chemistry of the Earth*, vol 27, pp805–813

Johnston, S. and Bernstein, A. (2007) *Voices of Anger: Protest and Conflict in Two Municipalities*, Centre for Development and Enterprise, Johannesburg

McKenzie, R. S., Mostert, H. and de Jager, T. (2004). 'Leakage reduction through pressure management in Khayelitsha: Two years down the line', *Water SA*, vol 30, no 5, pp13–17

Mwendera, E., Hazelton, D., Nkhuwa, D., Robinson, P., Tjijenda, K. and Chavula, G. (2003) 'Overcoming constraints to the implementation of water demand management in Southern Africa', *Physics and Chemistry of the Earth*, vol 28, pp761–778

Oberholster, P. J. and Ashton, P. J. (2008) *State of the Nation Report: An Overview of the Current Status of Water Quality and Eutrophication in South African Rivers and Reservoirs*, Parliamentary Grant Deliverable, Council for Scientific and Industrial Research (CSIR), Pretoria, South Africa

Postel, S. and Richter, B. (2003) *Rivers for Life: Managing Water for People and Nature*, Island Press, Washington, DC

Republic of South Africa (1996) *Constitution*, Government of the Republic of South Africa, Pretoria

Republic of South Africa (1998) *National Water Act* (Act No 36 of 1998), Government of the Republic of South Africa, Pretoria

Solanes, M. and Gonzalez-Villareal (1999) *The Dublin Principles for Water as Reflected in a Comparative Assessment of Institutional and Legal Arrangements for Integrated Water Resources Management*, Technical Advisory Committee, Global Water Partnership, June

Statistics South Africa (STATS-SA) (2007) 'South African population statistics: Census 2001', www.statssa.gov.za/census01.html, accessed 13 August 2007

Turton, A. R. (1999) 'Water Demand Management (WDM): A case study from South Africa', MEWREW Occasional Paper no 4, presented to the Water Issues Study Group, School of Oriental and African Studies (SOAS), London

Turton, A. R. (2003) 'The hydropolitical dynamics of cooperation in Southern Africa: A strategic perspective on institutional development in international river basins', in A. R. Turton, P. J. Ashton and T. E. Cloete (eds) *Transboundary Rivers, Sovereignty and Development: Hydropolitical Drivers in the Okavango River Basin*, AWIRU, Pretoria, South Africa, and Green Cross International, Geneva

Turton, A. R. (2008a) 'The Southern African Hydropolitical Complex', in O. Varis, C. Tortajada and A. J. Biswas (eds) *Management of Transboundary Rivers and Lakes*, Springer-Verlag, Berlin

Turton, A. R. (2008b) 'A South African perspective on a possible benefit-sharing approach for transboundary waters in the SADC region', *Water Alternatives*, vol 1, no 2

Turton, A., Nicol, A. and Allan, J. A. (2003) *Policy Options in Water Stressed States: Emerging Lessons From the Middle East and Southern Africa*, AWIRU, Pretoria, South Africa and London

Turton, A. R., Earle, A., Malzbender, D. and Ashton, P. J. (2006) 'Hydropolitical vulnerability and resilience along Africa's international waters', in A. T. Wolf (ed) *Hydropolitical Resilience and Vulnerability along International Waters*, Report no UNEP/DEW/0672/NA, United Nations Environment Program, Nairobi, pp19–67

Turton, A. R, Patrick, M. J. and Rascher, J. (2008) 'Setting the scene: Hydropolitics and the development of the South African economy', in M. J. Patrick, J. Rascher and A. R. Turton (eds) 'Reflections on water in South Africa', *International Journal of Water Resource Development*, vol 24, no 3, pp319–323 (special edition)

Van Wyk, E., Breen, C. M., Roux, D. J., Rogers, K. H., Sherwill, T. and van Wilgen, B.W. (2006) 'The Ecological Reserve: Towards a common understanding for river management in South Africa', *Water SA*, vol 32, no 3, pp403–409

Waddell, S. (2000) 'Emerging models for developing water systems for the rural poor: From contracts to co-production', Research and Survey Series, BPD Water and Sanitation Cluster, Business Partners for Development, London

Wall, K. C. (2005) 'Water and wastewater treatment works in South Africa: A study of the compliance and regulatory gap', Conference on Poverty Reduction through Better Regulation, CSIR, Johannesburg

Walwyn, D. and Scholes, R. J. (2006) 'The impact of a mixed income model on the South African CSIR: A recipe for success or disaster?', *South African Journal of Science*, vol 102, pp239–243

Woodhouse, P. (2008) 'Water rights in South Africa: Insights from legislative reform', BWPI Working Paper 36, Brooks World Poverty Institute, Manchester, UK

References – India

Ahmed, S. (2004) 'Sustaining peace, re-building livelihoods: The Gujarat Harmony Project', *Gender and Development*, vol 12, no 3, pp94–102, (reprinted in C. Sweetman (ed) *Gender, Peace-building and Reconciliation*, Oxfam, Oxford, 2004)

Ahmed, S. (ed) (2005) *Flowing Upstream: Empowering Women through Water Management Initiatives in India*, Foundation Books, New Delhi and Centre for Environmental Education, Ahmedabad

Brandes, O. M. and Brooks, D. B. (2007) *The Soft Path for Water in a Nutshell*, Friends of the Earth, Canada, Ottawa, ON, and POLIS Project on Ecological Governance, University of Victoria, Victoria, BC

Cleaver, F. and Franks, T. (2005) *Water Governance and Poverty: A Framework for Analysis*, Bradford Centre for International Development, Research Paper no 13, www.brad.ac.uk/acad//bcid/research/papers/ResearchPaper13CleaverFranks.pdf

Dubash, N. (2002) *Tubewell Capitalism: Groundwater Development and Agrarian Change in Gujarat*, Oxford University Press, New Delhi

GWA (2003) 'Tapping into Sustainability: Issues and Trends in Gender Mainstreaming in Water and Sanitation', Gender and Water Alliance, Dieren, The Netherlands, www.genderandwater.org

Iyer, R. R. (2007) *Towards Water Wisdom: Limits, Justice, Harmony*, Sage, New Delhi

Rocheleau, D., Thomas-Slayter, B. and Wangari, E. (eds) (1996) *Feminist Political Ecology: Global Issues and Local Experiences*, Routledge, London

Rowland, J. (1997) 'What is empowerment?' in H. Afshar and F. Alikhan (eds) *Empowering Women for Development*, Booklinks Corporation, Hyderabad

Shah, T. (1993) *Groundwater Markets and Irrigation Development: Political Economy and Practical Policy*, Oxford University Press, Mumbai

WASMO (2007) *Empowering Women for Improved Access to Safe Water*, Water and Sanitation Management Organisation, Government of Gujarat, Gandhinagar

WEDO (2003) *Untapped Connections: Gender, Water and Poverty – Key Issues, Government Commitments and Actions for Sustainable Development*, Women's Environment and Development Organisation, New York, NY, www.wedo.org

References – Middle East and North Africa

Attia, B. (2003) *Overview on Decentralisation and Participatory Irrigation Management: Comparative Analysis*, Paper presented at IDRC Forum on Decentralisation and Participatory Irrigation Management, www.idrc.ca/en/ev-44292-201-1-DO_TOPIC.html

Beaumont, P. (2002) 'Water policies for the Middle East in the 21st Century: The new economic realities', *International Journal of Water Resources Development*, vol 18, no 2, pp315–334

Brooks, D. B. and Wolfe, S. (2007) *Institutional Assessment for Effective WDM Implementation and Capacity Development*, Water Demand Management Research Series, no 4, International Development Research Centre, Ottawa, ON

Brooks, D. B., Thompson, I. and El Fattal, I. (2007) 'Water demand management in the Middle East and North Africa: Observations from the IDRC forums and lessons for the future', *Water International*, vol 32, no 2, pp193–204

de Châtel, F. (2007) *Water Sheikhs & Dam Builders: Stories of People and Water in the Middle East*, Transaction Publishers, London

Comprehensive Assessment of Water Management in Agriculture (2007) *Water for Food: Water for Life: Comprehensive Assessment of Water Management in Agriculture*, Earthscan, London and International Water Management Institute, Colombo, Sri Lanka

Doukali, M. R. (2005) 'Water institutional reforms in Morocco', *Water Policy*, vol 7, no 1, pp71–88

Elhadj, E. (2008) 'Dry aquifers in the Arab countries and the looming food crisis', *The Middle East Review of International Affairs*, vol 12, no 3, article 7 (on-line journal, no pagination)

Institute for Agriculture and Trade Policy (2007) 'Water crisis and food sovereignty from a gender perspective', Minneapolis, MN, www.tradeobservatory.org/library.cfm?refid=97668

Millennium Ecosystem Assessment (2005) *Ecosystems and Human Well-Being: Wetlands and Water – Synthesis,* World Resources Institute, Washington, DC

Oweis, T., Prinz, D. and Hachum, A. (2001) *Water Harvesting: Indigenous Knowledge for the Future of Drier Environments*, International Center for Agricultural Research in the Dry Areas, Aleppo, Syria

Pender, J. and Hazell, P. (2000) *Promoting Sustainable Development in Less-Favoured Areas: Overview*, International Food Policy Research Centre Policy Briefs on Promoting Sustainable Development in Less-Favored Areas; Focus 4, Brief 1, Washington, DC

Postel, S., Polak, P., Gonzales, F. and Keller, J. (2001) 'Drip irrigation for small farmers: A new initiative to alleviate hunger and poverty', *Water International*, vol 26, no 1, pp3–13

Saghir, J. (2002) *Reflections on Water Pricing and Tariff Design: Key Principles*, Paper presented at the Water Valuation Forum, Beirut, 26 June, www.idrc.ca/en/ev-44056-201-1-DO_TOPIC.html

Salman, A., Al-Karablieh, E., Regner, H.-J., Wolff, H.-P. and Haddadin, M. (2008) 'Participatory irrigation water management in the Jordan Valley', *Water Policy*, vol 10, no 4, pp305–322

Smith, L. E. D. (2004) 'Assessment of the contribution of irrigation to poverty reduction and sustainable livelihoods', *International Journal of Water Resources Development*, vol 20, no 2, pp243–257

Thirtle, C., Beyers, L., Lin, L., McKenzie-Hill, V., Irz, X., Wiggins, S. and Piesse, J. (2002) *The Impacts of Changes in Agricultural Productivity on the Incidence of Poverty in Developing Countries*, Department for International Development Report No 7946, London

Trottier, J. (1999) *Hydropolitics in the West Bank and Gaza Strip*, Palestinian Academic Society for the Study of International Affairs, Jerusalem

United Nations Development Program (UNDP) (2006) *Human Development Report 2006: Beyond Scarcity: Power, Poverty and the Global Water Crisis*, United Nations, New York, NY

United Nations Educational, Social and Cultural Organization (UNESCO) (2003) *World Water Assessment Program: Water for People; Water for Life*, Berghahn Books, New York, NY

van Hoffwegen, P. (2003) 'Decentralization and participation: Farmers' perspectives and incentives', paper presented at the Decentralization Forum, 2 February, www.idrc.ca/wadimena

Warner, J. F., Bindraban, P. S. and van Keulen, H. (2006) 'Introduction: Water for food and ecosystems. How to cut which pie?', *International Journal of Water Resources Development*, vol 22, no 1, pp3–15

Wolfe, S. E. and Brooks, D. B. (2003) 'Water scarcity: An alternative view and its implications for policy and capacity building', *Natural Resources Forum*, vol 27, no 2, pp99–107

World Bank (2007) *Making the Most of Scarcity: Accountability for Better Water Management Results in the Middle East and North Africa*, The World Bank, Office of the Chief Economist, Washington, DC

Zwarteveen, M. (2008) 'Men, masculinities and water powers in irrigation', *Water Alternatives*, vol 1, no 1, pp111–130

Conclusion

18
A Water Future Different from the Past

David B. Brooks, Oliver M. Brandes
and Stephen Gurman

At some point in every journey
by purpose or unawares
one arrives at a rag edge of water
> Patricia Lowther, 'In the Continent Behind My Eyes',
> in *Milk Stone*

As we write this last chapter of the book in early 2009, it appears that we are approaching a tipping point – perhaps several related tipping points as both our natural and our economic worlds are in a state of flux. The failure of both communism and capitalism, as ideologically constructed economic systems, is increasingly apparent, especially as we witness the financial meltdown occurring all around the globe. Both systems have benefits and limitations, but neither seems able to avoid jarring cycles of expansion and contraction nor increasing gaps between rich and poor, either within a state or between states. Both adopt ruinously exploitative practices toward natural resources and the environment by treating our finite and limited globe as if it can provide an inexhaustible source of materials and absorb an ever-greater volume of wastes. The impacts are increasingly visible even to non-scientists, as with rapidly melting glaciers, changing rainfall patterns and degraded and polluted rivers and lakes. Even our food supply, which once seemed able to expand fast enough to offset the fears of Reverend Malthus, is no longer assured in either quantity or quality, partially due to the real limits of water for agricultural uses being reached globally.

It would be colossally presumptuous to assert that water soft paths can prevent us from reaching any of these tipping points. The term *hydro-centricity* has been created to describe the hubris of water analysts who somehow jump from the necessity for water in human life to water as the determining factor in all decision-making and political choices (Brichieri-Colombi, 2004; Allan, 2007). We are more cautious in our assertions. We three editors, whose collective backgrounds include economics, ecological restoration, engineering, geology, international development and law, believe that the primary shift has to be towards a deeper, ecologically driven form of human activity that starts by assuring sustainable use of natural resources. We recognize that the conditions sufficient to assure ecological sustainability remain stubbornly uncertain and that the concept is far more often endorsed as a goal than actually adopted or put into practice. Nevertheless, we feel comfortable in suggesting that sustainability will depend on a total or near total reliance on the *renewable* part of resources and that there are indeed limits to growth, limits that appear to be more proximate than formerly thought.

So where do water soft paths fit into this broader concept of an ecologically sustainable and life-sustaining world? Water soft paths are the freshwater component of a sustainable society. A sustainable society is designed in ways that support its existing population and economy with enough water of appropriate quality to provide a high quality of life without prejudice to the ability of future populations and economies to have at least as high a quality of life. Though our concepts of soft paths in the context of sustainability start from ecological limits, they also incorporate the crucially important social goals of equality of opportunity, engagement and democratic politics, and equitable distribution of income and wealth among people, among peoples and among generations.

We see water soft paths as a 21st-century approach to water management. They embody what Peter Geick describes in Chapter 4 as the third age of water management. The concept we have developed here incorporates vision, method and a practical planning tool that together, we suggest, offer the promise of fundamental transformation. It is both prosaically simple and classically radical. On the one hand, it provides guidance on how to reduce water use and avoid water degradation, but, on the other, it also influences power relations, governance structures and institutions. For us, and as explored in Chapter 5, getting the water right is a crucial first step on the path to sustainability and must therefore be explicitly addressed as part of the broader societal evolution towards ecological governance. The soft path specifically provides transformative potential because it *depends* on human ingenuity to find ways to search for new approaches and practices and thus to embed an innovative character to the new institutions, planning practices and systems of natural resource governance. Equally important, in an era where, as shown in Chapter 2, climate change is no longer a threat in some distant future, but rather affecting us right now, the soft path builds resilience and provides the process to begin adapting to a changing water world.

The remainder of this concluding chapter will summarize briefly our thoughts at the end of what might be described as the first generation of water soft path studies. We will stand back from what has been said in earlier chapters of the book and reflect on two key questions:

- What are some of the important lessons that we have learned from water soft path analysis?
- What are some of the more important things that we still have to learn?

What have we learned?

Perhaps the most important thing that we have learned in the first generation of water soft path thinking is that it is possible to think holistically about water. Such thinking is not easy. Water is at least as ubiquitous in our society as energy, and every bit as complex. Even the concept of water varies from place to place, from time to time, and from activity to activity (Linton, 2009).

Major gains have come in water soft path analysis that build on the path-breaking work on energy by Amory Lovins (1977) more than a quarter century ago. Chapter 3 shows that it is possible to transfer the vision of soft paths from energy to water and to develop an analytical framework capable of yielding quantitative (at least reasonably so) methods. The research and conceptual exploration captured in the five chapters that make up Part II of this book also demonstrate that these methods indicate not just whether we are or are not using our water resources in a sustainable way, but also how specific constellations of technologies and policy choices could reduce our hydrological footprint (perhaps better dubbed our *watermark*) and begin moving our practices towards sustainability. When undertaken over time, this same analytical method provides signposts to indicate whether we are getting closer to a vision and a society living within its hydrological limits.

Many important differences exist between applying soft path analytics to water rather than to energy. Among other things, it is much harder to define cost effectiveness for water in a consistent and meaningful way across different uses and different regions. Even more important, in contrast to soft energy paths, which can be applied readily at the national scale, water soft paths are, more appropriately, applied at the local and, ideally, the watershed scale. This ecology of place is critical as the soft path quickly blurs from water management to broader issues of governance and collective social decision-making, which are more difficult to deal with at large scales and in complex economies. Finally, and perhaps most important, much more than energy, the notion of water as a service is not only a powerful driver of innovation and a way to open new creative avenues, but it also 'daylights' other aspects of water – water as a source of inspiration, an object of awe and of beauty, even something sacred (Suzuki with McConnell, 1997).

It is perhaps because water is so ubiquitous that we learned that inadequate technology is less of a problem than inadequate institutions. Technology offers a range of choices that, as shown in Chapter 14, range from the mundane to the radical, and that require, respectively, negligible change to major changes in water management systems. However, as elaborated throughout Part I and further developed in Chapter 12, a variety of imagined and real problems hinder the adoption of technologies and policies that promote water soft paths. Chapter 6 extends this discussion by looking at the interplay between policy and the role of technology and by exploring how soft paths can be assisted by the development of appropriate technology. Together, these thoughts lead to the conclusion that a significant contribution to a prosperous and sustainable society is only possible with institutional change, which takes us back to the crucial governance aspects of the soft path as introduced in Chapter 5 and policy aspects as introduced in Chapter 6.

More modestly, we learned that there is no one right answer to the question of how best to achieve sustainability in the use of water. To phrase the same conclusion in soft path jargon, there is not – indeed, cannot be – any one best soft path. As we knew from the start, soft path choices are inherently heavily value-laden. Some choices, such as improvements to end-use devices (toilets, sprinkler systems, cooling equipment) can be implemented quickly; others, such as grey water reuse, rainwater harvesting and changes in behaviour, only slowly; and still others, such as shifts to rain-fed agriculture, closed loop and cascading recycling of water and water-centric land use planning, more slowly still. Analysing the consequences of different paths can tell us something about the alternative choices, but there is no magic mirror on the wall that can tell us which path is 'softest of them all'.

Finally, we have learned, as have so many others, that communications and outreach are critical to move from concept to application. How one presents water soft paths is just as important as their content. Dissemination of information, and careful response to the inevitable critiques of soft path options and measures, is a critically important part of the process. Outreach and communication cannot take place too early; indeed, they should be present from the proposal stage onward; and, as demonstrated in Chapter 13, they must be presented in ways that are persuasive not just to the general public but to politicians and to water planners and practitioners themselves.

What do we still need to learn?

As is often the case when testing and applying new and evolving practices, the list of things still needed only seems to grow. Collectively, we in the water management and governance field have, in recent years, made significant progress but, it is increasingly obvious that, while we may see some light 'at the end of the tunnel', we have a long way to travel before we arrive at a place and time where the soft path approach is a normal part of the planning process.

In particular, we need to learn how to do better water soft path analyses. Some of the problems that soft path analysts and thinkers are facing are common to water issues in most places, for example insufficient data about use or implications of specific practices, such as farming, urban development or industrial practices on the environment, or finding ways to think in terms of watersheds when data and policy are framed by jurisdictional boundaries. Also common to many water issues is the need to learn how we can more accurately place values on water in its various uses and from various perspectives (Dupont and Renzetti, 2008). In particular, we need to learn more about the value of water in providing ecological services. We do not yet have widely accepted figures for the limits of stress that different ecosystems can accept at certain times or over certain periods of time. Although it is likely that we will never know enough, we do know that the values are large (see for example Millennium Ecosystem Assessment, 2005).

Dealing with the export of water is another aspect of the soft path that needs further exploration. Huge volumes of virtual water are transported in national and international commerce through trade in industrial and agricultural products. The issue for water soft paths is not (at least not generally) to limit such trade but to account for it. And the problem of accounting becomes even more complex when rainwater is included along with delivered water (Falkenmark and Rockström, 2005).

The most water-intensive sector of our society is agriculture, which directly affects the amount of virtual water that is traded in and out of any given watershed. The world is close to seeing serious gaps in the quantities of food demanded and the quantities that can be supplied, a problem that, as Sandford points out in Chapter 2, will become worse as a result of climate change. One of the most serious constraints will be the need to maintain ecological services and protect the environment while growing more food with less water. A recent report on water management in agriculture tersely answers the question, 'Will there be enough water to grow enough food?' with two words: 'Yes, if ...' (Comprehensive Assessment, 2007). The report contains many suggestions as to what might be included in that 'if' – some technical; most institutional – and many of them sound similar to what would be proposed by water soft path analysis. Clearly, water soft paths still have much to learn about the food–water–environment nexus.

The water–energy nexus is also rapidly mounting as an area of concern, particularly in an era when climate change is increasingly evident. The connection travels two ways. Saving water can save energy because of reduced pumping and treatment of water, and saving energy can reduce the volume of water needed to cool thermal electric plants or for hydroelectric generation. Although reduced use of heated water or steam saves both energy and water, in many cases water and energy trade off *against* one another. Notably, saline water and seawater can be made potable, but only with the expenditure of large volumes of energy; wastewater can be purified to any extent desired (as detailed in Chapter 14), but only with the expenditure of large volumes of energy. Industrial recycling of water requires energy for pumping and for additional treatment, and important energy–water trade-offs in the growing of food and its delivery to consumers exist. All of these areas where water saving and energy saving appear to be competitive need research to find ways to avoid or reduce the trade-off.

Finally, we must learn more about how to bring soft path approaches to bear on issues of equity, both within and between generations. Further analysis of equity will require that we link water soft paths to issues of budgetary allocations from government and to employment at all skill levels and in different regions. It will also require much more careful distinctions in choices between delivering a good quality of life and delivering a high standard of living. Such work depends on much closer linkages between economic variables, social goals and water use.

Water soft paths in your future?

Much more good news than bad exists for water soft path thinkers and analysts. The forces arrayed against changing from conventional top-down, supply-focused water policies to alternative bottom-up, demand-focused policies are numerous and established. However, interest in water soft path philosophy and approaches from those implementing policies is growing rapidly. For example, as shown in the third part of this book, communities and some regions are seriously exploring the soft path and making changes that are affecting water use and creating change for the future.

The research and application of demand management has done much to lay the foundation for a softer path, and users of water – from individual householders to large corporations – are changing their perspectives and practices. Perhaps a new global environmental understanding (probably driven by ongoing contentious debate around climate change and actions need to address it) coupled with a desire to reconnect to a sense of community and place is laying the foundation for a new water ethic. How else can one explain the declining rate of water withdrawals in the US as described in Chapter 15, or the applications of soft path thinking finding their way into water management around the globe as explored in the six case studies in Chapters 16 and 17?

Soft path concepts have come a long way since the mid-1970s, but they have much further to go before we achieve sustainability. A water soft path, just as with the elusive search for sustainability, is more a process than a goal, more an approach than a result, and more a verb – the act of doing – than a noun – a state of being. Early gains for water sustainability are possible by simply adding water soft paths to the water management options from which a community or a region can choose. While few jurisdictions are likely to completely adopt soft paths initially, this approach will start to look much more attractive in the future when, as is inevitable, they are faced with increasingly expensive conventional and more contentious environmental options.

Perhaps a tipping point is near. An old saying from the American West is that water flows uphill toward money. However, in much of the world today, government's ability to finance new infrastructure is so limited that the flow maybe reversing; water may now be flowing downhill away from large expenditures for front-end loaded and costly infrastructure. The greatest inducement to soft path thinking comes from communities in regions that are facing major expenditures to replace ageing infrastructure or to accommodate growth. The difficult task ahead will be the widespread implementation of full water soft path planning processes, including meaningful stakeholder involvement.

The challenge for the next generation of soft path thinkers and doers will be less in the individual technical concerns and more in the collective decision-making that enables it. How can we shift water soft paths from human vision and analytical method to a practical planning tool? How can we turn ideas into action? Those are the questions that must define the next wave of work in this field. Soft paths are designed to be ecologically desirable and socially acceptable, and evidence also indicates that they are economically feasible. The question now is whether they are, or can be made, politically attractive?

References

Allan, J. A. (2007), 'Beyond the watershed: Avoiding the dangers of hydro-centricity and informing water policy', in H. Shuval and H. Dweik (eds) *Water Resources in the Middle East: Israel-Palestinian Water Issues – From Conflict to Cooperation*, Springer, London, pp33–39

Brichieri-Colombi, J. S. (2004) 'Hydrocentricity: A limited approach to achieving food and water security', *Water International*, vol 29, no 3, pp318–328

Comprehensive Assessment of Water Management in Agriculture (2007) *Water for Food; Water for Life: A Comprehensive Assessment of Water Management in Agriculture*, Earthscan, London

Dupont, D. P. and Renzetti, S. (2008) 'Good to the last drop? An assessment of Canadian water value estimates', *Canadian Journal of Water Resources*, vol 33, no 4, pp369–380

Falkenmark, M. and Rockström, J. (2005) *Rain: The Neglected Resource*, Swedish Water House Policy Brief No. 2, Stockholm International Water Institute, Stockholm

Linton, J. (2009) *What is Water? The History and Crisis of a Modern Abstraction*, UBC Press, Vancouver

Lovins, A. B. (1977) *Soft Energy Paths: Toward a Durable Peace*, Ballinger/Friends of the Earth, Cambridge, MA

Millennium Ecosystem Assessment (2005) *Ecosystems and Human Well-Being: Current State and Trends*, vol 1, ch 7: Freshwater Ecosystem Services, World Resources Institute, Washington, DC

Suzuki, D., with McConnell, A. (1997) *The Sacred Balance: Rediscovering Our Place in Nature*, Douglas and McIntyre, Vancouver

Annex – How to Create a Soft Path Plan for Water

David B. Brooks and Oliver M. Brandes with Carol Maas,
Susanne Porter-Bopp and Jennifer Wong

The following steps serve as a basic guideline for creating a soft path plan. Many approaches and applications of the soft path exist; however this 'top 10' of steps provides the guideposts to any comprehensive process. The steps suggested here, and indeed any soft path planning process, can be undertaken at the community, regional, watershed and even senior government level (for example, provinces, states and even whole nations).

1   *Identify water services* – List all services provided by water (e.g. grass watering, toilet flushing, clothes washing, agriculture and food production, industrial cooling, manufacturing, energy development and production, etc.) and note the minimum quality of water that is needed to provide a particular service.

   Start thinking about the quality of water that is really needed to obtain a particular service. For example, do we need high quality water for toilet flushing, cooling, manufacturing or lawn watering? Or do we need to use water at all? If statistics are available on specific end-uses over time, collect them as well.

2   *Review water supply options* – Identify all current sources of water and determine whether any are being overused or degraded. Be sure to quantify the capacity of both surface water and groundwater, and both public and private supplies. In the absence of source capacity information, compile the rated capacity of all water supply plants. In addition, identify any water resources that might be reserved from use for religious, cultural or aesthetic reasons, and notionally set them aside from (further) exploitation. At the same time, the analyst must recognize the ecosystem services being provided by existing water resources, and make some estimate of how

much water has to remain *in situ* – that is, stream flow, lake volumes, minimum aquifer levels, and even patterns of flow – in order to maintain the level of those services. All of this water will be notionally unavailable in the soft path scenario. Also, exclude water that is found outside the region or watershed.

When reviewing available supply options, be sure to take account of normal climatic variations, that is the differences between wetter and drier years. In addition, start thinking about how water sources might change under the impact of climate change. This type of localized projection is very challenging, but water supply options must reflect future conditions of water availability for human use and for maintenance of ecosystem services.

3 *Adopt a projection for your community, region or watershed* – Create a business-as-usual (BAU) scenario for the community, region or watershed, at a time some 20–50 years in the future, based on applying current rates of water withdrawals and uses to the anticipated size of the population and the economy for that year. Though essentially a 'naïve' projection, do incorporate evident changes in living patterns (eg, a trend toward more multi-family dwellings) and in economic structure (eg, a decline in primary industry).

4 *Establish a desired future scenario* – Create a desired future scenario for water in the final year of your projection, including both soft and hard targets as appropriate. For example, a soft target could include establishing a 'culture of conservation' or 'to have the most efficient water use in Canada'. Hard targets should be quantitative, such as a maximum total future water use or 'no new water'. The target could also incorporate secondary targets based on the fraction of water that will be obtained from alternative sources, such as reuse and rainwater. In either case, most of the time should be spent on analysing water demands on an end-use-by-end-use basis. Almost all soft path analyses develop at least two distinct scenarios (in addition to the business-as-usual scenario) for the final year:

   (a) In one scenario, adjustments are explored to the fullest extent possible within the limits of what is, or what is expected to be, cost effective. This soft path scenario might suggest a policy mix including volume-based pricing, education and social marketing, rebates for low-flow toilets, and recycled water for parks and golf courses, and can be described as the preliminary Demand Management Scenario.

   (b) In a second scenario, the demand management scenario is supplemented by changes in personal habits, growth rates and economic structure. If the same region wanted to preserve as much land as possible in a natural state, farmers could be urged to return to rain-fed agriculture, urban planning could be adjusted to reduce runoff, and water-intensive industries could be discouraged or prohibited. Householders can be convinced to sweep rather than wash driveways, and to use native plants or xeriscaping in place of Kentucky blue grass for their lawns. This can be described as the preliminary Conservation Scenario.

5   *Adjust scenarios by matching water quality* – Establish the quality of water required to provide the services identified in Steps 3, 4a and 4b in order to distinguish those uses that require high quality water (notably, drinking, cooking, bathing and hand washing), and those that can be accomplished with lower quality water (toilet flushing, gardening, industrial applications). Modify the results achieved in Steps 4a and 4b by approaches that deliver water of the appropriate quality to each end-use. The result will be a final Demand Management scenario and a final Conservation scenario for the year of the projection developed in Step 3.

6   *Ensure desired future scenarios are sustainable* – The two final scenarios that emerge from Step 5 must now be compared with the water resources that are ecologically (and of course economically) available. Can the water demands associated with the final Demand Management scenario and the final Conservation scenario be met without negative impacts on the ecology? Can they be met in low rainfall years as well as in average rainfall years? Can they be met largely or exclusively from renewable sources? (This requirement does not preclude interim use of non-renewable aquifers and water stocked in lakes, but the limited quantities of such water must be taken into account.) Can they be met without inter-basin transfers? If not – that is, if acceptable water supplies are not sufficient to meet demands – one must go back to the scenarios in Step 4 and find ways to further cut (or change) the demands.

7   *Adjust for expected effects of climate change* – After having ensured the sustainability of the supply–demand match under current conditions, recalculate to further incorporate expected effects of climate change. Be sure to consider not only climate impacts on water resources, but also human activities, such as garden watering during longer drought periods or changing needs for irrigated agriculture needs. (Note that for this calculation, it is irrelevant whether climate change is attributed to natural cycles or the result of human actions.)

     The supply–demand conditions for that final year of your scenarios must be sufficiently resilient to operate in a future that has been affected by climate change. If not, once again return to Step 4 and find ways to reduce demands until they are.

8   *Backcast from a sustainable future to the present* – Create various soft paths by determining ways of linking the desired future patterns of water supply and demand to today's conditions. How does a community, a region or a watershed get from 'there' to 'here'?

     The analyst must determine reasonable (ie, economically, socially and politically acceptable) rates of building and replacing infrastructure. The analyst must also consider what policies or incentives would be needed to achieve those rates. Options could also include incentives for slower local population growth and, even more important, alternative (that is, less water-intensive) patterns of economic growth. Though the analysis goes backwards from the future to the present, the objective, of course, is to suggest what sorts of approaches will permit the society to get from the present to the desired future in ways that are simultaneously economically feasible, socially acceptable and politically achievable.

There is no one best result. The same future can be achieved in many different ways, some with more and some with less government intervention, some with higher and some with lower prices for water. The analyst can only suggest paths that work; he or she cannot judge which is preferable for the community, region or watershed. Backcasting is the most difficult and complex part of soft path analysis. How much backcasting is enough? It's enough when your results are at least reasonably persuasive – not to you, the analyst, but to the officials, planners, journalists and indeed the community who will (hopefully) read your report without having gone through all the previous steps.

9   *Write, talk and promote* – Now that you have developed a workable scenario, the next and very important step in soft path planning is to improve upon your conclusions by seeking broad public input. Almost certainly, this process will require revision of the analysis and modification of the scenarios. Most of the foregoing will have to be revised not just once but periodically. Soft path analysis is a process; it seldom reaches anything but an interim end. Still, it is incumbent upon the analyst to take the soft path scenarios to the public and to people who influence and make key decisions about fresh water. Gaining their understanding and acceptance of water soft paths is the only route to sustainable water management.

10 *Next iteration* – After you have rested a bit, and read a few novels and gone canoeing, played ball or whatever you prefer, start thinking about the next iteration of water soft path planning!

Index